THE POLITICS OF BROADCASTING

The Politics of Broadcasting

edited by Raymond Kuhn

ST. MARTIN'S PRESS
New York

Library of Congress Cataloging in Publication Data
Main entry under title:

The politics of broadcasting.

   Includes bibliographies and index.
   1. Broadcasting — Addresses, essays, Lectures.
2. Broadcasting — Political aspects — Addresses, essays,
lectures. 3. Broadcasting policy — Addresses, essays,
lectures. I. Kuhn. Raymond.
HE8689.4.P65   1985   384.54   84-15996
ISBN 0-312-62660-6

CONTENTS

TABLES AND FIGURES

Tables

Figures

For Anne

PREFACE

At a time when the broadcasting systems of a variety
of countries are in a state of flux, with many long-
standing principles as well as deeply-rooted preju-
dices now being questioned, *The Politics of Broadcasting* aims to introduce the reader to the politics
of broadcasting in selected countries of the western
world. With the advent of new telecommunications
and information technology, the development of which
is being actively encouraged by western governments
for industrial and economic reasons, broadcasting is
entering the most revolutionary stage of its history
since the introduction of television transmissions
to a mass audience. At the same time political
events, such as changes of government, are also
affecting the nature and quality of different national broadcasting systems. This book describes and
analyses the problems faced by politicians and
broadcasters in responding to these changing technological and political environments.
     Questions which the book seeks to answer with
reference to each of the different countries covered
include the following. What changes are taking
place or are about to take place, affecting the
structure of the broadcasting system? What elements
of continuity are still present? What are the terms
of the political debate on broadcasting and who are
the principal participants in that debate? How are
the relevant authorities reacting to and trying to
control technological developments in broadcasting?
What may be the likely consequences of changes in
the broadcasting system for programme content, scheduling policies and viewing habits?
     The book consists of a short introduction and
eight single country chapters, each written by a
specialist on broadcasting and politics of the respective country. No previous knowledge of the

Preface

subject has been assumed by the authors. The countries chosen are all major western political systems
of a liberal-democratic type: Great Britain, France,
West Germany, Italy, the United States, Canada,
Australia and Japan. A balance has been struck,
therefore, between European and non-European states,
as well as between Anglo-Saxon and non-Anglo-Saxon
cultures. While all eight countries differ in
several important respects including historical
background, cultural traits, territorial size, political traditions and broadcasting structures, many
of the political issues concerning the role and
development of broadcasting are common to them all.
The book emphasises both these national differences
and similarities.

    As the book is a collaborative venture, my
first debt of thanks must be to my fellow contributors. They all had to withstand my attempts to per-
suade, cajole and even bully them into amending
their individual contributions and meeting publication deadlines. Most cooperated willingly, others
capitulated reluctantly, while one in particular resisted tenaciously. All of them, however, deserve
my thanks. I should also like to express by grati-
tude to Professor Colin Seymour-Ure of the University
of Kent, Anthony Smith at the British Film Institute
and John Howkins of the International Institute of
Communications for their assistance in the early
stages; the Department of Political Studies at Queen
Mary College for its unwavering support; the Social
Science Research Council and Centre National de la
Recherche Scientifique for financial aid in respect
of my own chapter on France; and Teri Kalinka and
Evelyn Lockington for their typing of the manuscript.
Finally, I should like to thank my wife who as ever
has been a source of constant inspiration and com-
fort during the preparation of this book.

Raymond Kuhn

INTRODUCTION

Raymond Kuhn

Broadcasting is such a well-established feature of
contemporary western society that it is difficult to
appreciate just how recent an innovation is the
advent of radio and more especially television. In
the space of roughly seventy years, and nearer forty
in the case of television, broadcasting has assumed
a dominant role in our way of life and had incalculable consequences for the way we conduct our
affairs, whether in social, cultural, political or
economic matters.

     For example, with large sections of the popula-
tion in the West spending a major part of their
leisure time listening to radio or watching television, the broadcasting media have become the prime
sources of entertainment in the second half of the
twentieth century, overtaking, and for some people
wholly replacing, previously established leisure
activities such as reading books and going to the
theatre or cinema. At the same time radio and television have become major disseminators of culture to
the masses, opening up new horizons by introducing
many listeners and viewers to previously unheard of
cultural artefacts. They have also helped teach
people about events taking place outside their
immediate social and political environments, thereby
extending their level of general political knowledge. On the other hand, television in particular
has frequently been accused of encouraging a more
violent society, debasing moral standards and leading to the break-up of family life. It has also
been upbraided, for, inter alia, inducing passivity
on the part of the viewer, promoting political con-
formism and exalting consumerist values.

     Yet whether praised or blamed, receiving
plaudits or brickbats, the broadcasting media have
generally been attributed great importance as agents

which exercise a wide-ranging and profound influence on the way in which people perceive the world, internalise that perception and act upon it. Given their central position in contemporary western societies, radio and television, quite understandably, are deemed by many to exercise a great degree of power.

Not surprisingly, then, broadcasting is a topic which has attracted the interested and disinterested attention of both politicians and political scientists. Since information is a political resource and as radio and television constitute the primary sources of political information for the electorates of western democracies, most evidently, but by no means exclusively, through their news and current affairs output, it follows that the organisation of broadcasting and control of its output are subjects which often feature prominently on the political agenda. Moreover, in an era where a politician's image and style may be more electorally important than the substance of his or her views, no politician can afford to underestimate the electoral importance of radio and television.

This is not to argue that the broadcasting media are somehow all-powerful or that people's political views are determined solely by what they listen to on radio or watch on television. Research on evaluating the influence of broadcast output on the viewer-voter during election campaigns, for example, has shown that the determinants of electoral behaviour are many and varied. Neither partisan control of broadcasting nor the ability to perform well on radio and television guarantees electoral success, or vice-versa. Yet it would be jejune to argue convincingly that broadcasting exerted no influence on the electorate at all. While there is no agreement among political scientists (or researchers generally) about the influence of the broadcasting media, few would deny that broadcasting in western societies is a major agent of political socialisation, helping to shape people's political attitudes, beliefs and behaviour, in short a nation's political culture.

The political *effects* of broadcasting are not, however, the subject matter of this book. While no agreement has been sought, far less reached, among the various authors regarding its *degree* of political significance, all subscribe to the view that broadcasting is *to some extent* politically important. Minimally this is the case even if only because governments, political parties, pressure groups and

broadcasters behave as if it were. They may all be
performing a collective act of self-delusion, but
their motives, actions and the consequences of those
actions with reference to the role and development
of broadcasting require to be described, explained
and analysed nonetheless. This is one aim of this
book.

The present volume is an empirical study of the
politics of broadcasting in selected western countries. It is not a theoretical work. Each author
was asked to examine the relations between political
actors, particularly the government, and the broadcasting media, concentrating on those issues, such
as policy formulation, which seemed to them most
relevant to a political understanding of the development of broadcasting in the country concerned.

The authors have sought to maintain a certain
unity of approach. Each chapter contains some basic
introductory material, outlining the essential features of the historical development of broadcasting.
It then opens out into a treatment of contemporary
political/technological changes which have affected
(or may affect in the near future) the nature of the
broadcasting system. Every chapter, albeit to differing degrees, covers such items as the range of
broadcasting services on offer; the role played by
the state in establishing and regulating the organisational framework within which the broadcasting
media operate; the degree of political, and in
particular governmental, control exercised over
radio and television output; and possible consequences of any changes in the number and type of broadcasting outlets for viewing habits and programme
scheduling.

Because of varying national circumstances, the
eight chapters emphasise different aspects of the
general subject matter. Chapters 1 - 4 on the
western European countries (Great Britain, France,
West Germany and Italy) all focus on the way in
which the traditional broadcasting systems and
established organisations are at present going
through a period of transition, if not crisis, with
perhaps radical consequences for broadcasting in
these countries. The chapter by Muriel and Joel
Cantor on the United States (chapter 5) examines the
history and application of regulation in US broadcasting and in particular the contemporary regula-
tion/de-regulation debate. Richard Harding's
chapter on Australia (chapter 6) is largely concerned with the way in which broadcasting has been used
as a party political football over the last decade

or so, while Richard Collins argues that the main
issue in Canadian broadcasting (chapter 7) is the
extent to which it is dependent on US production to
fill up its schedules and the consequences of this
foreign penetration for Canadian culture and nation-
building policies. Finally, in his chapter on Japan
(chapter 8) Michael Tracey examines the reconstruction of broadcasting in the new post-war democracy
and outlines recent technological innovations which
are changing the nature of the broadcasting system
there.

No single conclusion, embracing the different
national broadcasting systems studied in this volume,
emerges as indisputably applicable to them all. Yet
certain themes and issues do cut across national
boundaries and appear relevant to more than one of
the countries included, even if not to all of them
equally. Of these the crisis of the public service
ethos, linked with, but not fully explained by, the
advent of new audiovisual technology, is the most
significant. The remainder of this Introduction
concentrates on this aspect of broadcasting's development in western democracies.

The crisis of the public service ethos is first
and foremost a crisis of certain public service
broadcasting organisations: the BBC and IBA in Great
Britain, RTF in France, ARD and ZDF in West Germany,
RAI in Italy, the CBC in Canada, the ABC in Australia and the NHK in Japan. All of these broadcasting
institutions, and the type of service they have
traditionally sought to provide, are increasingly
under threat, leading to a crisis of confidence
within these established broadcasting 'giants'.

Public service broadcasting is not a precise,
scientific term. Any working definition would,
however, comprise the following four elements:

   - a commitment to balanced scheduling across
   the different programme genres, with no undue
   emphasis on any one; hence public service
   broadcasting institutions have usually been
   statutorily required to educate and inform as
   well as entertain the audience. *One* institution has frequently had the task of satisfying
   all the audience's needs;

   - the broadcast institution is a public body,
   with normally a high degree of financial independence from both governmental and commercial
   sources;

- the service is provided to all (for example, outlying rural as well as densely populated urban areas) in return for a basic, initial payment, usually in the form of an annual licence-fee;

- political output is obliged to be balanced and impartial.

The tradition of broadcasting as a public service is strongest in Britain, where the classic embodiment of this approach was, and is, the BBC. The heavy hand of Reithianism ensured that the nascent BBC embarked on a programme scheduling policy which included a large quota of educational and information output, while programme content was designed not just to reflect tastes but to raise them through an emphasis, for example, on 'highbrow' culture. The new medium and its message were shaped under Reith largely and deliberately in ignorance of audience preferences. 'Look what happened to the Battleship Potemkin when the ratings took over' was an internal BBC 'catchphrase' of the 1920s. Benefiting from a state monopoly until the early 1950s, the BBC could afford to embark on this elitist, paternalistic approach to programming, preserved as it was from the threat of competition for listeners and viewers.
Established as a public corporation, the BBC was explicitly protected from commercial pressures. Advertising was (and remains) forbidden on BBC radio stations and television channels, with the Corporation being financed not out of general taxation or by block grant, but by a special licence-fee. Once the viewer has paid this licence, no further payment is required for the reception of the Corporation's various services. There is no link at the level of the 'consumer' between size of licence payment on the one hand and amount or quality of consumption on the other. (Even the introduction of a higher licence-fee for colour television sets in the 1970s did not break with the principle of a standard one-off payment for the reception of all services.) In addition, the BBC has considered that it has a public duty to provide its services to all parts of the national territory, even when the provision of such services was not commercially viable. One hundred per cent coverage of the country has been the goal.
With regard to its relations with the government and its political output, in theory the BBC is

politically independent, neither subject to governmental censorship or expected to follow a pro-
government line in programming content. As a
corollary of its political independence, the BBC's
news and current affairs output is obliged to be
balanced and impartial. The independence of the BBC
from political interference is ostensibly ensured by
the construction of filters and screens between it
and the political elites, including the government.
The Corporation's corporate ethos of public service
supposedly reinforces this pursuit of independence.
Balance and impartiality are imposed by a code of
practice, in this case the BBC Charter, which lays
down a variety of prescriptions regarding political
output. Independence and impartiality are interrelated in a liberal democratic double bind, the one
being the quid pro quo of the other:

> The state does not grant autonomy to the broad-
> casters to behave as they please: it grants
> autonomy only on the condition that broadcas-
> ters treat the controversial and problematic
> matters germane to their own sphere, and to the
> controversial sphere of the political system,
> which supports and creates the state, with a
> "due impartiality". [1]

There are, of course, still links between the
government and the Corporation, since it is the
former which fixes the level of the licence and
hence determines the BBC's annual revenue and it is
also the government which appoints to the BBC's
corporate guardian angel, the board of governors.
Nonetheless, the BBC is traditionally regarded as
the flag-bearer of the public service broadcasting
institutions, as Ralph Negrine shows in chapter 1.
Moreover, the strength of this commitment to public
service broadcasting was revealed in 1954 when ITV
was established. Though financed from commercial
advertising, the 'independent' television companies
were subject to similar public service provisions as
had been applied to the BBC when it enjoyed a state
monopoly.

This BBC model was admired and emulated by many
other countries when they were establishing their
own broadcasting structures. Not surprisingly the
BBC model was exported to British Commonwealth
countries such as Canada (chapter 6) and Australia
(chapter 7). It was also imitated by the main
continental western European states and by Japan
when broadcasting was being reorganised in these

countries after world war two.

In France, for example, the wartime role played by the BBC in relaying de Gaulle's speeches to the Resistance in France gave the Corporation a reputation in that country which it enjoys to this day. In Italy and West Germany too broadcasting was self-consciously set up on public service lines in reaction to the experiences of Fascism and Nazism. In none of these three major western European democracies was any private or commercial competition allowed. In France and Italy responsibility for broadcasting was accorded to state monopoly public bodies, the RTF and RAI respectively, while in West Germany it was devolved to the regions to prevent this apparently powerful propaganda weapon from falling into the hands of a strong, central state possibly controlled by political extremists. In Japan too the post-war reconstruction of the broadcasting structures was predicated upon a desire that the system, represented by the NHK, should have public service goals.

Only in the United States, with its stronger cultural attachment to individualism and belief in the virtues of the free market, was a very different commercial model adopted, as Muriel and Joel Cantor describe in chapter 5. With its emphasis on entertainment television, financed from advertising and sponsorship and responsive to consumer demands, this US commercial model is antithetical to the public service broadcasting ethos. Yet with this notable exception (plus some smaller western European democracies such as Holland), the BBC provided the blueprint for other western countries to copy: Britannia ruled the airwaves.

The crisis which first struck the BBC and its public service clones in the 1970s, calling their legitimacy into question, results from a combination of different strands: financial, political, technological and social. The confluence of these elements over the past decade has struck a blow, perhaps fatal, at the previously dominant position of these public service institutions and at the ethos which they embody. Let us try to disentangle the different elements of this crisis.

The first element is that the financial position of the public service broadcasting institutions has been eroded. In the case of the BBC, for example, as the television market became saturated in the 1970s and the transfer to colour sets lost its momentum, any increase in the total revenue of the Corporation depended more and more on the

government's willingness to raise the cost of the
individual licence-fee. This both Labour and
Conservative governments, as part of their counter-
inflation policies, were notably reluctant to do.
As a result, the BBC had in real terms static or
diminishing resources to cover the increasing costs
of its services. At the same time, the notion of
financial independence was exposed as a myth.
Government control of the licence-fee level became
a political issue, straining the BBC's claim to independence from government. Similar problems of a
shrinking financial base from licence revenue and/or
growing financial dependence on government for
licence increases affected other public service
broadcasting institutions. In some countries, such
as Italy in 1957 and France in 1968, advertising had
already been introduced on state monopoly public
service channels to help supplement licence revenue.
    At the same time as the growth in revenue has
slowed down or stopped, costs have escalated. The
cost of nationally produced television programming
is very high, especially in comparison with the cost
of programmes imported from the US. As Richard
Collins persuasively argues (chapter 6), Canada is a
prime example of the difficulties of maintaining a
high level of expensive national television production in a market dominated by the US. But the
other countries covered in this volume are suffering
as well, usually resorting to imposed quotas of
home-based production as a protectionist counter to
US imports. This is normally defended on the
grounds of maintaining programme standards and defending the national culture.
    Simultaneously the public service organisations
have built up and are continuing to extend huge
broadcasting empires: more television channels (a
second BBC channel in the late 1960s, three RTF
channels in France by the 1970s and three RAI channels in Italy by the same decade); the growth of
programming hours, including late-night, afternoon
and even breakfast television; and the creation of
local radio stations and regional television channels. All of these developments have led not just
to the public service institutions becoming large-
scale bureaucratic organisations, but also to resources having to be spread ever more thinly among
a host of worthy supplicants. Consequently, the
supply of revenue is now barely meeting the demand
of increased costs and services. Public service
broadcasting is in a financial mess.
    The second element of the crisis of public

service broadcasting derives from its links with
government and its political output. The success of
the public service broadcasters' claim to indepen-
dence/impartiality depends in part on the willingness of politicians to abstain from interfering in
the day-to-day running of broadcasting, partly on
the capacity of the broadcasters to resist such
interference where necessary by remaining in control
of the reporting and analysing of news and current
affairs and partly on elite and mass acceptance that
the goals of independence and impartiality are being
attained or are at least attainable. These pre-
conditions are by no means universally fulfilled.
Moreover, the feasibility of attaining them is increasingly open to question.

The independence/impartiality couplet has never
been applicable to the public broadcasting organisations of all of the relevant countries studied in
this volume. For example, in France and Italy
partisan political control of broadcasting output
has been the norm in the post-war period. As
Raymond Kuhn shows (chapter 2), since the second
world war France has suffered from a broadcasting
system controlled by the governing political
authorities, who have consistently appointed political symphathisers to the important decision-making
posts in state radio and television. Frequently,
and usually systematically, the government has
directly manipulated and even censored political
output to further its own political ends, while at
the same time resisting any challenge to the legal
framework of the state monopoly which allowed the
authorities to run broadcasting as an integral part
of the executive branch of government.

In Italy, as Don Sassoon demonstrates (chapter
4), a similar state of affairs has been evident.
Here the state monopoly broadcasting organisation
was for a long time after the second world war under
the control of the dominant political force, the
Christian Democrats. As a result, broadcast output
was designed to serve Christian Democrat interests,
while the party in turn used broadcasting for
clientelistic purposes as part of their giant web of
patronage. With the inclusion of the Socialists in
the governing coalition in the early 1960s, and the
legitimation of the Communists and their co-optation
into a pro-system defence alliance in the 1970s as
Italy was buffeted by economic, social and political
crisis, the hegemonic position of the Christian
Democrats has been severely modified. However,
though appointments to the RAI are no longer

9

monopolised by a single political party, the state
service is still the object of party political control and patronage.

While France and Italy are the two most out-
standing examples of partisan political control of
broadcasting, it does not follow that in the other
countries with public service traditions included in
this volume broadcasting is independent or impartial.
In West Germany, as Arthur Williams shows (chapter
3), while the post-war constitutional arrangements
excluded the federal government from any role in
broadcasting policy, this has not meant that broadcasting has been immune from illegitimate political
control. The two main national political parties,
the Christian Democrats and the Social Democrats,
have exercised undue influence in the decision-
making bodies of the broadcasting houses, sharing
out administrative and managerial posts in a system
of *proporz* which reflects their electoral strengths.
This system has often led to acrimonious party
political battles over news and current affairs output.

Similar party political conflict over output,
this time at the federal level, is the subject of
Richard Harding's chapter on broadcasting in
Australia (chapter 7), where despite public service
norms governments in the 1970s, particularly the
right-wing government of Malcolm Fraser, intervened
to have politically critical programmes banned from
the air. Both Richard Collins in his chapter on
Canada (chapter 6) and Michael Tracey in the chapter
on Japan (chapter 8) make passing references to the
transgression of public service provisions regarding
political output in the broadcasting systems of
these two countries.

Again the BBC can be used to exemplify the
types of difficulties public service broadcasting
institutions have encountered over the past few
years concerning their relations with political
elites and their political output. Traditionally
the object of hostility from certain sections of the
Labour party and the trade union movement, the BBC
has also come under attack recently from the Conservative party and government, notably over its coverage of the Falklands war. The creation of a new
political force in British politics in the 1980s,
the SDP, has also posed the Corporation problems regarding its statutory commitment to political
balance. For one reason or another it seems that
all the established political parties in Britain
have been becoming more critical and demanding of

the BBC.

Various aspects of the Corporation's political coverage have come in for criticism recently: the reporting of events in Northern Ireland, which for many observers stretched the BBC's commitment to impartiality beyond credibility; the Grunwick dispute; the Healey-Benn deputy leadership contest in the Labour party; the Corporation's coverage of the nuclear weapons issue, including its refusal to screen *The War Game* and its retracted invitation to E P Thompson to present the unilateralist case in an annual Dimbleby lecture; and most recently a *Panorama* programme on right-wing infiltration of the Conservative party.

As Ralph Negrine shows, the Goldilocks view of the BBC's political output, 'not too Conservative, not too Labour, just right', has always been a misleading description. The BBC has never been ideologically neutral. Moreover, in the past it has been the subject of fierce political controversy, most notably over its role in the 1926 General Strike and the 1956 Suez crisis. The present situation differs from past experience, however, in two important ways.

First, political complaints about the BBC's coverage have been reinforced by much academic output. The development of media studies in British higher education over the past decade or so has led to the publication of a growing number of critical works on the BBC and British public broadcasting in general. Given that within this field, 'the most productive controversies have been located *within* Marxism rather than *between* the Marxist and liberal-pluralist approaches',2 the BBC has often found itself without support in the academic community. Intellectually, the critics of the public service tradition as practised by the BBC have been in the ascendancy. They have dominated the debate, encountering only limited and beleaguered opposition. The battle of ideas has been one-sided.

Secondly, dissatisfaction with the BBC's political output is more widespread and more visible than it has ever been in the past. Attacked by all the mainstream political parties, the trade unions and a whole host of minority groups, the Corporation is finding it increasingly difficult to respond to a multiplicity of conflicting demands, while at the same time striving to maintain its 'independent/impartial' stance. The re-ideologising of British party politics with the breakdown of the post-war elite consensus, the growth in the number of groups demanding access to broadcasting and the salience of certain 'difficult' issues, such as the nuclear defence controversy, are not just isolated events in a sea of relatively untroubled calm. They combine to present an image of an institution stretched and twisted this way and that, less and less the master of its fate, more and more the victim of external forces.

The third element of this crisis in public service broadcasting is the expansion of broadcast outlets coupled with advances in broadcasting technology. New developments in broadcasting such as satellite, fibre optics cable and the video cassette recorder promise (or threaten) to increase the number of programme outlets available to the viewer, fragmenting the traditional mass audience by changing apparently ingrained viewing habits. In the longer term television will be used not just for the reception of programmes, but as an integral part of the hardware in the information technology revolution, providing a wide range of interactive services. The traditional public service organisations are having to cope as best they can with such technological changes and the different broadcasting possibilities they offer the viewer.

Not all the expansion in outlets has been the result of *technological* change. For example, the growth of privately controlled radio and television in Italy over the past few years was caused by a *legal* decision by the Constitutional Court, removing the RAI's monopoly over broadcasting at the subnational level. Moreover, in some of the countries studied in this volume the ground for the advent of the new technology has been long prepared. For instance, in both Canada and the United States cable television has been a feature of the broadcasting system for many years.

In other countries, however, including Britain, France and West Germany, the new technology, particularly cable, will not only provide competition for the traditional public service broadcasting organisations, but will also undermine many of the principles (such as balanced scheduling) which they have taken for granted as desirable and necessary. The regulations governing cable television operators in these countries are likely to be much less strict than those applied to the public service organisations, both with regard to political coverage and output generally. Potential cable viewers will have to pay more directly for the 'consumption' of the broadcast product, with subscriptions varying

depending on the range of services required by the
viewer. 'Pay as you consume' rather than the one-
off generalised licence will become a standard means
of financing television. Finally, while urban areas
will be comparatively profitable terrain for cable,
sparsely populated rural areas will not. Consequently, the number of broadcast outlets available will
vary from locality to locality. In short, the
development of cable will run counter to essential
aspects of the public service ethos. It is scarcely
surprising, then, that the public service organisations usually view the advent of cable with alarm,
since it poses a major threat to their previously
unchallenged domination of the audience.

The final element in the crisis of public
service broadcasting stems from the changing nature
of western society. The increase in leisure time,
the explosion in leisure interests and the differen-
tiation in moralities, tastes and expectations have
contributed to the fragmentation of the old-style
mass audience. The traditional public service
broadcasting organisations, restricted by statute
and hidebound by convention, have often found it
difficult in the past to respond to this growing
cultural and moral pluralism. These difficulties
can only increase in the future as audiences further
disperse among the different broadcast outlets.

What then does the future hold for broadcasting
in the countries included in this volume? The trend
would appear to be towards more numerous broadcast
outlets than in the past, including more television
stations at the local and regional level. Some of
the output of these stations will be produced
locally, particularly news and sport. At the national level with increased production costs for certain genres, such as drama, there will be greater
emphasis on imports, especially from the US, and
more coproductions. Broadcasting output will
probably be de-regulated. The consumer will have to
pay more directly for the product consumed, as
broadcasting becomes another good to be sold in the
marketplace. The emphasis will overwhelmingly be on
television as entertainment. In short, it seems
that broadcasting systems in other western countries
will increasingly conform to the US commercial model.
Reithian values are not dead. Not yet. The media
are not American. Not yet. But the omens for public service broadcasting have scarcely looked less
favourable.

Introduction

REFERENCES

1.   S. Hall, 'Broadcasting, Politics and the State: the Independence/Impartiality couplet', paper presented to the IAMCR conference, Leicester, 1976, p.6.
2.   M. Gurevitch, T. Bennett, J. Curran and J. Woollacott (eds.), *Culture, Society and the Media,* London, Methuen, 1982, p.8.

Chapter One

GREAT BRITAIN : THE END OF THE PUBLIC SERVICE
TRADITION?

Ralph Negrine

Broadcasting in Britain is at the crossroads. After
sixty years of gradual and regulated expansion, it
is now exposed to a number of external political and
technological forces which may overturn the previously generally accepted view of its role. In the
last decade the emergence of a new ideological basis
to political conflict, more open and frequent criticism of the broadcasting media from politicians and
academics, rapid social change and economic decline
have all contributed to a reassessment of the status
and functions of broadcasting in the social, cultural and political life of the nation. At the same
time, the advent of the new information technologies
poses a real threat to the broadcasting institutions
by exposing their traditionally established relationships with politics, culture and the audience
to a brash and vigorous commercial challenge.
      Two features of the traditional system seem
particularly at risk. First, British broadcasting
has in the past been heavily regulated. The broadcasting institutions of the BBC (British Broadcasting Corporation) and IBA (Independent Broadcasting
Authority) are licensed by Parliament, which has
decreed the purposes of both the publicly and commercially funded sectors along broadly similar lines.
Each has 'a duty to provide radio and television
services for the dissemination of information, education and entertainment' and to ensure and maintain
programme quality and standards.[1] This regulatory
framework has compelled both institutions to pursue
the ideal of 'public service broadcasting' rather
than respond simply to the desires of the audience
and dictates of the market. Secondly, because
broadcasting has played an important part in social,
political and cultural life, fundamental changes to
its structures have tended to emerge out of a long

15

and involved process of discussion both inside and outside Parliament. Taken together these two features have until recently resulted in a fairly precise, shared conception of the role and duties of the broadcasting media in Britain. Both features are now under threat.

While social, economic and political change will necessitate a continuing process of negotiation and accommodation between the broadcasters, politicians and the audience, the pace of the technological developments may produce an entirely new set of structures and facilities which could undermine the founding principles of the existing services and of themselves precipitate large-scale change over an extremely short period of time. The introduction of direct broadcasting by satellite and of local cable television, accompanied by an expansion in the use of video cassette recorders, may well revolutionise broadcasting without the scope and implications of that revolution being adequately debated or fully appreciated. The maintenance of the public service tradition, the relationship between the broadcasters and the state and the challenge posed by the introduction of new technology to the existing broadcasting institutions are three interrelated facets of the current concern about the structure and role of British broadcasting in the 1980s. This chapter examines each of these three aspects in turn.

THE RISE AND DECLINE OF PUBLIC SERVICE BROADCASTING

The decision of the Post Office to set up the British Broadcasting Company in 1922 as a cooperative of set manufacturers was an attempt to overcome a series of essentially technical and organisational problems: the need to satisfy set manufacturers by ensuring that all participated in the birth of broadcasting, the desire to avoid chaos on the air waves on the American scale and the wish to guarantee an efficient and satisfactory service to all listeners. It was only later that the Company came to acquire a social and political direction; in its inception it was an 'expedient solution to a technical problem.'[2]

There was, nonetheless, one distinctive element in this particular solution. This was the decision to finance the service out of a licence fee payable by all those in possession of radio sets and not out of some form of advertising revenue. The Company was thus guaranteed a yearly income and could pursue a programme policy that was developed with little regard for the wishes of the audience.

This approach to the role of broadcasting in British society was more than matched by authoritative official interpretations of its duties. Radio, many argued, was a scarce national resource and should therefore be developed and regulated in the interests of the nation. As the Crawford Committee recommended in 1926, 'the broadcasting service should be conducted by a public corporation acting as trustees for the national interest, and its status and duties should correspond with those of a public service.'[3] It is here that one can trace the foundations of public service broadcasting with its emphasis on public duty, on providing for all and on informing, educating and, not simply, entertaining. John Reith's part, both in his capacity as the Company's Managing Director and as the Director General of the Corporation, in the creation of this ideal-type model of public service broadcasting has been amply documented and he was undoubtedly able to exploit such thinking in a way not equalled elsewhere or since.[4]

In order to ensure that broadcasting was ultimately accountable to Parliament and at the same time free from direct government control in its day-to-day affairs, power was delegated to a broadcasting Authority to run the service along the lines decreed by Parliament. The Authority, 'a body of people acting as trustees for the public interest',[5] does not have executive control over broadcasting but in theory acts as a means of distancing broadcasting from government. This arrangement has been used for the BBC since 1927 when it was set up under Royal Charter and for the commercial broadcasting sector from 1954 onwards.

Thus, the Governors of the BBC - who are constitutionally the BBC - have to ensure that it is run in the public interest by reviewing the work of the institution. In the past, this has involved both reprimanding broadcasters and offering them support when under attack. This dual role, which contains glaring contradictions, also applies to the IBA whose duties include the allocation of broadcasting franchises to the regional television companies and local radio stations, the building of transmitters and the overall supervision of broadcasting output in the commercial sector. Since both bodies are appointed by, or on the advice of, government they have come to be seen either as a buffer between the state and the broadcasters or as an indirect mechanism by which the state can exert control over broadcasting. The membership and strengths or weaknesses of these two authorities, as well as their working relationship with those in executive control of broadcasting, have obvious and significant repercussions for broadcasters and their autonomy.

The state's ultimate authority over broadcasting exemplifies one of the deficiencies of 'public service broadcasting', though paradoxically Reith would not have been able to develop the BBC as he did, had he not had the full support of the state. His vision of broadcasting which was based on four major principles - assured sources of funding, the brute force of monopoly, the public service motive and national coverage - could not have been put into practice unless it had received the tacit approval and support of the state. When faced with threats to its broadcasting monopoly or to its programme policy from, say, either wireless exchanges or overseas commercial radio stations, it was only natural that Reith should turn to the state to underwrite the BBC's monopoly. The 1920s and 1930s provide many examples of appeals to the state and Reith's large measure of success in retaining the broadcasting monopoly.[6]

This dependence on the state was well appreciated by Reith. Though it created severe problems at times of crisis, it was the price to be paid for pursuing high ideals in matters of broadcasting. With domestic competition effectively prohibited, the BBC became the main instrument of broadcasting in Britain. Reith developed it into:

> A kind of domestic diplomatic service, representing the British - or what he saw as the best of the British - to the British. BBC culture, like BBC standard English, was not peculiar to itself but an intellectual ambience composed out of the values, standards and beliefs of the professional middle class, especially that part educated at Oxford and Cambridge.[7]

Reith's departure from the BBC in 1938 and the expansion of the BBC television service from 1945 onwards did little to undermine these established practices and principles. The continuity in British broadcasting stems in part from the BBC's broadcast monopoly in radio and television from 1922 to 1954 and it also owes much to the commitment of the broadcasters to the ideals of public service broadcasting.

Nevertheless, as the above quote makes clear, there was much dissatisfaction with the BBC's total control of broadcasting and its output. All previous attempts to introduce alternative broadcasting services had met with failure, but the election of a Conservative government in 1951 saw the start of a concerted campaign in favour of commercial television.[8] After much powerful lobbying the Television Act was passed in 1954, setting up the Independent Television Authority to supervise a federal structure of commercially funded television companies, each one serving a different region. To offset the allegedly harmful effects of sponsorship or reliance on major advertisers, a system of spot-advertising was introduced. This intervention was seen as a way of minimising harmful and unwanted practices in commercially funded broadcasting systems and of protecting the public service ideals of British broadcasting.

The introduction of commercial television, even within the public service framework, directly threatened the position and security of the BBC. The immediate popularity and novelty of the former's programmes forced the BBC to review its output and made it aware of the need to survive in an increasingly competitive environment. As long as the BBC had remained a monopoly, television viewers had had no programme choices nor, for that matter, could there be any dispute as to which institution should be allocated the television licence fee. Independent Television (ITV) undermined the BBC's historical sense of privilege and security. With less than 30% of the national audience - it went down as low as 27% in the 1950s - the BBC's position as the main instrument of broadcasting in the UK was clearly threatened, as were its claims to the full licence fee. Since the early 1960s, therefore, the BBC has aimed to reach a 50% share of the audience as a means of supporting its claims to the licence fee and ensuring its continued survival.

With the two institutions in competition for viewers, their programming policies converged to meet audience demands. Indeed, many critics have since maintained that the process of competition eroded the differences between a commercial and a publicly funded television service as the BBC became more market-oriented.[9] Further additions to the existing radio and television services would become deeply contested as efforts were made to detach them from this duopoly. As the case study of

Channel 4 amply demonstrates (see pp.25-27 below),
there was a determined attempt on the part of many
groups in society to keep it out of the competitive
struggle between the two giants of broadcasting.

Though some of the effects of competition were
beneficial, others were not. The process of competition stretched the finite resources of the BBC
and was to highlight one of the major differences
between the two structures and their sources of
funding. While commercial television could meet its
costs out of a pool of advertising revenue that was
continually growing even if only at the rate of inflation, the BBC had to finance its expenditure out
of a licence revenue that was fixed at long intervals and depended on government approval for its
increases. As a result, the licence fee was too
often seen as a political issue since increases -
albeit much needed by the BBC - were believed to be
an electoral liability. In recent years, the
licence fee has been fixed at three yearly intervals
and this has reduced, though not eliminated, its
political sensitiveness.

In the 1960s broadcasting slowly began to
change. A new television channel was allocated to
the BBC (BBC 2) in 1964 and by the end of the decade
it was joined by a large number of local radio
stations, commercially and publicly funded under the
supervision of the IBA and BBC respectively. In
addition to these important structural alterations,
the nature and content of broadcasting was also
changing. Indeed, the 1960s have come to epitomise
'public service broadcasting in its finest hour of
liberation',[10] at its most provocative, irreverent
and challenging.

It is possible to identify three processes at
work during this period of transition. First, the
structural changes identified above were acknow-
ledgements of the heterogenous nature of the national audience and, in themselves, vehicles to serve
and exploit sections of it. BBC 2, for example, was
a 'high brow' service aiming to attract a different
audience from the more down-market BBC 1 and ITV,
while many of the new radio stations, such as Radio
1, were pop music stations directed at the burgeoning youth market. Secondly, there was a growing
feeling that the Britain of the 1960s was socially,
politically and economically different from previous
decades and that the broadcasting services had somehow failed to reflect this. Lastly, broadcasting
practices, whether in politics or drama, were often
criticised for their inability to cope with these

changes or explain them. They had been designed in, and for, a different era and were now inappropriate. Although the first process opened up broadcasting structurally and culturally, to new voices and new needs, the last two were by far the most significant since they exposed broadcasting to major criticisms and were to form the basis of future debates about broadcasting in Britain.

Of these last two processes, the social and political changes were the most difficult to pinpoint or quantify largely because one was looking at trends and sometimes isolated incidents within a broad historical sweep. Nonetheless, the perception of change became a cornerstone of contemporary critiques of the media and society. Even the Annan Committee on the Future of Broadcasting - the only committee appointed by the Home Secretary in the last two decades to look at this subject - found it appropriate to devote a whole section to 'The Change in the Climate of Opinion' in Britain. It observed that:

> The new vision of life (from the 1960s on-
> wards) reflected divisions within society,
> divisions between classes, the generations and
> the sexes, between north and south, between the
> provinces and London, between pragmatists and
> ideologues ...11

One immediate result was that in contrast to the work of the previous Committee of Enquiry[12] in 1960 the

> questions which the public were now asking
> about broadcasting were vastly different from
> those which concerned that Committee. They
> were more critical, more hostile and more
> political.[13]

This catalogue of divisions, the questioning of society which it gave rise to, the increasing lack of confidence and self-doubt and the 'erosion of cohesion and unity'[14] were now important features of the British scene. The 'ideals of middle class cul-ture'[15] which had informed British broadcasting in the past were now at odds with a divided Britain.

Other commentators have similarly remarked on these changes and their consequences. Asa Briggs, the foremost historian of British broadcasting, has noted how changes in society - and other events such as professionalisation and unionisation within the

BBC - made 'governing the BBC' more difficult in the
1970s than at any other period.[16] This view was
echoed by Alasdair Milne (Managing Director, BBC TV
and Director General designate) who remarked that
the prescriptions for broadcasting set out in previous eras - even only a matter of ten years ago -
were of little value in a rapidly changing social
and political environment.[17]

Changes, for example, in the political system
(and one could just as easily concentrate on changes
in British society and social mores during the same
period) were seemingly making the task of the broadcasters more difficult than hitherto. For instance,
throughout the early years of radio and television
broadcasting, the two-party system had reigned
supreme, with power changing hands at frequent intervals. In such a political context broadcasters
could comfortably balance opposites and feel able to
survive in the middle-ground. However, the practice
of judiciously balancing the two major political
parties could no longer be adequately employed when
the polarisation and fragmentation of British politics had undermined the legitimacy of this middle-
ground. The BBC had tended to gravitate towards the
centre and towards consensus in terms of politics
and values; in fact, it took a perverse pride in
being accused by both the Labour and Conservative
parties of favouring the other, in the belief that
by pleasing neither on occasions it achieved a high
degree of impartiality. By the 1970s this impartiality and the Corporation's occupation of the
middle-ground were suspect. In 1981 Milne admitted
that the BBC was

> besieged from both sides by people who feel
> that there is no middle-ground. The Liberal-
> SDP Alliance now seems to be seizing that, but
> from the traditional political parties there
> has apparently in the last four or five years
> been a tendency to argue that we move to
> extremes and the BBC may be left representing
> something which may not exist.[18]

Though Milne was making specific references to the
birth of a new political party, the Social Democratic Party - itself evidence of political change - he
was acknowledging the new 'climate of opinion' and
its effects.

A variety of political changes called into
question the traditional working ethos of the broadcasting institutions. The fragmentation of the

22

political centre, the breakdown in the post-war
elite consensus regarding the management of the
mixed economy along Keynesian lines and an increasingly ideological response from both Right and Left
to political and economic problems in the 1970s were
all part of this changed climate of political debate. By the late 1970s the modest economic growth,
affluence and full employment policies of the 1950s
and 60s had given way to stagnation, inflation and
an unprecedented increase in the post-war level of
unemployment. The election in 1979 of the Thatcher-
led Conservative government signalled a break from
the commonly accepted reference points of British
politics since 1945.

At the same time as the two main political
parties moved towards their respective extremes, new
issues and forces made their appearance in British
politics. The rise of Celtic nationalism in Scot-
land and Wales in the 1970s was an early indication
of the structural weaknesses of the two-party
system. Moreover, the response of the traditional
parties to the phenomenon of nationalism was not
reducible to the classic left-right dichotomy. The
nationalist issue cut across party lines. So too
did other issues forcing themselves on to the political agenda. Britain's membership of the EEC,
government policy on Northern Ireland and the debate
regarding the maintenance of Britain's nuclear de-
terrent were other examples of issues where new
lines of division were superimposed on the Conserva-
tive-Labour split, cutting across the established
two-party cleavage. At the same time a multiplicity
of social and political groups, including ecologists,
feminists, ethnic minorities and unilateral nuclear
disarmers among others, demanded access to broadcasting both to put their case and to demonstrate
their legitimacy. Though seeking to stem this unwanted tide, the broadcast media were compelled, if
not always successfully, to include more issues and
groups in political debate.

In this new climate, the public service concepts of balance, impartiality and objectivity in
political coverage proved increasingly inadequate.
In practice, they failed to reflect the political
spectrum in its entirety and tended to exclude or
marginalise all those who strayed outside the
accepted central boundaries of political argument.
The notion of balance was too narrow to explore
divergent opinions and their subtleties. It necessarily divided and exaggerated differences for the
sake of political television. Similar criticisms

have been levelled against the notions of impartiality and objectivity. By interpreting events from
within the processes of parliamentary government and
through the eyes of its representatives, television
easily silences those who dissent.

Such criticisms of the broadcasting media became rather commonplace in the 1970s. As academic
interest in the field of media studies grew, so the
critiques of media output became more sophisticated
and wide-ranging. All areas were now exposed to the
academic scalpel, which revealed broadcasting's
partial and incomplete account of power, social
change and conflict in British society. Broadcast
output was alleged to misrepresent black people[19]
and radical groups[20]; its news content was accused
of bias against the political Left, the trade union
movement and the working class in general[21]; and its
coverage of Northern Ireland was at best satisfactory.[22] In other words, there were significant
omissions which produced a distorted picture of
society. Claims to impartiality, objectivity and
even fairness were criticised as unjustified since
they were not fulfilled in television's output.
Although the broadcasters vehemently denied these
accusations, they recognised the need to respond and
so became more aware of the shifting political environment and its consequences for political broadcasting.[23]

These changes in the socio-political system,
together with the academic criticisms of the broadcasting institutions, highlight the rather difficult
position which they have come to occupy. The BBC
and IBA remained in control over the means of mass
communications, but those whose work or views they
had long ignored were now clamouring for access. The
artist resented the duopoly for its restricted and
middle-of-the-road media fare and the political
activist for its narrow political outlook, while
professional guardians of the nation's moral welfare
objected to the broadcasting institutions' alleged
irreverence and irresponsible use of power. However,
the institutions of the 1970s were too rigidly set
within the competing duopoly to be able to meet
fully the demands made upon them. Nor were they
able to serve new needs in radically different ways.
Television was still too scarce a resource - and
perhaps too important a political weapon - to be
granted the freedom to exploit the richness and
diversity of contemporary life.

The challenge to broadcasting in the 1970s was
to create new vehicles for a different era. It is

for this reason that the case of Channel 4 is of interest, since it is a good illustration of the way new types of services can be designed to cater for needs previously overlooked in the competitive struggle for the mass audience.

During the ten or so years leading up to the opening of Channel 4 in 1982, there was much discussion about this fourth and last available over-the-air national television channel. The opposition to a commercial channel was based on the fear that it would only 'complete the symmetrical strait-jacket of broadcasting in Britain and continue it forever: two public institutions would each supervise two channels and they would compete, two by two, for parallel audiences in perpetuity.'24

Successive governments appeared to accept the objections to the proposals for a second commercial television service and the 1974 Annan Committee of Enquiry into the Future of Broadcasting saw those proposals as both inappropriate and undesirable. The Committee recommended that the fourth channel should allow for diversity, new ideas and experimentation. It advocated the setting up of an Open Broadcasting Authority whose aim would be to satisfy new needs and whose existence 'would lead to better programmes, more diverse programmes, more socially useful programmes and more enjoyable programmes for hundreds and thousands of people'.25

In proposing this Authority, the Committee was attempting to come to terms with changes in society and in the climate of opinion. It was also trying to satisfy a whole series of demands that were being made of the broadcasting institutions: that they should be more accountable, more open to outsiders and more representative of a widening range of social and political views. As these demands suggest, the campaign for a new type of broadcasting service was informed by the intellectuals' and professionals' critiques of broadcasting. As always, the general public 'hardly made any suggestions for the use of the fourth channel'.26

In the event, the 1980 Broadcasting Bill, drafted by the newly elected Conservative government, allocated the fourth channel to the IBA, the regulatory body for the commercial sector, on the grounds that a new authority would either make demands on the public purse or have to compete with the existing ITV services for advertising funds.27 The IBA would regulate Channel 4 and ensure that its output would 'contain a suitable proportion of matter calculated to appeal to tastes and interests not

generally catered for by Service 1 (i.e. ITV 1)'.[28]
Unlike the ITV 1 system, Channel Four would act as a
commissioning agent and not as a production company.
Its output would come from independent producers (up
to 35%), major ITV companies (up to 40%), regional
ITV companies (up to 20%), ITN (15%) and from
foreign sources. Wales was to have its own version
of Channel Four, a Welsh language service SC4.

Channel Four's funding was so organised as to
enable it to survive in the broadcasting marketplace
as a minority service. It is funded by the existing
commercial television companies through a system of
subscriptions; in 1982-3 Channel 4's total revenue
from these sources was about £100m. In return, the
ITV companies sell the advertising time on Channel
4 in their own regions and retain the advertising
revenue. If, as was likely, the subscriptions exceeded the advertising revenue, the ITV companies
were given permission to charge these losses against
the advertising levy which they pay annually to the
Exchequer. In effect, their losses would be reim-
bursed out of public funds. This method of funding
supposedly insulates Channel 4 from the direct pressures of advertisers in search of large audiences,
but it has left it exposed to pressure from its
subscribers, the ITV companies. On paper then the
plans for Channel 4 were intricate and ingenious.
In practice, there was one basic problem, namely,
could a national television service aimed at minority audiences - the 'tastes and interests not
generally catered for' - survive in a highly commercial sector? Since the size of the audience is
critical for a commercial television medium, would
there be enough viewers to justify Channel 4 both
financially and culturally?

Executives at Channel 4 expected the audience
to grow slowly but reach a 10% share of the total
audience - equivalent to BBC 2's share - within a
few years. This view was premised on the assumption
that the ITV companies would be willing and ungrud-
ging subscribers to Channel 4. It was possible, as
some companies made clear, that this funding would
be in jeopardy if their own problems were aggravated
by the subscription charge or, equally likely, if
the subscription charge reduced their own funds for
production.

Channel 4 has survived the first year of its
existence though not without considerable criticism
and heart searching. It has been criticised for its
programmes and their quality, for their controversial nature and also for the small audiences that

they reach. The major problem remains the low
audience rating and this has produced pressure from
the ITV companies that it should popularise its programmes, though, as Channel 4 executives point out,
it is not that an audience does not exist but that
it does not exist as a mass audience created for the
benefit of the advertisers. In April 1983, for
instance, Channel 4 executives claimed that over the
period of one month, 35 million viewers turned to
Channel 4 at some time.

How Channel 4 will resolve this problem is too
early to say - it needs an audience to survive but a
mass audience would run counter to its philosophy.
Whether pressure will eventually force it to move in
the direction of mass audiences will depend on its
attraction to advertisers who are in any case not
willing to pay the rates commensurate with a mass
audience television service.

Channel Four can count on many successes and
failures across a whole range of programmes. Since
broadcasting institutions are constantly evolving,
it is likely that there will be a continuous review
of its position and financial viability, and some
fine tuning. To date, however, it remains an
attempt to open up broadcasting services to those
many voices which previously lacked regular access
to the medium of television. In many ways it represents a latterday attempt to emulate the rather
battered Reithian ideals of public service broadcasting.

BROADCASTING, POLITICS AND THE STATE

Television is now probably the single most important
medium for the communication of political information. For many, it is the crucial source of
information about the outside world. But its importance also derives from its role in industrial
societies. Unlike many other institutions, television is implicated in processes of change: it is
both the creator and the product of change in
society. In the field of politics, its treatment
and coverage of war, elections or nuclear arms has
had enormous consequences for political organisation and behaviour. Similarly its treatment of
social issues has provoked many questions about its
role in creating, and not merely reflecting, a changing society.

The growing awareness of the nature of the
television medium and its far reaching, if unquanti-
fiable, effects has contributed to a major re-

assessment of its work. Television's output has
ceased to be 'a mirror' of society; a subtler view
sees it as a

> heavily selected interpretation of events, one
> which structures reality for us, which shapes
> and frames a world for us to inhabit and accept
> as real and legitimated, one which sets the
> agenda within which ... we are led to discuss
> the terms of our lives.[29]

By raising these issues, it has become possible to
see television as one of the core political and
ideological institutions of any society. It has
also opened the way to a fuller analysis of its
work: an analysis of its agenda-setting function,
its part in re-enforcing cultural norms and, most
crucially, its work in relation 'to those who rule
dominant institutions...'.[30] For if the broadcast
media are not reflecting some already achieved consensus, or given 'reality', but tend to select and
reproduce those definitions of 'reality' which
favour and legitimate existing structures in society,
then their work is part of a process of legitimation
and consensus formation.

This major reconceptualisation of the role of
television has made its political output, that is,
mainly news and current affairs programmes, a highly
controversial and contested area. It has raised
questions about television's capacity and willingness to accurately reflect the wide range of views
present in contemporary Britain; instead, it has
highlighted its prior commitment, and allegiance, to
a specific political perspective and its treatment
of all political issues from within the ideological
framework of a liberal democratic polity.

One effect of this analysis has been to shift
attention away from specific fields of enquiry and
to a closer examination of the location of the
broadcasting institutions in the political system.
A central issue here is the relationship of the
broadcasting institutions to the state and the ways
in which this sets real limits to the work and
autonomy of the broadcasters. Since these institutions have 'a responsibility to (the) political
process and political environment, not merely to
serve it but to sustain it...',[31] their freedom of
action and interpretation are circumscribed. There
are certain limits and constraints which are set by
the terms of the relationship between the state and
the broadcasting institutions and by the articu-

lation of professional practices within that political system.

In exploring these broader issues in the relationship between broadcasting and politics, it becomes necessary to abandon the simpler views of the location of broadcasting in British society. Concepts such as 'pressure and resistance' and even 'autonomy' are inadequate as explanations of the work of these institutions. As Stuart Hall has argued:

> The question of "external influence" (on broadcasting) is a thoroughly inadequate way of framing the problem. It is predicated on a model of broadcasting which takes at face value its formal and editorial autonomy: external influences are then seen as illegitimately encroaching upon this area of freedom ... the real relationship between broadcasting, power and ideology is thoroughly mystified by such a model.[32]

Yet the model criticised has had widespread currency in Britain because of a combination of deficient alternative conceptual frameworks and much anecdotal evidence which continually breathes life into it. Thus, the many instances when the broadcasting institutions have stood their ground in the face of 'illegitimate encroachment' lend support to the cruder forms of analysis. The conflict surrounding the BBC's treatment of the 1956 Suez Crisis and such programmes as *Yesterday's Men* (BBC, 1971) and *The Question of Ulster* (BBC, 1972)[34] all contribute to the 'pressure and resistance' model by demonstrating the ability of the broadcasting institutions to withstand pressure from governments. Similarly, because the Home Secretary's power of veto over all television programmes - a power contained in the broadcasting licences - has never been used, it is still possible to claim, if disingenuously, that the power 'has always been treated as a reserve power and the Corporation (i.e. the BBC) has enjoyed, and enjoys, complete freedom in the handling of its programme activities'.[35] In this way, everyday compromises are marked by some notable and exceptional instances of resistance.

But as studies of the relationship between broadcasting and the state demonstrate, it has never been necessary to exercise this power of veto because the broadcasting institutions themselves are well aware of the practical limits to their

theoretically wide freedom. As one student of the
BBC has written, 'the kind of arrangement arrived at
between the government and the BBC at the time of
the General Strike (in 1926) provided the mould for
the kind of compromise solution and understanding
which has prevailed since then.'[36]

What is this 'solution and compromise' and why
does it remain unchanged? The answers are to be
found in an examination of the broadcasting institutions' location within the political system and the
broadcasting practices that grow out of this.

The broadcasting institutions have always defined their position as being within the liberal
democratic political system and, therefore, they
endorse its main principles. Despite having to
acknowledge and reproduce alternative and radical
viewpoints in order to ensure that most views are,
to an extent, represented they recognise that they
are 'part of the nation, and the constitutional
creation of Parliament'. The BBC 'could not pretend
to be impartial between the maintenance and dis-
solution of the nation. Nor could it be impartial
about those things which Parliament had decided
were unacceptable by making them illegal.'[37]

This statement of the BBC's location within the
political system - and it is one with which the IBA
concurs - exposes the contradictions inherent in the
practices of broadcast journalism. Though claiming
to be 'impartial' and 'objective', the BBC nonetheless sees itself as 'an institution within the constitution'[38] - the phrase used by Reith in 1926 to
explain his actions over the General Strike. Claims
to detachment and disinterestedness in the context
of controversy therefore rest uneasily next to a
commitment to the existing social and political
order.

The consequences of this commitment have long
been apparent to those who persistently question the
very nature of that political system. Whereas
parliamentary forms of political activity fall
easily within the purview of the broadcasting institutions, extra-parliamentary political behaviour
appears both illegitimate and a threat to parliamentary democracy. It is then not surprising that many
groups in society, most notably trade unions and
minority groups, feel aggrieved by their treatment
in the media.

Broadcasting has also accepted Parliament as
its natural pole and has interpreted its task as one
of reproducing 'a picture of the political discourse
dominated by Parliament. (it) is ... not part of a

"fourth estate" ... but rather operates impartial
brokerage within a prevailing political system.'39
And, despite numerous lapses, it has attempted to
apply an even hand mainly in relation to the major
protagonists in the political system. The resultant
practice of balancing opposites, perhaps the only
satisfactory way of handling governments and their
oppositions in Parliament, has come to be seen as an
operational solution to the need for impartiality in
all matters of political broadcasting.

Such practices are linked, in turn, to certain
rules and agreements which govern political broadcasting by Ministers of State and political parties
during and outside of election periods. Many of
these rules and agreements, set out in the late
1940s in a BBC aide-memoire in order to define the
terms of the relationship between politicians and
the broadcast (radio) media, remain relevant today.
Their origin is of no specific interest here though
it is worth noting how they were accepted by the BBC
television service (and in due course commercial
television) to become key practices and points of
reference.

Writing about the 1950s programme *In the News*,
Goldie recalled how attempts to achieve some balance
between the political forces failed to please them.
Instead, they put pressure on programme makers so as
'to ensure that some solid party men were included
in the ... (programme) team'.40 As she later observed, 'we (BBC producers) were under the general
obligation to be fair and impartial. We interpreted
this as meaning that we ought to preserve an overall
political balance...'41

At times, these attempts to preserve a political balance create their own difficulties. In the
run up to the June 1983 General Election, the broadcasting institutions were criticised for their
willingness to include the Social Democratic Party
in their election programmes. The SDP had been
created in 1980 by a number of defectors from the
Labour and Conservative Parliamentary parties. Its
national electoral support was unknown since it was
formed during the life of a Parliament, though
opinion polls rated its popularity very high. This
situation did not fit easily into that governed by
the rules of election broadcasting which allocated
time to the different political parties according to
the votes cast for them in past elections, the number of seats contested, the number of MPs each had
and so on.

Critics of the SDP (and the media) felt that

its enormous popularity and coverage were the result of its attraction for journalists who favoured its middle-of-the-road, pragmatic approach to politics. Rather than seeing it as a clear rejection of class politics, they saw the SDP as the creation of the media. In such an atmosphere it was unlikely that there would be general agreement between the political parties as to the allocation of broadcasting time between them. The SDP - now in Alliance with the Liberals - was hungry for media exposure, particularly because it appreciated its value and importance for maintaining support, but the major political parties were unwilling to have their share reduced. They saw no reason to treat a party that had never fought a general election as an equal.

In the event, a compromise solution was struck with the two major parties and the Alliance dividing up the total time devoted to election broadcasts in the ratio of 5:5:4, as opposed to 5:5:3 in past elections. The importance of this compromise lies in the fact that the broadcasting institutions forced the decision on the political parties. This is in the tradition of party political broadcasting where the broadcasters take the initiative and offer the parties media exposure. In this case, as on previous occasions, the broadcasting institutions had interpreted their task as one of ensuring that there is a degree of formal equality between the major parliamentary contestants and guaranteeing the proper functioning of the democratic and electoral processes.

The key to understanding these practices and other rules or agreements is that they reflect, particularly in the case of the BBC, what it has imposed on itself in the past while also reasserting their continuing importance in the present. Indeed, the Royal Charter of the BBC and the Television Acts for Independent Television contain little that relates directly to programme policies apart from several general injunctions to ensure due impartiality, balance and fairness. Their translation into actual practices was undertaken by specific institutions in specific political contexts. These mirror the self-definition of a broadcasting institution within a certain political system and the repeated use of particular practices tends to reinforce this self-definition.

Broadcasters are aware of their location within the political system and are sensitive to the views of those who wield political power, since their comments or criticisms cannot be easily ignored.

This sensitivity can produce a timidity which results in submission in the face of threats. The
last decade has witnessed numerous instances when
broadcasters have readily responded to calls, mainly
from politicians, to alter or delete programme
items. In addition to a catalogue of programmes on
Northern Ireland, programmes about Zimbabwe, Welsh
nationalism and state secrets have also been affected. Even more recently, in January 1983, the
Prime Minister's press secretary warned the BBC that
it could face 'incalculable damage'[42] if it did not
share its film of Mrs. Thatcher's visit to the
Falklands with the commercial television news
service. As one BBC journalist recently remarked,
'It's getting to the stage where we don't dare upset
authority or the establishment in any form - not
just the government but other governments, even individual politicians.'[43]
     One of the root causes of conflict in the
relationship described above is that the broadcasting institutions do not - and perhaps cannot -
always passively reproduce the agendas and definitions of 'reality' favoured by those in power to the
total exclusion of other perspectives. For broadcasters, the avoidance of conflict with those who
rule amounts to the abdication of their responsibilities and professional duties as journalists.
Furthermore, their work is to a large extent premised on such professional imperatives as 'news
values' and these cannot be ignored without a loss
of credibility. This helps to explain the existence
of many programmes or programme items which create
problems for broadcasters. Whether their concern is
nuclear power or nuclear arms, those who dissent
from the actions of the state may need to be represented. When the form of their dissent is dramatic,
e.g. demonstrations, they are even more newsworthy
and so more likely to obtain media coverage. The
result of this is that broadcasters and 'those who
rule' are imprisoned in an unequal relationship
which inevitably produces tensions.
     There are two notable examples of the many
forces at play in this tense relationship. During
the 1956 Suez Crisis and the 1982 Falklands Conflict
broadcasters attempted to represent fairly those who
dissented from the actions of the governments of the
day. In both instances, the BBC was heavily criticised for its actions. Clearly, those in political
power are reluctant to devolve full control over the
most powerful medium of mass communication to those
who have the power to oppose them or cast doubts on

their claims. Both examples illustrate not only the actions of the broadcasters, but also the mechanisms of control over broadcasting.

The 1956 Suez Crisis offers possibly the best post-war example of BBC resistance to overbearing pressure from a government. During the crisis both its internal radio and television services and its external radio services came under attack from a Prime Minister who felt that at times of conflict, especially foreign conflict, opposition and dissenting views ought not to be broadcast. The duty of the external broadcasting services was to present a united front to the outside world.

The BBC, on the other hand, did not feel able to distinguish between internal and external needs. It could not abandon its attempts to be consistent in its internal and external news and current affairs programmes: if there were major divisions of opinion in the nation then they ought to be broadcast. But the government saw the matter differently and, in an effort to silence criticism, it placed one of its liaison officers at the BBC (radio) and also took action to reduce its financial help to the BBC's external services.[44]

In television, the position was somewhat different. Political opposition to the government's actions had been incorporated into a number of current affairs programmes and towards the end of the crisis the leader of the Labour opposition was able to respond to the Prime Minister's second ministerial (television) broadcast. The BBC's insistence that at times of controversy and disagreement between the major political parties each should be granted some access to the broadcast media allowed a more open discussion of policy to take place. Needless to say, this stand exposed it to considerable pressure and for a time its own long-term survival was in doubt. Nevertheless, the contrast with the BBC's debacle in 1926 when the government of the day exercised direct editorial control over its radio output is very sharp.

There is, however, a danger in exaggerating the importance of the Suez Crisis as an instance when broadcasting asserted its formal independence from government. Though the BBC did withstand many attempts at intervention, it is important to take into account those circumstances which permit an institution to retain a degree of formal independence. Unlike the events surrounding the Falklands conflict in 1982, there was violent political disagreement over the Suez Crisis both in, and outside,

Parliament. There was no single acceptable solution
to the crisis and hence no single definition of the
'national interest'. With an opposition party
offering an alternative view of, and solution to,
the crisis it would have been difficult not to grant
it access to the media. Indeed, the BBC's rules of
political broadcasting were designed with the purpose of ensuring that such opposition could not be
ignored or overlooked.

The BBC's handling of the crisis was an attempt
to guarantee access to the major political parties
when there was disagreement. It was upholding the
practices it had helped formulate a decade or so
earlier. Clearly, had there been no political party
in opposition to the government's actions or widespread disquiet nationally and in the press, the BBC
would have found it much more difficult to pursue an
impartial line. The reproduction of the parliamentary struggle, though it does expose broadcasting to
numerous threats, does not ultimately place it in
mortal danger since it is only balancing competing
and legitimated parliamentary views. So long as it
employs those general principles which had been
established in order to govern the relationship
between broadcasters and the political parties in
Britain, its independence is secured.

In contrast, during the Falklands conflict
there was little parliamentary opposition to the
government's decision to send a task force to the
South Atlantic. The opposition Labour party was in
broad agreement with the Conservative government and
it was left to a small group of MPs to voice criticisms. It was therefore likely that with so little
parliamentary opposition or opposition in the
national press, any attempt to question the wisdom
of British policy would prove immensely difficult.
Two BBC programmes came in for major criticism: one,
a current affairs programme, *Panorama* (May 10 1982);
the other, a news programme *Newsnight* (May 8 1982).
The *Panorama* programme was intended to be a minority
view of the conflict, while the *Newsnight* programme
merely maintained an air of objectivity by using
such phrases as 'British troops' and 'the British'
and not, to the chagrin of its critics, 'our troops'
and 'we'.[45]

Both programmes provoked an immediate reaction.
A jingoistic Fleet Street accused the BBC of being
unpatriotic and these accusations were repeated by
the Conservative party in Parliament. As the Prime
Minister stated on May 6 1982,

> Many people are very concerned indeed that the
> case for our British forces is not being put
> over fully and effectively. I understand that
> there are times when it seems that we and the
> Argentines are being treated almost as equals
> and almost on a neutral basis.[46]

The subsequent row between the government and the
BBC left it in no doubt as to its duties at times
of conflict. As in 1956, it could not question
policies; its duty was to report the actions and
sayings of the government in the best possible light.
   The most curious aspect of the Falklands episode is that the BBC overwhelmingly accepted the
British government's case. That certainly is the
evidence contained in leaked confidential minutes of
the BBC news and current affairs team.[47] The furore
was probably the result of two unpopular programmes
being transmitted at a time when British troops had
suffered losses and morale was waning. The BBC's
behaviour, then, was perhaps not as extreme as its
detractors make out. There is much evidence to
support the view that its coverage of the conflict
was based largely on official sources of information
and minimally on public feeling or public debate.
Unlike the Suez Crisis, the BBC did not even have
the national press with which to highlight criticisms of government policy. When Parliament and the
press is at one, the BBC lacks any external points
of reference with which to present a different view
of a particular situation. As with its new practices more generally, it merely reacts to and reports
events.
   These two major national crises also demonstrate the general reluctance to tamper explicitly
and publicly with the freedoms that the broadcasting
institutions allegedly enjoy. They do not disguise,
however, the readiness with which those in authority
express their displeasure and this, of itself, can
act as a brake against future indiscretions. Calls
to the broadcasters 'to put their houses in order'[48]
- the phrase used by the Prime Minister after the
BBC filmed the IRA in Carrickmore, Northern Ireland
- fulfil a number of immediate and future functions.
They question the widsom of existing practices,
define the limits of broadcasting's freedom, warn of
possible consequences and usually have direct
effects on future programming policies. In these
ways, traditional and established practices are
maintained and reinforced and those that are likely
to cause problems discouraged. This (sometimes)

subtle, informal and indirect process of control retains and lends support to the public image of autonomous broadcasting institutions. As Reith wrote in his diary during the General Strike, 'they (the members of the government) will not say that we are to a considerable extent controlled and they make me take the onus of turning people down.'49

The relationship between broadcasting, politics and the state is necessarily fraught and made up of compromises and accommodations on the part of the broadcasters and the politicians. The means of voicing displeasure or exercising censure may be different today than in the past, but the underlying motivations remain unchanged. Nor will they be different in the future.

It is therefore unlikely that any crisis in broadcasting will be the direct outcome of political tensions or recriminations. Though not unfeasible, the consequences of destroying a largely credible and politically important means of mass communication may far outweigh the cost of tolerating an occasionally irritating medium. It is, rather, in an *indirect* way that the political process currently poses threats to broadcasting. By encouraging a certain form of technological development, the present government may propel the broadcasting institutions into a situation where their supremacy and established relationship to the audience, culture and politics are severely undermined.

BROADCASTING IN THE NEW AUDIOVISUAL ERA

It was argued in the introduction to this chapter that the traditional method of regulating British broadcasting and the established view of its role in society were now the object of a number of direct and indirect challenges. As Britain enters a new audiovisual era in the 1980s, it is becoming clear that the traditional method and established view, both of which have a long, impressive and enviable record of success, are under attack. While historically broadcasting has always been in a process of transition, the contemporary attack on the system and the public service values it seeks to embody poses a new set of problems to the corporate structures of the existing broadcasting institutions.

A broad historical perspective of broadcasting in Britain would reinforce this view as well as highlighting two important points. First, more often than not, it is the BBC rather than commercial television which is under threat. A corporate

structure running two television channels, four
national and twenty local radio services cannot
easily fund itself out of a licence fee that fails
to keep up with increasing costs and inflation. New
services, rising costs and the chill wind of competition for viewers all contribute to instability.
Adaptation and accommodation then become a fundamental part of the art of management. While commercial television is itself not immune from similar
problems (e.g. the recent fall in audience ratings
due to an increased use of video recorders has sent
shivers down the spines of commercial television
executives as advertisers demand a reduction in
advertising rates), it is the BBC which is in the
front line.

Secondly, and more significantly, systems of
communication need to be analysed as evolutionary
structures. Too often, commentators and critics
have interpreted media institutions as static and
immune from change. Such a perspective not only
distorts the real history of broadcasting but also
the necessarily evolutionary nature of organisations
that exist in the public domain. Moreover, to argue
as some have done that the BBC needs to be protected
from, say, the ravages of the commercialism of cable
television is to condone acts of undiscriminating
preservation. Such moves would fail to distinguish
the good from the bad and may prevent the incorpor-
ation of new elements so as to create new systems of
communication.

The origins of the present threat to the established broadcasting order can be traced directly to
the election of the Conservative government in 1979.
Central to its approach to governing Britain in the
1980s has been the belief in competition and the
power of 'market forces' to determine the shape of
economic structures. This very same approach has
been applied to the new information technologies,
and it is through the government's pursuit of these
technologies that the established broadcasting institutions now face some formidable competitors. By
'opening up' broadcasting to market forces, the
government has sought to expose previously insulated
and regulated institutions to competition mainly
from cable television, whose power they may be unable to challenge.

The new information technologies will replace
scarcity in broadcasting with plenty. Optical
fibres will enormously increase the potential of
cable television systems, satellites will increase
the number of national and international services

available and the convergence of the new information technologies will completely revolutionise the nature and potential of the television screen. By increasing the range of television services available from the present four to a possible twenty or more, cable would easily undermine the duopoly which was founded on the principle of scarcity. Furthermore, by splintering the audience, it could damage the corporate financial structures built around the concept of the mass audience.

In practice, the nature and the extent of the impact of cable television, or indeed all the information technologies, will depend on the policies adopted to direct their growth and development. Different policies will create different possibilities and it is therefore crucial to consider the present Conservative government's approach. The government's approach is based on primarily industrial considerations - hence cable is part regulated by the Department of Industry and part by the Home Office, the traditional repository of broadcasting affairs - and a belief in encouraging private entrepreneurial initiative. To achieve maximum growth in a short space of time the government has imposed a minimum of restrictions on would-be cable operators and granted them a great deal of freedom to exploit cable systems, including permission to run subscription or pay-TV services. Many see the latter concession as possibly the most profitable part of any cable operation and so likely to lead to, or initiate, other less profitable developments, e.g. telebanking.

Though this approach aims to speedily exploit the emergent technologies, it also reveals an unwillingness to insulate the existing broadcasting institutions from the more dire consequences of the new technologies and a readiness to permit the criterion of profitability to override socially and politically desirable ends. Although applicants for the currently available twelve licences will be encouraged to employ the newest technologies, particularly optical fibres, in the most adventurous ways, there will be no compulsion on them to do so. It is also, at present, unclear what mechanism will exist to make cable operators accountable. The Cable Television Authority has not yet been formed and its terms of reference have not been set out. Finally, licences will only be available for cable systems with a maximum of 100,000 subscribers.[50] The likely outcome of this approach to cable television is a rather patchy development with different technical specifications in use across the country.

Unregulated cable television contrasts sharply with both the BBC's and ITV's catalogue of duties and assumed responsibilities. Cable television, an entertainment medium par excellence, will be concerned with certain types of programmes and even subscription television will only tolerate the popular and the profitable. Injunctions to inform and educate are unlikely to prove meaningful with reference to cable television. In these ways, cable television will expose the existing broadcasting institutions to a market-oriented view of the television-audience relationship and will prove to be a radical departure from the founding principles and practices of broadcasting in Britain, the ethos of the public service. Though Reith's missionary zeal may have been extreme, it did attempt to provide 'the best' for the nation and not simply what would reach the greatest audience. As the BBC remarked in its evidence on cable television, unregulated cable television will be 'socially divisive, (it will) sacrifice hard-won programme standards and coarsen the popular taste which has been painstakingly developed by public service broadcasting.'[51]

Despite the imminence of these future battles, current developments indicate that the growth of cable television may be slower and patchier than anticipated. The costs of wiring city areas are being continually revised upwards and this has raised doubts about the profitability of cable systems. In addition, there is little evidence to suggest that subscription television will be as popular or as profitable as first thought, while there are also growing doubts about the media industries' ability to find sufficient material to fill up the new channels. Cable television's future has undoubtedly been affected by the enormous popularity of video cassette recorders in Britain - a paradox when it has the 'least worst television in the world' - which have proved to be a cheaper and more flexible form of home entertainment. In this respect, the monthly charge or fee for cable television subscribers will be a critical determinant of its popularity and success.

At present there are too few cable systems in Britain to cause concern to the broadcasting institutions. The 13% of the population covered by cable systems are ill-served by a combination of out-dated and unsophisticated technologies that provide four or six television channels. Furthermore, as they are required to transmit all four BBC and ITV services, this reduces their competitiveness.

The twelve new licences to be issued in November 1983 will add approximately another million subscribers at some stage in the near future. These new systems are likely to be far more advanced than the existing ones and to prove more of a challenge to the broadcasting institutions.

In responding to the challenge posed by cable television, it is inconceivable that broadcasting will not itself change in some way. There are signs already that this is happening. The BBC's plans for the 1980s include direct broadcasting by satellite (dbs) both as a national distribution system and as the sharp end of a competitive struggle against cable television. It could be argued that the BBC's efforts at competing commercially by providing subscription television on its dbs services of itself alters the character of public service broadcasting as it has developed in Britain. Though valid, this interpretation ignores the powerful and overwhelming corporate objective of survival that has produced accommodations and adaptations, historically and in the present. The sale of television programmes, teletext, co-productions and subscription television on dbs are all means of ensuring greater longevity. Though they also signal danger by, for example, tipping the balance away from a licence fee system, their primary purpose is to guarantee survival in a rapidly changing political, social and technological environment.

Dbs offers the BBC a new lease of life and a new outlet for its wares. With two subscription channels on which to show its own material as well as first-run films, it could succeed in remaining at the forefront of British broadcasting. But, as with most well laid plans, there are problems. First, dbs may need to be linked up to cable television systems if it is to find a sizeable audience. Although meant as a 'public service' rival to cable television on the grounds of its universal availability, the high cost of dish aerials and the low angle of the satellite, which may make the signal out of reach to many, have forced them closer together.[52] Secondly, the BBC is likely to face severe competition from other commercial dbs services on other satellites. Thirdly, BBC dbs may not be compatible with European broadcast standards and so lose a substantial part of the potential audience.

As a result of these three main factors, the BBC may have over-reached itself. What appeared initially as a lucrative and promising development for the BBC has turned out to be a costly and far from advantageous enterprise. So much so, that it has yet to commit itself formally to the future development of dbs; the need to sign an agreement which would commit the BBC to an expenditure of £24.4 million a year over seven years has provoked a major re-assessment of the potential benefits of dbs for the BBC. If it pursues its original plans of using a high powered satellite, it will risk the above crippling costs; if it uses less powerful satellites, it might encourage its cable television rival by forcing people to subscribe in order to take advantage of dbs. The BBC is caught in an argument it cannot win.

It is becoming clear that economic viability is only one aspect of the future 'media revolution'. Rapid technological change and an increasing number of technical options - as in the case of satellite broadcasting - give rise to uncertainty and panic. Should the BBC or commercial broadcasting companies invest in high, medium or low powered satellites? And, more specifically, what are the consequences for broadcasting, for the public and for cable services? Is the development of subscription channels reconcilable with the concept of public service? What are the real costs and benefits?

Such questions are easy to pose and (almost) impossible to answer. They are illustrative, however, of the possible changes that are likely to take place in the next decade. The continuing desire on the part of commercial institutions to reach profitable audiences and the response of public institutions to meet these challenges is propelling them into an era characterised by uncertainty. Despite the much heralded 'media revolution', the nature of its development is not easy to discern. The example of satellite broadcasting highlights a small part of a more complex whole. Cable television may, or may not, be able to offer full interactive systems; if forced to carry the BBC's two proposed dbs services and the commercial broadcasting companies' counterparts, the much advertised era of plenty may be no more than the existing services plus a half dozen or so other services offering sports, children's programmes, first-run films and music. Whether any of these will prove financially profitable is not known.

That so many are willing to take part in the 'media revolution' - there have, for example, been thirty-seven applications for the twelve advertised

pilot cable television licences - suggests that the
prospects look good. But this commitment is a commitment to the technology and its potential profitability; programming, and more generally content, is
of secondary importance. Yet as more and more services compete for a finite audience with a limited
number of leisure hours (as well as existing services extending their viewing hours with morning and
afternoon programmes) questions of content should be
paramount. What new sources of programming will be
developed to fill ten or even five new television
services? What libraries will be raided for old
films and serials? The danger is that the 'media
revolution' will only offer the public new ways of
catching up on old material. For many the prospect
of new services running (most probably) American
soap-operas round the clock is worrying: first, it
exposes Britain to a vast influx of foreign programmes with its attendant consequences and, secondly, if attractive to the public, it could draw
audiences away from the established broadcasting
services and their balanced programme schedules. In
the ensuing competition for the audience, the costly
drama series, the challenging play and the complex
current affairs programme may be sacrificed. *Dallas*,
or British equivalents, will become the norm, as
programming schedules become Americanised. Such
dangers will face the BBC as well as commercial
television whose fortunes are more immediately linked
to the size of the audience.

This is part of the present crisis in British
broadcasting. Technological change in the form of
cable, dbs and even video cassette recorders will
bring other changes in their wake: changes in culture, in the economics of broadcasting and in
leisure patterns. The task for the 1980s and beyond
is to retain the very best in broadcasting and to
discard, or avoid, the worst. This requires the
integration of the existing institutions of broadcasting into the communication structures of to-
morrow. Otherwise, their distinctiveness as institutions with roots in a public service broadcasting
tradition will no longer be visible and they will
merge into the market-oriented television of the
future or, more dramatically, wither away.

References

1. BBC's Royal Charter, article 3 (a) and IBA Act, 1973, section 2 (2).

2. P. Eckersley, *The Power Behind the Microphone*, London, Cape, 1941, p.18.

3. Crawford Committee of Enquiry, 1926, quoted in the *Report of the Committee on the Future of Broadcasting*, (Chairman: Lord Annan), HMSO Cmnd. 6753, 1977, p.9. Hereafter referred to as *The Annan Report*.

4. A. Briggs, *The History of Broadcasting in the United Kingdom*, vol. 1, *The Birth of Broadcasting*, Oxford, OUP, 1961. T. Burns, *The BBC: Public Institution and Private World*, London, Macmillan, 1977.

5. *The Annan Report*, p.33.

6. R. Negrine, 'From Radio Relay to Cable Television: an historical approach', *The Historical Journal of Film, Radio and Television*, 1984 (forthcoming).

7. Burns, *The BBC: Public Institution and Private World*, p.41.

8. H.H. Wilson, *Pressure Group: The Campaign for Commercial Television*, London, Secker and Warburg, 1961.

9. See J. Curran and J. Seaton, *Power without Responsibility*, London, Fontana, 1981, ch. 11.

10. R. Lusty, quoted in M. Tracey, *The Production of Political Television*, London, Routledge and Kegan Paul, 1977, p.164.

11. *The Annan Report*, p.14.

12. *Report of the Committee on Broadcasting*, (Chairman: Pilkington), HMSO Cmnd. 1753, 1962.

13. *The Annan Report*, p.8.

14. J. Morgan in R. Hoggart and J. Morgan (eds.), *The Future of Broadcasting*, London, Macmillan, 1982, p.64.

15. *The Annan Report*, p.14.

16. A. Briggs, 'Governing the BBC', in R. Hoggart and J. Morgan (eds.), *The Future of Broadcasting*.

17. A. Milne, *The Communicators*, BBC Radio 4, 1981.

18. *Ibid.*

19. P. Hartmann and C. Husband, 'The mass media and racial conflict', in D. McQuail (ed.), *Sociology of Mass Communications*, Harmondsworth, Penguin, 1972.

20. S. Hall, 'A World at One with itself', in S. Cohen and J. Young (eds.), *The Manufacture of News*, London, Constable, 1973.

21. Glasgow University Media Group, *Bad News* (1976) and *More Bad News* (1980), London, Routledge and Kegan Paul.
22. P. Schlesinger, *Putting Reality Together*, London, Constable, 1978.
23, *The Man Alive Debate*, 'Bad News', BBC2, July 28 1982. *Newsweek*, 'Does television tell the truth', BBC2, November 13 1981.
24. A. Smith, quoted in *The Annan Report*, p.231.
25. *The Annan Report*, pp.239-241.
26. *The Annan Report*, p.230.
27. *Broadcasting bill*, Bill 139, HMSO, February 4 1980.
28. *Ibid*, clause 3.
29. R. Hoggart in Glasgow University Media Group, *Bad News*, London, Routledge and Kegan Paul, 1976, p.x.
30. T. Gitlin, *The Whole World is Watching*, Berkeley, University of California Press, 1980, p.10.
31. A. Smith, *The Politics of Information*, London, Macmillan, 1978, p.98.
32. S. Hall, 'External Influences on Broadcasting: the external-internal dialectic in broadcasting: television's double bind', Occasional Paper, Centre for Contemporary Cultural Studies, Birmingham, 1972, p.8.
33. M. Tracey, *The Production of Political Television*, ch.10.
34. Lord Hill, *Behind the Screen*, London, Sidgwick and Jackson, 1974.
35. BBC Yearbook 1976, BBC, London, p.272.
36. T. Burns, *The BBC: Public Institution and Private World*, p.16.
37. BBC evidence to *The Annan Report*, p.268.
38. J. Reith, quoted in M. Tracey, *The Production of Political Television*, p.151.
39. A. Smith, *Television and Political Life*, London, Macmillan, 1979, p.21.
40. G.W. Goldie, *Facing the Nation: Television and Politics*, London, The Bodley Head, 1977, p.71.
41. *Ibid*, p.116.
42. B. Ingham, quoted in the *Guardian*, January 11 1983.
43. 'When the heavy hand of Auntie comes down too hard', *Guardian*, January 31 1981.
44. A. Briggs, *Governing the BBC*, London, BBC, 1979, p.215.
45. R. Harris, *Gotcha! The Media, the Government and the Falklands crisis*, London, Faber and Faber, 1983.

46. M. Thatcher, quoted in R. Harris, *Gotcha!*, p.75.

47. *Sunday Times*, January 30 1983.

48. M. Thatcher, quoted in the *Guardian*, November 9 1979.

49. J. Reith, in C. Stuart, *The Reith Diaries*, London, Collins, 1975, p.96, entry dated May 11 1926.

50. White Paper, *Cable Systems and Services*, HMSO Cmnd. 8866, 1983.

51. BBC, *The Cable Debate The BBC's reactions to the Hunt report*, 1982, p.34.

52. 'Cable will undermine the BBC', *New Scientist*, May 5 1983.

Chapter Two

FRANCE: THE END OF THE GOVERNMENT MONOPOLY

Raymond Kuhn

The two most salient features of broadcasting in
France since the end of the second world war have
been, first, its *legal* status as a state monopoly
and, secondly, its use for partisan *political* purposes by the government of the day. The organisational framework of the state monopoly has meant
that television in particular has not had to contend
with any commercial competition, even of the regulated, public service variety which breached the BBC's
monopoly in Britain in the 1950s. While in certain
frontier regions, such as Alsace, viewers have been
able to receive programmes from foreign television
stations, in general the state television channels
have enjoyed the freedom to decide what the captive
French audience would watch in all areas of programming.
    During this same period (1945-81) a close
political control was maintained over broadcasting
to ensure that news output reflected and reinforced
the views and policies of the government. Appointments to key decision-making posts in broadcasting,
especially in the news departments, were made
largely on the basis of political rather than professional criteria, while at times direct ministerial censorship was also common practice. As a
result, French broadcasting was characterised by
'government control, more extensive and more political than is usual in Western Europe'.[1]
    This is not to argue that since 1945 there have
been no changes in the structure of French broadcasting or lack of reforms intended to give the
broadcasters greater independence from the government.
The development of television in the 1950s, the
establishment of a second television channel in 1964,
the introduction of commercial advertising on the
two state channels in 1968, the creation of a third

channel with an allegedly regional vocation in 1973
and the attack on the state monopoly by localised
pirate radio stations in the late 1970s were all
evidence of a broadcasting system growing in size
and seeking to satisfy new demands. To help cope
with these and other chançes a succession of broadcasting reforms were introduced either by ordinance
(1959) or more usually by statute (1964, 1972 and
1974). All of them had as one objective the reduction of government control over broadcasting.
However, the willpower required to achieve this goal
was sadly lacking. In short, neither the principle
of the state monopoly, nor the practice or partisan
political control was ever seriously challenged, far
less abandoned.

There are signs, however, that this description
of French broadcasting as a government-controlled
state monopoly is no longer wholly accurate. As far
as radio is concerned, the state monopoly has never
been completely effective, even though the state
owns a large, and frequently majority, shareholding
in the popular 'commercial' stations such as *Europe
1, Radio Luxembourg* and *Radio Monte Carlo*.[2] In any
case since 1981 the state's monopoly in the provision of radio services has been definitively
abandoned. Privately owned local radio stations
have been legalised to compete with the national and
local services of the state radio company, *Radio
France*, and with the 'commercial' stations (more
commonly known in France as the peripheral radios
because to comply with legal requirements their
transmitters are usually situated just outside
French territory). These small, private stations
are now an integral part of the French broadcasting
system.

With regard to television, a fourth channel,
Canal plus, is due to begin transmissions towards
the end of 1984. This will be the first channel not
to be managed by a state broadcasting company. In
addition, local cable television services will be
established in various parts of France over the next
few years as the government implements its policy on
the new information technologies. The programmes
of the established state television companies will
form only a small part of the multi-channel facility
available to cable subscribers. Other options will
include satellite-beamed programmes from foreign
stations, community programmes, teletext and, in the
future, a whole range of interactive services. The
introduction of satellite television across western
Europe and the advent of the video cassette recorder

will further weaken the state's ability to control
the 'programme diet' of French viewers.

The political side of the broadcasting/politics
equation has also recently undergone a significant
change. The presidential and parliamentary elections of 1981 marked the end of the dominance of the
present political system of the Fifth Republic by
the Gaullist-Giscardian Right, with the Socialist-
Communist Left winning national political office for
the first time since the creation of the regime in
1958. By the autumn of 1981 the Socialists, who now
dwarfed their electorally declining Communist *frère-
ennemi*, had a firm grip on the offices of the presidency and premiership, occupied the most important
posts in the Council of Ministers, enjoyed an
absolute majority in the National Assembly and were
placing supporters in selected key posts in the administrative and para-administrative sectors of the
French polity.

The election of a Socialist President and
government has encouraged hopes that the tradition
of political control over broadcasting can now be
abolished and, like the guillotine, relegated to the
annals of history. In opposition the Socialists,
and none more than the new President, François
Mitterrand, were fierce critics of Gaullist and
Giscardian interference in broadcasting, with the
result that they are under strong pressure to break
with this practice. The content of the 1982 broadcasting statute, the fifth major piece of legislation in twenty five years, gives grounds for cautious optimism in this respect. Again the question
is whether the political willpower is there to enforce the spirit of the law.

Broadcasting in France, as in many other
countries in western Europe, is, therefore, in a
process of transition. The established system is
gradually giving way to another, as yet barely defined, where the viewer will ostensibly have a
greater choice of programmes than ever before, while
also, it is to be hoped, benefiting from a less
government controlled news output. The penury of
the early 1960s, when France had only one television
channel, will be replaced by an apparent *embarras de
richesses* scarcely conceivable a few years ago.

Yet the break with the past is not quite as
extreme as it may appear, at least in the short term.
The state remains the predominant influence in the
shaping of the French broadcasting system of the
future. The government is still accused of exercising political control over news output, and not

just by the opposition. Moreover, the extension of
broadcasting hours and of programme outlets, accompanied by an increasing Americanisation of the
product, is scarcely an innovation of the 1980s.
While French broadcasting is undoubtedly changing,
very radically in many respects, it is also marked
for the moment by an element of continuity. To
appreciate this present mixture of change and continuity, it is first of all necessary to examine the
history of state/broadcasting relations in France
from the end of world war two to the victory of the
Left in 1981.

THE TRADITIONAL SYSTEM: THE GOVERNMENT-CONTROLLED
STATE MONOPOLY 1945-81

While prior to the outbreak of the second world war
there had existed in France private radio stations,
after the Liberation the provisional government
headed by General de Gaulle retained the principle of
the state monopoly in broadcasting which had been
established by the collaborationist Vichy regime. The
various centrist coalitions which governed France
during the Fourth Republic (1946-58) used their
political control of state broadcasting, in effect
radio, to the detriment of the regime's opponents:
the Communists, isolated in a cold war ghetto
following their expulsion from government in 1947,
and the Gaullists, critics of what they regarded as
a weak, parliamentary system of government.[3]
    Following the ignominious collapse of the
Fourth Republic over its failure to resolve the
Algerian problem, a completely new political system
was established in 1958 (the Fifth Republic), headed
by a powerful President - de Gaulle. However, the
change from one regime to another did not result in
a loosening of the close links between the government and the broadcasting services. In fact the
reverse was the case, with the new Gaullist political elite entrenching the practice of politicisation
and firmly defending the state monopoly against in-
frequent commercial onslaughts.
    After the foundation of the Fifth Republic the
Gaullists willingly adhered to the tradition whereby
governmental control of state broadcasting was regarded as a legitimate spoil of electoral victory.
From the earliest days of the new regime Gaullist
sympathisers were placed in key managerial and
editorial posts at the *Radio Télévision Française*
(RTF).[4] Though scarcely innovatory, this practice
was to be of much greater political importance after

1958 than previously. First, in sharp contrast to
the short-lived coalition governments of the Fourth
Republic, the Gaullists were to enjoy sixteen years
of uninterrupted rule. The governmental instability
of the Fourth Republic was replaced by a system of
party government in which the Gaullists steadily
occupied the principal offices of the politico-
administrative system. Secondly, the establishment
of the Fifth Republic coincided with the implanta-
tion in France of television as a mass medium.
While before 1958 television was slow to make much
market impact, after that year the sales of television sets soared to reach near saturation level by
the end of de Gaulle's presidency. Thus, the start
of the prolonged period of Gaullist domination of
the political system was contemporaneous with the
advent of television as the primary means of national mass communication in France.

During the early years of the Fifth Republic
the war in Algeria and the possibility of the conflict spreading to metropolitan France were used by
the Gaullist government to justify its close control of the RTF's news output. However, the
successful resolution of the Algerian problem in
1962 did not provide the occasion for a reduction
in direct ministerial control. The experience of
the wartime resistance had demonstrated to de Gaulle
at an early stage in his political career the importance of broadcasting as a political weapon, as
well as providing him with the opportunity of developing his own expertise in the use of the broadcasting media. On several occasions during his
presidency (for example, during the attempted putsch
by army generals in Algeria in 1961) de Gaulle used
the broadcasting services to his own political advantage, while his opponents were systematically
kept off the air. Moreover, the hostility of the
traditional governmental parties of the Fourth
Republic to the Gaullist regime, the presence of a
strong, well-disciplined Communist party and the
virulent, not to say violent, antagonism of the
ultra-right to de Gaulle's decolonisation policy
impressed upon the Gaullist government the advantages to be gained from strict control of broadcasting.

In addition, broadcasting was an impeccably
Gaullian device. While according to Gaullist doctrine direct election of the President of the
Republic and the use of the referendum permitted the
general will of the sovereign people to be expressed
without the deforming influences of intermediary

bodies such as Parliament, political parties or
pressure groups, in similar fashion radio and television allowed the head of state to address directly
le pays réel.   Finally, Gaullist ministers argued
that their control of broadcasting could be justified
as an attempt to balance the anti-Gaullist forces
which allegedly dominated the French press.   One-
sided presentation of news by the state broadcasting
organisations, far from infringing the public service norms of balance and pluralism, was designed,
the Gaullists argued, to ensure the observance of
these principles across the totality of the French
mass media - broadcasting *and* the press.
   Whatever the reasons, justifications or sheer
sophistry employed to defend the close, direct control of broadcasting's political output by the
government during the de Gaulle presidency, the
facts are not in doubt.   From 1958 to 1969 radio and
television news content was decided upon by
Gaullist appointees within the broadcasting services
working in close liaison with top officials at the
Ministry of Information and even the Minister in
person.[5]   News bulletins were constructed with reference to political rather than professional considerations, while, particularly before 1965,
election and referendum campaigns were blatantly
one-sided.   An illustration of the nature of the
relationship between the government and the RTF
during the early years of de Gaulle's presidency is
provided by Alexander Werth:

> During de Gaulle's visit to the United States
> in April 1960 the French radio seemed to think
> it quite natural to start one of its news bul-
> letins with the words: "In the absence of
> General de Gaulle, there is no political news
> in France today."[6]

The passing of a new broadcasting statute in 1964
did little to improve this state of affairs.
Modelled on the BBC charter the 1964 statute, which
set up the *Office de Radiodiffusion Télévision
Française* (ORTF), was to remain more honoured in the
breach than in the observance.   The avowed intention
of the government was that the 1964 statute signi-
fied a step towards greater autonomy for state
broadcasting, with the establishment of a board of
governors to act as a buffer between the politicians
and the broadcasters.   Alain Peyrefitte, the Minister of Information responsible for drafting the
legislation, stated in the National Assembly that

'the fundamental defect which we intend to remedy
by the present statute is the permanent confusion
which has taken root in the minds of the public between RTF and the government.'[7] This did not prevent him, however, from appointing several members
of his ministerial *cabinet* to key posts at the ORTF
and running the news services from his ministry.

The events of May 1968 fully exposed the short-
comings of the 1964 reform. Broadcasting staff,
including journalists, came out on strike in protest
against the government's directives regarding the
reporting of the events and more generally against
the way in which the government had manipulated the
state broadcasting services over the previous ten
years. The strikers demanded a new ORTF statute to
guarantee the independence of broadcasting, freedom
from ministerial pressure and an impartial news
service. Naturally the government could not accept
these demands, since in theory they were already
guaranteed by the 1964 statute. Taking advantage of
the climate of reaction which followed the May
events, the government quelled the strike by dis-
missing or demoting its leaders and making only
token concessions to the strikers' demands.[8]

After de Gaulle's resignation from the presidency in 1969 and Pompidou's election as his successor, broadcasting became the responsibility of the
new Prime Minister, Jacques Chaban-Delmas. Like all
Gaullists Chaban-Delmas had been shocked by the up-
surge of protest which had taken place in May 1968
and from which the de Gaulle presidency had never
fully recovered. Rejecting purely repressive measures as inadequate for the resolution of the problems 1968 had brought to the surface, he launched
his project to transform what he diagnosed as
France's 'stagnant society'.

Included in the new Premier's wide-ranging
proposals for the construction of a 'New Society'
was a reform of broadcasting. The Ministry of
Information was abolished and responsibility for
news programming given to professional broadcasters
of sound reputation. New directors of news were
appointed and given complete financial and editorial
responsibility for the work of their departments.
As a result, they were able to choose journalists
without interference from the government or the
politically tainted ORTF management. In a controversial move one of the 1968 strikers, Pierre
Desgraupes, was even appointed by Chaban-Delmas as
director of news on the widely viewed channel 1. As
a result of this reorganisation at the ORTF, news

programmes were more openly critical of government
policy while opposition and trade union leaders made
more frequent appearances on screen than before.[9]

However, the 1969 reform did not fundamentally
alter the ingrained attitudes held by a large section of the political elite, most notably within the
Gaullist party, on the issue of government-broad-
casting relations. The Chaban-Delmas reform was
vigorously opposed by many Gaullist deputies and
never received the unequivocal support of President
Pompidou, with the result that the 'liberalisation'
depended on the Prime Minister's ability to remain
in office. When in the summer of 1972 he was dismissed by Pompidou in the run-up to the important
1973 parliamentary elections, a new tougher line on
broadcasting was initiated.

A second ORTF statute was introduced to mark
the end of the Chaban-Delmas experiment. The
Ministry of Information was reconstituted and placed
in the hands of the ultra-conservative Philippe
Malaud, a supporter of President Pompidou. The news
departments lost their highly-prized but precarious
independence, some journalists were sacked and
Desgraupes resigned in protest. Another personal
supporter of the President, Arthur Conte, was appointed director general of the ORTF with the task of
ensuring that broadcasting output would serve the
interests of the many Gaullist deputies who, elected
in the backlash elections of 1968, would be hard
pressed to defend their seats against candidates of
the recently formed Union of the Left. The 1972
statute represented the alignment of the state broadcasting organisation with Pompidou's publicly affir-
med view of the ORTF as 'the voice of France', the
official mouthpiece of the French state.

This concept was specifically rejected by his
successor to the presidential office in 1974, Valéry
Giscard d'Estaing, the first non-Gaullist President
of the Fifth Republic. A reorganisation of broadcasting formed part of a reformist package introduced in the early months of the Giscard presidency
to give the new President a liberal, humanitarian
image and to differentiate his septenate from the
previous years of Gaullist rule. By the provisions
of the 1974 statute the ORTF, a major edifice of the
Gaullist state, was dismantled and replaced by a new
broadcasting structure of seven separate companies
organisationally independent of each other.

There were sound administrative reasons for implementing a reorganisation of state broadcasting at
this time. The ORTF was in severe financial diffi-

culties, had been crippled by a series of strikes
and was the object of a vehemently critical parliamentary report drafted by a close associate of the
new President.[10] Apart from an improvement in programme quality, the principal aim of the 1974
statute was to cut the umbilical cord linking government and broadcasting. The Ministry of Information
was again abolished as part of a presidential pledge
that he would tolerate no interference with the independence of the professional broadcasters. More
generally, the 1974 broadcasting reform formed part
of a wider objective of replacing the authoritarian
face of Gaullism with the liberal mask of Giscardism,
which, the President hoped, would enable France to
be governed from the centre in a more consensual
fashion than had previously been the case.

In practice, however, while the 1974 reorganisation modified the form of governmental control, it
barely affected its substance. This became particularly clear from 1976 onwards when the Giscardian
regime came under fire not only from the Socialist-
Communist Left, but also from the Chirac-led
Gaullists, who though formally supporters of the
governing coalition were becoming increasingly
hostile to the policies and style of the President.
The act which clearly showed that the 1974 reform
was a false dawn was the appointment of Jean-Pierre
Elkabbach as director of news in one of the new
television companies, *Antenne 2*. Imposed on the
company management by the Elysée in January 1977,
only a few weeks before the municipal elections and
just over a year before the crucial parliamentary
elections which the Left were expected to win,
Elkabbach was only one of various Giscardian appointees given key posts in the state broadcasting media
and peripheral radio stations at this time.[11]

The final years of the Giscard presidency were
to make a mockery of the claims made by government
spokesmen with regard to the 1974 reorganisation.
News coverage was manipulated to favour the Giscardian component of the governing coalition at the
expense of both the Gaullists and the Left. Television interviews with the President, including the
one in which he was questioned about the Bokassa
diamonds, were to Anglo-Saxon observers reminiscent
of the sycophancy of the *ancien régime* court. The
principal innovatory force in broadcasting management in 1974, Marcel Jullian (head of *Antenne 2*),
who had been sufficiently naive to take at face
value the President's pledge to defend the independence of the broadcasters, was the most important

victim when the first wave of management contracts
came to be renewed at the end of 1977. Challenges
to the state broadcasting monopoly by pirate radio
stations, including one set up by the Socialist
Party, were savagely repressed once the 1978 parliamentary elections had been safely negotiated.
Stronger anti-strike legislation was introduced in
1979 to counter trade union activity. Even much
heralded improvements, such as the introduction of
a right of reply to ministerial broadcasts for
opposition parties and the creation of a daily
access programme for minority groups *(Tribune
Libre)*, remained largely cosmetic operations.

If the history of the Giscard presidency is one
of abandoned reformism, nowhere is this more evident
than in the field of broadcasting where the practical limits of Giscard's espousal of the advanced,
liberal society became increasingly apparent. The
Gaullist emphasis on direct control of political
output via the Ministry of Information was replaced
by a system of control through presidential appointments. Opposition politicians were now allowed to
appear on the screen to an extent which would have
been unthinkable in the early 1960s, particularly if,
as in the case of the Communist party leader Georges
Marchais, their appearance was designed to highlight
the divisions within their ranks. However, news
editorials and commentaries remained predominantly
one-sided. While the crude, external intervention-
ism of the de Gaulle presidency had given way to a
slightly subtler internal manipulation during
Giscard's septenate, by the time of Giscard's
electoral defeat in 1981 the government-controlled
state monopoly was in its essential aspects still
alive and well.

Yet control of news and political output by the
government, though important, was by no means the
only noteworthy feature of French broadcasting
during this post-war period. Elsewhere in the
broadcasting system significant changes were taking
place. The most obvious was the replacement of
radio by television as the principal mass medium, a
trend common to all western societies. Watching
television now became a major pastime for large
sections of the French population. Given the low
level of newspaper readership in France and the
dominance of the regional over the national press,
television was by far the most important source of
national and international news for the majority of
people.

It was also the major provider of entertainment

and culture. During de Gaulle's presidency, it has been argued, an elitist view of broadcasting's role resulted in a high standard of programming. In the 1960s the state television service acted self-consciously, rather as the BBC had done in a previous era, as the medium par excellence for the dissemination of 'highbrow' French culture both to viewers in metropolitan France and to the wider audience in the Francophone countries.

> Until the 1969 reshuffle (the Chaban-Delmas reform mentioned above - author) ... French television at least tried to keep up a certain cultural and moral tone, however uninspired the results. State monopoly did seem to carry one advantage: there was no need to compete with commercial television for audiences ... and therefore the proportion of serious or cultural material could be kept fairly high. So long as de Gaulle and Malraux remained in charge of the spiritual well-being of the French, the ORTF bought little of the American pulp material so common on British screens ... Television was didactic in the true French pedagogic manner.'[12]

Moreover, despite news censorship, magazine programmes with a political content, such as *Cinq Colonnes à la Une*, largely escaped ministerial control and, though they tended to deal with foreign rather than French issues, represented a creative breakthrough for French television.[13]

After 1969 this elitist concept gave way to a more populist approach. Financial constraints as the television sales market peaked, extended programming hours, a new third channel, competition for viewers between the two main national channels and rising costs of programme production led inexorably to a greater emphasis on popular entertainment programmes. French television was managed less like a civil service department (the majority of broadcasting employees had lost their status as civil servants during the 1960s) and more like a commercial company. The high cultural aspirations of the de Gaulle era were abandoned.

This trend towards entertainment television became more noticeable after the 1974 Giscardian reform. Dismantling the ORTF into its constituent parts exposed the production services, now a separate state company - the *Société Française de Production* (SFP), to the chill winds of competition. The new

programme companies (TF1, *Antenne 2* and FR3), in
effect the old ORTF television channels, preferred
either to produce their own programmes or buy more
cheaply elsewhere, most notably from the USA. As a
result, the SFP came close to bankruptcy and the
government was forced to intervene to compel the
television companies to purchase a quota of their
programmes from the SFP. While this exercise was
enough to save the production company from extinc-
tion, it did little to reverse the established trend
away from large-scale home-based production.

The economic logic of the 1974 reform was at
odds with the pious hopes of Giscard and his ministers that competition between the channels would
result in higher quality programming. The reverse
proved to be the case. Unlike at the ORTF, there
was after 1974 no single authority in overall charge
of state broadcasting to balance out the needs and
interests of the various sectors: transmission, programming and production. Consequently, each separate company fought to defend its own corner, with
drastic effects for some companies, like the SFP,
and adverse results for the system as a whole.

In addition, the dependence of the two main
national television companies, TF1 and *Antenne 2*, on
revenue from commercial advertising for over half
their income reinforced the competitive ethos of the
1974 reorganisation by inducing the two companies to
pursue the mass audience. The result was an
effusion of American or American-style trivia and
low-budget French productions punctuated with the
occasional 'big' production or cultural programme.
The number of feature films shown on television rose
to the alarm of the French cinema industry, who also
complained about the low levels of compensation paid
by the channels if they exceeded the already generous quota of films allowed in their operating conditions drawn up by the government *(cahiers des
charges)*. Ad hoc measures taken by the government
in response to criticisms from the Committee on
Programme Quality, the High Audiovisual Council,
annual parliamentary reports and various television
directors and producers, such as Jean-Christophe
Averty, failed miserably to redress the balance.[14]

The 1974 reform was not wholly to blame for
this state of affairs. The shift towards entertainment television in France was part of a much wider
western trend. Other national broadcasting systems
were being exposed to cheap American imports and
finding it difficult to sustain domestic production
on a large-scale. The malaise was international.[15]

Moreover, it could be argued that entertainment
television in the form of films, serials and American soap operas and detective stories were popular
with the French audience, however much certain sections of the political and intellectual elites might
rail against this 'cultural imperialism' and decline
in programme standards.

On the other hand, the sharp decrease in the
number of cultural and educational programmes during
the 1970s[16], the growing emphasis on films, foreign
series and repeats and the lack of any counterbalan-
cing, upmarket 'cultural ghetto' channels such as
exist in Britain (BBC2 and most recently Channel 4),
when taken in conjunction with government manipulation of news output, meant that the public service
norms enshrined in the 1974 statute were far from
being achieved in practice. The question in 1981
was whether a Socialist government by introducing a
new statute could do any better.

BROADCASTING DURING THE MITTERRAND PRESIDENCY: THE
1982 REFORM

On their election to government in 1981 the Socialists found themselves faced with a multiplicity of
challenges in the broadcasting field. Not only was
the traditional system of the government-controlled
state monopoly proving increasingly unsatisfactory,
but in addition French broadcasting was highly
centralised, technically inferior to its counterpart
in Britain, frequently unimaginative and barely responsive to the changing demands of French society.
A new statute, accompanied by a change in attitudes,
was more than ever necessary if French broadcasting
was to remedy these defects and prepare the way for
the advent of the much-vaunted audiovisual revolution. The 1982 broadcasting reform, the spirit and
content of which marked a clear break with the
traditional system, was designed with these factors
in mind.[17]

The first feature of the 1982 reform which
should be stressed is the abandonment of the state
monopoly with regard to programming. While in
theory French broadcasting is to continue to be run
as a public service, the state has given up its
jealously guarded exclusive rights to controlling
all sources of broadcasting output, though it still
retains overall charge of frequency allocation.

With regard to *radio* the abandonment of the
programming monopoly had been on the cards since the
1981 election victory. Sympathetic to the flourish-

ing of pirate radios during the latter half of the
Giscard presidency, and even setting up a pirate
station of their own, *Radio Riposte*, the Socialists
could scarcely have continued for long the repressive policy of their predecessors. Legislation of
the pirate stations was, therefore, an early priority for the new administration. This was initially
accomplished by legislation in the autumn of 1981
and confirmed in the main statute of July 1982.

Since 1981 the floodgates have been opened to
an apparently infinite number and astonishing
variety of small, privately run, local radio stations, so that by the end of 1983 it was estimated
that up to 850 were operating quite legally.[18] As a
result, many different groups in French society now
enjoyed privileged access to local radio. These include politically marginal groups, previously largely ignored by the state broadcasting services:
ecologists, feminists, immigrants, and so on.
Religious bodies, ethnic minorities, newspaper and
magazine publishers including *l'Humanité*, *le Matin*,
l'Unité and *l'Express*, community associations,
scouts and music lovers have all taken advantage of
the new freedom. While municipal radios as such are
not allowed, town councils have also joined in,
though they must be careful not to contribute more
than 25% of the revenue of the relevant station.
Radio Tour Eiffel, backed by the Gaullist mayor of
Paris, Jacques Chirac, is probably the best-known
example of this type of station. Like the pop music
pirates in Britain in the 1960s, the new local
stations are satisfying a demand previously left un-
fulfilled by both the state radio company and the
peripheral stations. Not surprisingly they are
proving extremely popular with French listeners.

The government has not been content to leave
the development of private local radio to market
forces. On the contrary, it has sought to organise
(some would argue limit the effectiveness of) the
new stations. For example, while not having to conform to any public service obligations regarding
programming, the stations have been restricted to a
maximum transmission capacity of up to 30 kilometres.
Two aspects in particular of the Socialist government's policy on private radio have come in for
criticism: financing and frequency allocation.

The first, and most controversial, decision was
to ban commercial advertising as a possible source
of finance. This has meant that many stations have
had to eke out a hand-to-mouth existence helped by
voluntary subscriptions and donations. Conscious of

their financial plight, the government is also allocating funds taken from the advertising budgets of the state radio and television companies.[19] Nonetheless, some radios have had recourse to secret advertising of commercial products, a practice which at present the authorities have great difficulty in controlling.

The government argued initially that to allow advertising would be to run the risk of a commercial ethos, ideologically hostile to the Socialist regime, dominating this non-state sector of the media. However, more prosaically the government were also concerned to protect the departmental and regional press from yet another competitor for advertising funds. It is also likely that the Socialists were worried about the possible effects on the state broadcasting sector if advertising were allowed on private radio. With the introduction of advertising on the regional state channel, FR3 (previously immune from advertising because of the opposition of the regional press lobby), all three state channels now derive some income from advertising. The government may well have feared the deleterious effects on the finances of state television if advertising revenue had to be spread too thinly among a host of recipients. Paradoxically, therefore, while most of the state broadcasting sector is supported by advertising, the private radio sector is not. One of the classic dividing lines between a public and private service, the source of finance, has been fudged.

The second problem facing the government after the legalisation of private radio was that the demand for licences to broadcast far outweighed the supply of available frequencies, especially in the Paris region. Responsibility for the allocation of frequencies was given to the newly created High Audiovisual Authority (see below), which has tried to satisfy as many demands as technically feasible. In Paris this has involved grouping radio stations together, placing them on the same frequency and dividing broadcasting time up between them on an equitable basis. While in general this task has been completed with remarkable smoothness, there have been some difficult cases. The most notorious has concerned a station entitled *Radio Solidarité*, whose president is the former Minister of Information, Philippe Malaud. Originally *Radio Solidarité*, which has strong political sympathies for the right-wing opposition, was allocated a frequency at the very edge of the spectrum. After a series of vociferous complaints, however, the High Authority allocated the station a frequency more acceptable to it. Immediately other radio stations protested against this alleged favourable treatment. As a result, in trying to act impartially and counter charges of political bias, the High Authority has been accused of partisanship![20]

The main problem facing the private stations is that of finance. Once the initial flood of enthusiasm evaporates and audiences tire of the amateurism of many of the local stations' programme output, it is likely that some stations will cease functioning, particularly as advertising revenue is forbidden them. On the other hand, many will survive and no doubt new ones will be established. Moreover, since the law forbids concentration of ownership, there will still be a great deal of diversity in programme output. Unlike in television where usually the more channels there are available the more similar is the output as each channel pursues the mass audience and caters for the lowest common denominator of taste, radio, with its lower overheads and production costs, can multiply its outlets while still offering the audience a wide variety of choice. In a country where the people have in the past been often deprived of choice by an untrusting state, the spread of private radio must be deemed on balance beneficial.

In the field of *television* the abandonment of the state's programming monopoly has not as yet had an impact on the French public. However, the ramifications of the government's decision will soon be apparent as France prepares to launch a fourth television channel to join the present three state television companies. Channel 4, christened *Canal plus*, will begin transmissions towards the end of 1984.

Unlike the other three channels, *Canal plus* will not be managed by a state broadcasting company. Rather it is to be run by the multi-media conglomerate, Havas, which besides having a stake in *Radio Télévision Luxembourg* is also active in the fields of advertising and travel. While the French state owns just over half of the shares in Havas, the company is run on a strictly commercial basis. But it also enjoys close links with the government. One of its former chairmen, Yves Cannac, was an ex-member of President Giscard's *cabinet* at the Elysée and had been largely responsible for drafting the 1974 broadcasting statute. Its present chairman, André Rousselet, was director of Mitterrand's presi-

dential *cabinet* until the summer of 1982 and is re-
puted to be a close associate of the President.
While at the Elysée he was actively involved in
helping draw up the 1982 broadcasting reform and
supervised the top appointments to the broadcasting
companies made by the Socialists in the aftermath of
the 1981 election victory. A key figure in determining Socialist attitudes towards broadcasting,
Rousselet was given responsibility for the establishment of the fourth channel and it was under his
personal guidance that the proposals for *Canal plus*
took shape.

These proposals are unashamedly commercial in
their outlook. The options of a cultural, educational or 'alternative' channel were soon rejected
in favour of a pay-television service.[21] In return
for a monthly subscription of around 120 francs
(about £10) on top of the annual television licence
fee, viewers will be able to watch programmes not
available to audiences of the three state channels:
by far the major attraction will be recently released feature films. By concentrating on major
urban areas in the first instance (Paris, Lyons,
Marseilles and Lille), Havas hopes that the necessary one and a half million subscribers will be
found to make the new service commercially viable.
According to market surveys this objective is likely
to be realised.[22]

Predictably, the programming of feature films
by *Canal plus* aroused the greatest controversy,
since it provoked a worried response from the French
cinema industry which, through its lobbying organisation - the Bureau de Liaison des Industries
Cinématographiques (BLIC), sought to have its interests defended in a series of discussions prior to
the establishment of the new channel. While Havas
wanted the least possible interval between the release of new films in the cinema and their transmission on *Canal plus*, BLIC opposed anything less
than a 12 months' minimum delay, fearing that otherwise the extra service would have seriously adverse
consequences for the cinema industry, already
suffering from a variety of difficulties. In addition, concern was expressed about the total number
of films to be screened and about the quota of
French produced as opposed to imported films.

After prolonged discussions between the interested parties, it was in the end the government
which imposed a decision. *Canal plus* will be able
to show films six months after their general release
if they have not been a commercial success in the

cinema. For more popular films it will have to wait
between nine and eighteen months. No films will be
programmed on Tuesdays or Fridays before 10 pm, on
Saturdays before 11 pm and on Sundays until 8.30 pm.
At least half of the films will have to be French
produced. Finally, twenty five per cent of the new
channel's income will go to help the French cinema
industry.[23] It remains problematic, however,
whether these provisions which form part of the
channel's operating conditions will be adequate to
allay the fears expressed by the cinema lobby.

Why is the French government so keen to establish a fourth television channel, particularly of
this type? As with the development of cable, *Canal
plus* forms an integral part of the government's
policy to build up the national electronics industry
as a principal growth sector in the economy. The
device which subscribers will have to rent to un-
scramble the transmission signal of the new channel
will be manufactured in France. Moreover, as some
older television sets (just under half of the 14
million colour sets used at present) will be unable
to receive *Canal plus* even with an unscrambling device, the government is expecting an increase in the
sale of television sets, most of which it hopes will
be French-made.

The government is also gambling that quotas of
home-produced programmes will aid the ailing French
production sector, dominated by the state managed
SFP but also including a host of independent production companies. Both the SFP and the private
companies have suffered recently from a lack of
orders from the established state channels. In addition, since *Canal plus*, once established, will be
self-financing on a voluntary basis, no extra strain
is placed on the licence fee. The operational cost
to the state is, therefore, nil. At the same time
the channel makes no demands on the commercial advertising sector, which is so important for the
budgets of the state channels. Even the capital
costs have been reduced by the fact that the new
channel will use an already existing transmission
network.

Nonetheless, it may seem odd that a Socialist
government, which in opposition stoutly defended the
principle of the state monopoly as the best guaran-
tor of public service broadcasting and attacked the
alleged deterioration in programme standards during
the 1970s, should be presiding over the creation of
a channel which, while still nominally subject to
public service guidelines, will in practice be run

on the market principle of satisfying consumer
demand. There is nothing Socialist or politically
progressive about *Canal plus*, which could well have
been established under a Gaullist or Giscardian
President. In fact in terms of programming *Canal
plus* will be less radical than the British Channel 4
which, set up under a right-wing Conservative
government, has gone some way to cater for minority
tastes in its programming policies and not just pursued the mass audience in a commercial fashion.

France's fourth channel may pose a whole series
of problems for the broadcasting system as a whole.
For example, what will be the effects of the new
service on the audience figures of the existing
state channels? If, as seems likely, these tend to
drop, the legitimacy of the state channels will be
called into question with the result that requests
for an increase in the licence will not be regarded
favourably by the government. Funds and audiences
may then decline in a vicious downward spiral, pre-
judicing the range and quality of the state service.
It seems clear then that France is moving towards a
two-tier broadcasting system: one service for those
who can and choose to pay extra and another for
those who either will not or cannot pay the subscription in addition to the licence. It is ques-
tionable whether such a system can still be called
a public service.

The abandonment of the state monopoly in programming marks the first step away from the traditional system described in the first section. The
Socialist government also intended that the 1982
reform take a second step by breaking with the
practice of a government-controlled political output
used for partisan ends. One objective of the recent
reorganisation of broadcasting was to reduce its
links with the government (yet again!) by making the
professional broadcasters responsible for news and
current affairs output. This involved limiting the
freedom of the government to intervene in the running of the companies, for example by changing the
method of appointment to key decision-making posts.

The achievement of this objective necessitated
the establishment of a buffer between the government
and the state broadcasting companies: the High
Authority for Audiovisual Communication. This new
body has taken over from the government responsibility for appointments to the top managerial posts,
notably director general, and also selects a minority of the governors on the different company
boards. The main function of the High Authority is

to ensure that the companies respect their public
service obligations as laid down in their operating
conditions, for example with regard to news coverage
and harmonisation of programme schedules.

The composition of the High Authority is,
therefore, of crucial importance. It has nine members, of whom three each are chosen by the President,
the Speaker of the National Assembly and the Speaker
of the Senate. Since the first two office-holders
are both Socialists (Mitterrand and Mermaz), the
government could have immediately infringed the
spirit of the 1982 reform by packing the High Authority with unconditional political sympathisers. In
fact, however, this does not seem to have taken
place, even though the majority of the appointees
have political leanings to the left of centre.[24]

In its first year of operation (September 1982-
83) the High Authority managed with some considerable success to establish itself as an independent
agent in the broadcasting system. Unlike the board
of governors at the ORTF, for example, it did not
automatically assume a pro-governmental stance in
political disputes. It upheld complaints of partial
treatment from opposition politicians, most notably
by the Gaullist party leader - Jacques Chirac.
During the municipal election campaign of Spring
1983 the High Authority ensured that the television
and radio companies maintained a party political
balance in their output, though on one occasion it
did have to compel *Radio France* to transmit a statement from a Gaullist candidate in Paris as a counter
to a previous interview with a Socialist party rival.
In the allocation of local radio frequencies the
Authority's decisions have not been determined by
political considerations.

The High Authority has now become the focal
point for complaints from political parties, interest groups and individuals, which in turn relieves
the pressure on the managements and staffs of the
separate broadcasting companies. On the other hand,
the interventions of the Authority have themselves
not always been welcomed by the channels, especially
the journalists, who through their union representatives have voiced their resentment at what they
regard as illicit trespassing on their professional
territory.

Overall, however, the new institution has been
a relative success. Somewhat belatedly the French
have managed to create a body which supervises
broadcasting output without at the same time enjoying close or subordinate links with the authorities,

a feat which defied previous right-wing presiden-
cies. But unfortunately given the development of
new media in France and the resultant changing
nature of the system as a whole, the establishment
of the High Authority may well have come too late to
enable it to exercise a preponderant influence in
shaping the future of French broadcasting. Its role
is limited by statute, while in the future it may
well be constrained by the creation of new services
outside its jurisdiction.
     Even in the present system the existence of the
High Authority has not led to the emergence in
France of anything approaching a consensus regarding
the political independence of the channels or the
balance of their political output. For example, the
right-wing opposition has contended that prior to
the enactment of the 1982 reform the Socialists
appointed their own sympathisers to the top broadcasting posts, appointments which for the most part
the High Authority later confirmed. Moreover, the
Right argue that appointments made since the establishment of the High Authority, such as that of
Hervé Bourges as director general of TF1, have been
politically motivated.
     Certainly the Socialists clumsily handled the
problem of removing Giscardian collaborators, thus
laying themselves open to the right-wing charge of
indulging in a political witch-hunt.[25] However,
this accusation came oddly from the mouths of
politicians who when in power themselves had systematically removed staff from their posts on political grounds in major purges such as those which took
place in 1968 after the strike at the ORTF and in
1974 during the implementation of the Giscardian
broadcasting reform. Moreover, in the context of
Fifth Republic politics it was inconceivable that
those implicated most closely with the Giscardian
presidency should remain at their posts after
Giscard had been decisively rejected by the electorate. *Le changement* required their removal, as the
crowd who celebrated the Socialist victory in the
place de la Bastille knew only too well.
     In any case the right-wing complaints of poli-
ticisation of the broadcasting media via the new
appointments were exaggerated. Communist sympathisers are few and far between in the top managerial and
editorial posts, as the Communist party leadership
has been at pains to point out. Moreover, while
persons with Socialist sympathies are more numerous,
the political colonisation of broadcasting since
1981 is no more extensive, and arguably less so,

than that which took place during the Peyrefitte
era in the 1960s or the Giscardian presidency in the
1970s.

This is not to deny the accuracy of some of the
opposition criticisms. In the early honeymoon
period of the Mitterrand presidency when the Right
were politically weak and in organisational dis-
array, the policies of the new government were
favourably presented on television. Socialist
spokesmen and ministers, clearly enjoying the fruits
of power, seemed never to be off the screen.[26] After
the introduction of the economic austerity measures
in the summer of 1982 the government used commercial
breaks to defend its economic policies. Presented
as public information and not party political broadcasts, these governmental appeals were not balanced
by any reply from the opposition. Finally, the
amount of coverage given the President, the government and the parties of the governing coalition
(Socialists, Communists and Left-Wing Radicals) far
outweighs that accorded to the opposition parties
(Gaullists, Giscardians and assorted centrists),
though at least the government now makes public the
amount of time given to the respective political
forces.

Again many of the arguments of the opposition
critics fail to be totally convincing because they
are overstated and hypocritical.[27] Even if news
coverage is biased towards the Socialists as they
contend, this cannot be said to be comparable with
the manipulation of the media by the Red Guards in
China during the 'Cultural Revolution', as one
right-wing politician has argued.[28] The preferential treatment given the government and its supporters over the opposition is already evident from the
official figures without the disproportion having to
be magnified by recourse to unofficial, opposition-
sponsored surveys.[29] Political output is not nearly
so crudely one-sided as it was in the 1960s under
the Gaullists, nor is there any reason to believe
that the Right would act much differently than the
Socialists are doing at present if they were in
power. Moreover, one should not forget that most of
the French press is sympathetic to the Right, an
advantage which the Left did not enjoy when it was
in opposition.

Even allowing for the natural hyperbole of
French opposition parties, however, it is clear that
despite the good offices of the High Authority
political output on the state broadcasting channels
is by no means impeccably balanced or impartial. It

has proved very difficult for the Socialists to make a clean break with this feature of the traditional system, since their support in principle for the application of public service ideals to political broadcasting clashes in practice with their desire to have their policies presented in a favourable light, particularly at times of economic crisis and electoral decline. Giscard in 1976 opted for favourable publicity when his regime came under fire. There are signs that, however reluctantly, the Socialists may have made a similar choice.

The third feature of the 1982 reorganisation which sought to differentiate broadcasting under the Socialists from the traditional system was the attempt to decentralise responsibility for a significant share of programming and production from Paris to the regions. Since the second world war French broadcasting has been highly centralised: until relatively recently there was no local radio in France, public or private; regional radio was regarded as an ancillary service to the national networks; regional television production was not encouraged and few regional television programmes were broadcast, with the infamous exception of the progovernmental nightly evening news bulletin screened just before the main national news; finally, regional cultures and languages found little expression on the state broadcasting services. The Napoleonic tradition of centralisation, buttressed by the Gaullist/technocratic commitment to a powerful, centralist state, ensured that broadcasting was used as a 'nation-building' weapon against the possibility of the 'one and indivisible Republic' fragmenting. Thus prior to 1981 state broadcasting was not just synonymous with government broadcasting; it also meant national (ie Parisian) broadcasting as well.[30]

Attempts had been made before 1981 to remedy this state of affairs. In January 1973 a regional television channel was established. After the 1974 Giscardian reorganisation regional television became the responsibility of a separate company, *France Régions 3* (FR3), while regional radio was controlled by the national, state radio company, *Radio France*. The headquarters of both companies were, of course, in Paris. Giscard was no more in favour of devolving political power to the regions than his Gaullist predecessors had been, with the result that the regionalisation of broadcasting, like so many of Giscard's reforms, flattered to deceive.

The 1982 reform sought to reverse this centralist tide. Apart from confirming the legalisation of private local radio, the new statute built upon the tardy Giscardian commitment to state-run local radio under the control of regional radio companies and ultimately *Radio France* itself. The intention was that these local radios would have a considerable measure of autonomy with regard to programming. While as yet relatively few of these public local radio stations exist (only 16 by the end of 1983), the government is committed to the establishment by 1987 of at least one in each department, ie 96 in all. Unlike the private stations, public local radio has to abide by a number of public service obligations, including the normal ones of political pluralism and balanced output. From the inauspicious beginnings of barely audible pirate broadcasts by *Radio Verte* in 1977, France has quickly acquired a system of local radio, public *and* private, but mostly outside state control.

The 1982 statute also converted the regional units of FR3 into separate regional, television companies, initially twelve in number. While a company has also been created at the national level to co-ordinate some of the activities of these regional companies, programming and production policy is now to be decided at regional level. These regional companies began transmissions in September 1983 with programmes in the early evening non-peak period. While to help attract viewers an episode of the American soap opera *Dynasty* was included in the weekly schedule of each region, approximately 90% of programming was to be regionally produced. On the other hand, as most of these programmes are of the cheap, 'talking heads' variety, there must be some doubt about the capacity of regional television to attract viewers in sufficient numbers to make it a success.[31]

It will be some time before definite conclusions can be drawn about the success or failure of regional broadcasting in its new guise. It is already apparent, however, that a decentralist broadcasting policy is not without problems, particularly as regards television. Even with the introduction of commercial advertising on the regional channel it is open to question whether there will be sufficient financial support forthcoming to put the ambitious regional broadcasting policy into practice. It is also not certain, despite early favourable ratings, what level of demand exists for regional programmes. Perhaps when all is said and done even

the Breton nationalist will prefer *Dallas* to programmes about Celtic bagpipe music. If funds are in
short supply and viewing figures low, then the argument stated above regarding the unfavourable position of the state channels vis-à-vis *Canal plus* will
apply with even more force to the regional companies,
who run the risk of becoming the Cinderellas of the
broadcasting system with no Fairy Godmother or
Prince Charming to rescue them from their plight.

THE 'NEW' MEDIA

Despite elements of continuity, the traditional
system of broadcasting in France is undoubtedly
changing, quite noticeably in some respects, as yet
imperceptibly in others. However, the most revolutionary changes still lie ahead. One additional
television channel, the advent of private local
radios, the establishment of the High Authority and
the decentralisation of some production and programming constitute relatively minor alterations when
compared to the possibilities at present being explored with regard to the introduction of new broadcasting services, notably via cable and satellite.
It seems certain that in a few years the average
French viewer in an urban area will be able to receive a multiplicity of television channels on a
scale undreamt of until fairly recently. What consequences this media explosion will have for viewing
habits, programming policy, leisure patterns, the
conduct of politics and a variety of other features
which go to make up 'the French way of life' are by
no means evident as yet. What is clear, however, is
that the introduction of the 'new' media sounds the
death knell for the traditional system.
   The key element in this expansion of television
channels is cable. Not that cable television is
strictly speaking a new medium. It has long been
exploited in the USA and Canada, while even in
France pilot projects were given the go-ahead in the
early 1970s. At that time cable was regarded by
many progressives in western Europe, including France,
as the ideal technology to bring to an end the centralised control of broadcasting by the state. Cable,
it was argued, by encouraging participation in the
life of the local community would revivify inter-
personal communication in a society characterised by
individual alienation and anomie.
   However, the French government at the beginning
of the 1970s was sceptical about the benefits to be
derived from cable television and its instinctive

response was cautious. While in July 1973 cable
experiments were authorised in seven towns, only the
project in Grenoble transmitted programmes on a regular basis. Moreover, after Giscard's election to
the presidency in 1974 the potential of cable as a
local alternative to the national state networks was
not developed. On the contrary, cable was discouraged, with even the Grenoble experiment grinding to a
halt in 1976.[32]

Various reasons can be put forward to explain
the failure of cable to take off in France at this
time. First, and most importantly, the political
will was lacking. Giscard could accept the utility
of cable in its minimalist role as an aid to transmission in areas of poor programme reception, ie as
a relay for the programmes of the state channels.
However, he was totally opposed to its use as an
alternative source of programming.

> I think that at the moment we should think
> about whether we have to keep on multiplying
> *ad infinitum* the range of mass media. The risk
> is that the media destroy each other, as we can
> see happening with the present difficulties of
> the press. The three state television channels
> have not yet reached a stage of full develop-
> ment. Therefore, we have to wait for the full
> use of the present media before asking the
> question about the future role of alternative
> media.[33]

Giscard's opposition to the development of cable as
a local medium was based partly, therefore, on the
difficulties such a measure would create for the
regional press and the competition it might generate
for the state channels. Both of these media stood
to lose out as disseminators of information and
beneficiaries from advertising revenue. The opposition of the influential regional press lobby was
particularly important in strangling the infant
cable at birth. Secondly, given the lack of state
backing, private enterprise was reluctant to invest
in a technology which showed limited capacity for
profitability. Finally, in the absence of fibre
optics technology, the potential of cable as an
interactive medium was not yet apparent.

Under President Mitterrand the government's
attitude to cable has changed quite dramatically.
Far from being regarded as an unwanted ancillary
service or unnecessary competitor, cable has now
been elevated to the status of essential component

in the so-called communications revolution. As such
the implications of its development extend far beyond its capacity to extend viewers' programming
choice by acting as the carrier for numerous television channels. In fact, the television side of
cable, which is being used at present as the carrot
to entice people to subscribe to the new service,
will in future be of relatively minor importance.
In the longer term the development of a whole range
of interactive services such as teletext, videotext,
telebanking, teleshopping and so on will be of much
greater significance as France embraces the new information technology, which brings together the
previously discrete services of the telephone, the
television and the computer.

The present enthusiasm of the Mitterrand government for cable has, therefore, very little to do
with broadcasting as traditionally conceived or with
local community television, though the ramifications
of cable will be felt in both these areas. Rather
cable is being pushed in France because the development of fibre optics technology is seen as an essential element in France's adjustment to the changing
world economy. With the downgrading of the traditional manufacturing industries such as steel, ship-
building and heavy engineering, the French government believes that if France is to compete in the
international marketplace it must concentrate on
certain key industrial sectors, including the new,
high technology, 'sunrise' industries. Thus France,
which has never fully completed its industrial
revolution, is already seeking to ensure its place
in the communications revolution of the 1980s.[34]

There are other reasons too why cable is now
being positively encouraged. The installation of
cable networks will help provide much needed jobs
(though exactly how many is at present uncertain) in
a country with an unemployment total of around two
million. In addition, with the development of
satellite broadcasting in Europe the cabling of
households will do away with the need for each householder to purchase the special receiving device, the
'dish', otherwise necessary to receive programmes
directly by satellite. Instead, each cable network
can have a central reception station which will receive the satellite broadcasts and transmit them via
cable to households. If this solution is adopted by
the French government, then no additional expenditure will be required on the part of the householder
over and above his regular cable subscription. It
will also mean that lower powered telecommunications

satellites could be used for television transmission
in preference to the more complex direct broadcasting satellites (DBS). At the same time regulation
of programme material will also be made easier,
since satellite output can then be controlled at the
central reception station. The relevant controlling
authorities, the government for national programming
and the High Authority for local broadcasts, will be
able to monitor what the French viewers watch. As a
result, undesirable output or offensive material can
be kept off the screen.

In the autumn of 1982 the government announced
its strategy on cable.[35] It is intended that one
and a half million households will be linked to a
cable system by 1986, with one million additional
households being connected every year after that. In
Paris alone it is hoped that 500,000 households will
receive cable by the end of 1989, while an experimental phase to cable 10,000 households should be
completed in 1984. Lille, Lyons, Montpellier, as
well as those towns which experimented with cable in
the 1970s, have jumped on to the cable bandwagon.
The cabling of France in the 1980s is reminiscent of
the government's drive to install a modern telephone
network in the previous decade: a strong technocratic commitment on the part of the state to the
development of an up-to-date communications system.

In contrast to Britain, where the government is
relying on private investment to cable the nation,
in France the state through the Ministry of Posts
and Telecommunications is responsible for supervising the installation of the technical infrastructure which then remains its property. However, the
initiative to cable a particular area and the
management of the cable telvision network are the
responsibility of the local authorities, who bear up
to 30% of the initial investment costs. With regard
to control of programming, each participating
authority has been asked to set up a body specifically designed for this task (*société locale
d'exploitation commerciale*) composed of representatives from the public and/or private sectors, but
usually including members from the state transmission company. A variety of interests may be involved at this stage, including press groups and
commercial enterprises intent on securing a stake in
the new multi-media future. No person or company
can, however, have a financial interest in more than
one cable service.

As far as the television programmes themselves
are concerned, it seems clear that while in some

towns the proposals give some weight to local
community services, in the first instance at any
rate the emphasis will be on entertainment television so as to attract subscribers. These will pay
an initial capital sum to be linked up to the network and then a monthly subscription. For example,
the municipality of Paris has proposed that cable
subscribers should receive programmes from the
following sources in the short term: the three state
channels (TF1, *Antenne 2* and FR3); two peripheral
television channels, so-called because like the
peripheral radio stations they operate from just
outside French territory, *Radio Télévision Luxembourg* and *Télé Monte Carlo*; one British channel,
either BBC or ITV; two local channels, both run by
private companies, one of which will concentrate on
a specific target audience such as young people or
sports enthusiasts; the new fourth channel, *Canal
plus*; and finally, programmes from the recently
established Francophone satellite service, TV5,
which shows the best programmes from the three
French state companies, the Belgian broadcasting
services and the Francophone Swiss service.[36] To
help pay for these programmes, up to a maximum of
80% of the necessary operational finance of any
service can come from commercial advertising. In
the longer term it is intended that subscribers will
be able to order their own television programmes
from a 'menu' they can consult on their screens. The
interactive services will follow later.

Apart from cable, other changes are taking
place or being considered which contribute to the
overall picture of a system in flux. For example, a
new company entitled *la Régie Française des Espaces*
(RFE), is to be set up to manage the utilisation of
spare programming capacity on TF1, *Antenne 2* and
FR3. RFE will hire out time on these channels outside of their own normal transmission hours to companies, associations, community groups and so on.
Trade unions and political parties, however, will
not be allowed to rent the available television time.
For anything between five minutes to an hour the
groups who have purchased this facility will be able
to use it for public information programmes, staff
training, company communication, educational or
cultural purposes.[37]

Finally, for industrial reasons the government
may decide to maintain its interest in operating a
direct broadcasting satellite for fear of leaving
this potential export market to its rivals. The
French and West German governments agreed to combine

forces on the construction of direct broadcasting
satellites back in the late 1970s. The French DBS,
named TDF1, is due to be launched in 1985 and was
intended to carry TF1, *Antenne 2* and a peripheral
television channel, providing better reception to
all areas of France. At the moment, however, the
French commitment to DBS is being reviewed, with the
powerful Ministry of Posts apparently favouring the
cable/telecommunications satellite option at the expense of DBS.[38]   However, even if the government
does decide to bow out of DBS, sufficient innovations will already have been introduced to change
radically the nature of the French broadcasting
system in the space of a few years.

CONCLUSION

The main theme of this chapter has been that broadcasting in France is at present going through a
period of flux and transition after many years of
relative stability. Whereas previously the established system was modified or adapted in an incre-
mental fashion, now the nature and scope of the
changes being introduced point to the emergence of a
wholly different set-up. In Kuhnian terms French
broadcasting is undergoing a paradigmatic shift,
with the long-standing traditional system giving way
to a successor.
      As far as the viewer is concerned, the major
innovation lies in the multiplication of channels
and the increase in programming hours: more television will be available for consumption more frequently. As the number of outlets expands in geo-
metric progression, no longer will the viewer be
restricted to the programme output of one, two or at
most three channels. Rather he will have a wide
variety of programme sources from which to choose.
At the same time the individual schedules are increasing in length to fill up previously neglected
time-slots as France moves ineluctably to all-day
(and in the future presumably round-the-clock)
television. Already the state companies are considering emulating the British channels in importing
the horrendous American practice of breakfast television. Moreover, as in other western countries,
albeit more slowly than in the US or Britain, the
spread of video cassette recorders will free the
viewer from externally imposed scheduling constraints
and allow him to exercise greater control over his
own programme intake. The era of the undisputed
dominance of the state channels is undoubtedly at an

end. The age of viewer sovereignty is apparently
beginning.
   This brave new broadcasting world is not without its own problems, however, particularly for the
state sector which seems destined to become the poor
relation of the system. The implementation of the
1982 statute, including notably its commitment to
regionalised broadcasting output, has resulted in
the employment of more staff with a consequent increase in operational costs. At the same time home-
based television production is fiercely expensive
and uncompetitive. As a result, the state channels
are having to operate within very tight budgetary
constraints as regards programming policy. Much of
the output, therefore, already consists of low
budget studio programmes, such as game shows or
debates, feature films and imported material, especially from the US. The screening of French produced television fiction, whether it be the adaptation for television of a classic novel or a new
drama specially written for the small screen, would
appear to be on an unstoppable decline: 19.5% of
total programme output in 1978, only 12.7% in 1982.[39]
There is little reason to expect a reversal of
this trend in the future as the state channels engage in severe competition for audiences with restricted resources.
   What may the situation be like in the longer
term? Some of the new channels will appeal to
specialised markets and cater for tastes from 'high'
to 'lowbrow' which the state channels with their
statutorily imposed balanced schedules could never
hope to satisfy fully: opera lovers as well as pop
music addicts may eventually have their individual
television channels just as they have their separate radio stations now. Many channels, however,
will not be specialised, nor will they carry balanced schedules. They will be mere distributors of a
standardised, predominantly American-style product:
offending few people, pleasing many, inspiring none.
As French production companies, both state and
private, are squeezed by American producers who can
spread their costs over a larger domestic and international market, French television will almost
certainly become even less of a vehicle for the
spread of the national culture than it is today.
   Will the changes mean that broadcasting output
will be of lower quality than, say, twenty years
previously? There can be no undisputed answer to
this question, since any response will be based on a
subjective assessment of programme standards. There

may be a natural tendency on the part of some to
hark back to an alleged golden age of French television: where are the shows of yesteryear? Some
will bemoan the new system as a move away from
public service ideals, while others will welcome the
enlarged choice of channels.

It seems clear, however, that there will in
future be a closer link between the size of payment
made by the viewer on the one hand and the type and
quality of product available for consumption on the
other. There will no longer be a flat-rate licence
payable by all equally.[40] Viewers will not only pay
more for television, but the cost will vary depending on what they want, or more importantly can
afford, to watch. The audience will fragment, with
many viewers consuming more of what they want from
television, provided they can pay. Others, notably
the less well-off, will be deprived of what in the
past might have been provided by the state channels
as part of their public service obligations. In
short, there will be different classes of viewer.

At the systemic level, some types of programming may well not be affordable by any single channel, since none can be assured of securing a large
enough audience. Fragmentation of the audience will
result in certain diseconomies of scale. If so, the
short-term satisfaction of individual consumer
choice will lead to the elimination of some options.
Inevitably some types of programme, such as expensive documentaries, will no longer be made, not due
to lack of demand, but rather because no single
channel will be willing and able *on its own* to
attempt to satisfy the demand. The new channels
will not take the financial risks the traditional
public service channels might have accepted in the
past, while the state companies will now lack the
necessary finance themselves. If this scenario is
correct, the multiplication of channels will lead to
some reduction in programme choice for *all* viewers,
as consumption and programming decisions which are
perfectly rational at the level of the individual
viewer and separate channel have unintended and undesirable consequences at the level of the system.
French viewer sovereignty will not be limitless or
without costs.

Good or bad, desirable or undesirable, enlarg-
ing or reducing choice, opening up new horizons or
reinforcing American cultural imperialism, the
change to a new broadcasting system is taking place.
Moreover, there is now no going back, since even if
a return to the traditional system were still

possible, which is doubtful, it is in any case not considered desirable by any of the major political parties in France which might reasonably expect to influence policy in this field. The previous commitment to a state monopoly broadcasting system, which cut across the right-left party divide, is now regarded as anachronistic by most sections of the political elite, with the possible exception of the electorally declining Communist party which as ever wants to fight the present war on the same lines as the previous one. Whether the future works or not, it is here to stay.

References

1.   R. Thomas, *Broadcasting and Democracy in France*, London, Crosby Lockwood Staples, 1976, p.1.
2.   R. Kuhn, 'Government and Broadcasting in France: the resumption of normal service', *West European Politics*, vol.3 no.2, May 1980, p.205.
3.   J. Montaldo, *Dossier ORTF 1944-74: Tous Coupables*, Paris, Albin Michel, 1974.
4.   P. Viansson-Ponté, *Histoire de la République Gaullienne*, (vol.1), Paris, Fayard, 1970, p.70.
5.   J. Thibau, *Une télévision pour tous les français*, Paris, Seuil,1970. C. Durieux, *La Télécratie*, Paris, Tema, 1976, pp.31-37.
6.   A. Werth, *The De Gaulle Revolution*, London, Robert Hale, 1960, p.396.
7.   Alain Peyrefitte's speech in *Journal Officiel, Débats Assemblée Nationale*, May 27 1964, p.1377.
8.   On broadcasting during the 1968 'events' see R. Louis, *L'ORTF un combat*, Paris, Seuil, 1968 and A. Astoux, *Ondes de Choc*, Paris, Plon, 1978.
9.   J. Thibau, *La télévision, le pouvoir et l'argent*, Paris, Calmann-Lévy, 1973, pp.17-46.
10. *Journal Officiel, Documents Assemblée Nationale*, 1973-74, no.1072, June 20 1974. (The Chinaud report).
11. R. Kuhn, 'The presidency and the media, 1974-82', in V. Wright (ed.), *Continuity and Change in France*, London, Allen and Unwin, 1984.
12. J. Ardagh, *The New France*,(2nd edition), Harmondsworth, Pelican, 1973, pp.614-615.
13. J.-N. Jeanneney and M. Sauvage, *Télévision, Nouvelle Mémoire*, Paris, Seuil, 1982.
14. J. Siclier, *Un homme averty*, Paris, Jean-Claude Simoen, 1976, pp.192-201.
15. R. Kuhn, 'Judging French TV by its programmes', *Intermedia*, vol.6 no.1, February 1978.
16. M. Souchon, *Petit Ecran, Grand Public*, Paris, Documentation Française, 1980, p.152.
17. For a summary of the main provisions of the 1982 reform see R. Kuhn, 'Broadcasting and Politics in France', *Parliamentary Affairs*, vol.36 no.1, 1983.
18. First annual report of the High Authority for Audiovisual Communication, Paris, 1983, p.37.
19. *Le Monde*, September 25 1982.
20. *Le Monde*, October 21 1983.
21. This option caused some disquiet within the French Socialist party. For example, see the article

on Didier Motchane's criticisms of government
policy in *Le Monde*, July 20 1983.
    22. *L'Express*, no.1689, November 25 1983.
    23. *Le Monde*, February 17 1984.
    24. R. Kuhn, 'Broadcasting and Politics in
France', p.77.
    25. *Observer*, June 21 1981.
    26. J.-F. Revel, *La grâce de l'Etat*, Paris,
Grasset, 1981, ch.7.
    27. See, for example, M. Poniatowski, *Lettre
ouverte au Président de la République*, Paris, Albin
Michel, 1983, pp.121-133.
    28. A. Peyrefitte, *Quand la rose se fanera ...*,
Paris, Plon, 1983, chs. 19-22.
    29. M. D'Ornano, *La manipulation des médias*,
Paris, Albatros, 1983, pp.52-56.
    30. D. Descollines, 'Propos sur la télévision
régionale', *Projet*, no.112, 1977.
    31. *Le Monde*, September 3 1983.
    32. *Presse Actualité*, nos. 81-82, March-April
1973 and F. Barbry, *La télévision par câbles*, Paris,
Cerf, 1975.
    33. *Télé-7-jours*, no.821, February 1976.
    34. H. Pigeat, *La télévision par câble commence
demain*, Paris, Plon, 1983.
    35. *Le Monde*, November 5 1982.
    36. *Télédistribution*, no.5, 1983.
    37. *Le Monde*, October 27 1983.
    38. *Connections*, no.1, October 1983.
    39. First annual report of the High Authority
for Audiovisual Communication, Paris, 1983, p.64.
    40. This statement should not be interpreted
too literally. Since the mid-1970s there have been
two licence-fee rates, one for colour and the other
for black and white sets. In 1983 the rate for the
former was 471 francs (approximately £40) and for
the latter 311 francs (approximately £25).

Bibliographical note

In general there are few works published in English
on broadcasting in France. The basic book, contain-
ing much factual information, is R. Thomas, *Broadcasting and Democracy in France*, London, Crosby
Lockwood Staples, 1976. In addition, the reader
might usefully consult the following: A. de Tarlé,
'France: the monopoly that won't divide', in A.
Smith (ed.), *Television and Political Life*, London,
Macmillan, 1979; J. Ardagh, *The New France*, Harmondsworth, Pelican, 1973 (second edition) and 1977
(third edition); J. Ardagh, *France in the 1980s*,

Pelican, Harmondsworth, 1982; and the articles by myself, which are mentioned in references 2, 11 and 17.

Chapter Three

WEST GERMANY: THE SEARCH FOR THE WAY FORWARD

Arthur Williams

When Helmut Kohl made history in October 1982 by
ousting Chancellor Helmut Schmidt in the first successful 'constructive vote of no confidence'[1], he
made much of the idea that he was the first Chancellor of the postwar generation. There was a sense in
the air that the SPD-FDP[2] alliance had run out of
ideas and lost the will to act; the new regime would
bring fresh minds and fresh energy to the task of
getting the economy moving again and setting the
country to rights. Kohl lost no time in demonstrating that any doubts about the strength of popular
support for the change were ill-founded when he
reinforced his position in the general election of
March 1983. Although some doubts may remain both
about the morality (though not the legality) of the
constructive vote of no confidence and about the
legality (though not morality) of the way the early
election was engineered[3], there can be no doubts
about the strength of purpose demonstrated by both
of these actions.
     Although it is still much too soon to judge the
impact of the change of regime and the qualities of
Kohl's chancellorship, it is possible to see the
ultimate smoothness with which the change-over was
accomplished, together with the naturalness of
Kohl's decision to seek ratification from the electorate and the ease with which the Greens took their
place in the *Bundestag* for the first time, as clear
confirmation that West German parliamentary democracy works perfectly well in practice. Indeed, it
might be argued that continuity through change is
emerging as one of the principal characteristics of
West German politics and one of which the principal
political actors are explicitly aware.
     One of the major themes in Willy Brandt's first
declaration of government policy in 1969[4], when the

SPD became the senior partner in the governing coalition for the first time, was 'continuity and renewal' coupled with the desire to 'venture more democracy'; Helmut Kohl marked the CDU's return to power in his first declaration of policy[5] by entitling it 'Coalition of the Centre: For a Policy of Renewal', dwelling on the continuities with earlier CDU-FDP governments and ending with a strong statement of the principles on which the renewal of the country's energies would be based - in effect, a reaffirmation of the West German democratic order. Many of the points made in his statement could have been made equally well by an SPD-FDP coalition; his second policy statement[6], coming as it did only a few months after the first, maintained the same pattern.

It is hardly surprising, given the constraints facing any West German government - German history, the geo-political situation, constitutional structures, nationally and internationally established policies and a continuing coalition partner (FDP) - that there should be little sign of major changes of course between governments of different colour.[7] However, between Brandt and Kohl, despite similarities of formulation, much had changed on the political agenda; Kohl's immediate problems may be unemployment and the social budget, but he is also facing questions about the shape of society in an age of new technologies (for example, cable and satellite), new environmental concerns and new awareness of the vulnerability of individual privacy.

In his second policy statement, Kohl pointed to three areas of technological development which hold both opportunities and dangers for the future: new production techniques, biotechnology and new information and communications technologies. He referred to the latter also in his first policy statement. On both occasions he spoke of the opportunity to stimulate the economy and of the potential contribution to the development of West German democracy offered by an increased variety of opinion presented to the public. While the two ideas were kept well apart in the earlier speech, in the second speech they were closely linked; furthermore, in the second speech, he saw the federal government seeking an early opportunity to enter a dialogue with the federal States (*Länder*) about the media system of the future - an idea suggested only tentatively in his first statement.

There is no evidence to show that Kohl planned to introduce a comprehensive, tightly-knit scheme for

he media as part of his policy and there is some
evidence[8] that his ideas on the broadcasting component were more circumspect; however, the basic ideas
and the position they occupy in his policy statements do provide clear indications of what was
generally held to be a new major area of development.
The second statement in particular shows how easy it
is to link together ideas that are, in fact, barely
related and how readily questions long resolved are
reopened in the belief that the new communication
technologies are really new media requiring new
legislation.

It is important, if one is to understand developments in the West German broadcasting system in
the mid-1980s, to disentangle some of the confusions
of which Helmut Kohl's policy statements are only a
very public reflection and, more importantly, to
uncover the continuities in these developments, thus
pointing up any really new factors.

Clearly, fibre optics is the technology which
could draw all the various elements together, and it
is the anticipation of this that lies at the root of
the confused thinking about the changing media; yet
the technology itself does not have the power, and
even its potential may not imply the necessity, to
change basic, established relationships within the
media of communication and information. Nor, inci-
dentally, does it necessarily imply an increase in
jobs, but rather the opposite.[9] Similarly, the im-
pression that it has been left to the CDU to open
the gates to the brave new world of the modern media
tends to disregard many of the facts: the time-scale
involved, projects already in progress and the
eagerness of the business world and the public for
the new technologies. What is new is the wholly
positive attitude of the new government to the new
technologies.

The SPD, not least Helmut Schmidt himself[10],
had very serious reservations about the possible
effects on society, individuals and the family, of
the multiplication of the number of available television programmes. The SPD did not believe, as Kohl
does, that an increase in the forms taken by broadcasting and a greater number of programmes necessarily implied improvements in the information of
the citizen and the facilitation of better opinion
formation. However, while the SPD did tend to take
a more cautious approach, they did not close their
minds to the new technologies: almost all of the
developments currently in progress and which might
become linked in fact as well as in people's minds

because of the versatility of optical fibre owe
their initial impetus to the 'Report of the Commission on the Development of Technical Communcations
Systems' (KtK).

The KtK commission was constituted at the behest of the SPD-FDP government in November 1973 and
presented its report at the end of 1976. The range
of developments since then has been bewildering.
They include: projects in Berlin and Düsseldorf to
test *Bildschirmtext* (Btx - teletext) based on the
British viewdata system, organised by the federal
Post Office and due to finish in late 1983[11]; large-
scale optical fibre cabling in seven cities (Berlin,
Hamburg, Hanover, Düsseldorf, Stuttgart, Nuremberg
and Munich) to improve local telecommunications
(known as BIGFON), which it is intended later to
integrate via long-distance links using fibre optics
(known as BIGFERN), the first of which (Hamburg-
Hanover) was sanctioned by the last government for
1983-84; new experiments in Berlin by six companies
to raise the long-distance communication potential
of optical fibre, commissioned by the federal Post
Office as part of the government's 'communications
technology' programme; satellite feasibility studies
relating to both telecommunications and broadcasting;
field studies with videotext on the two main television channels - mainly so far of programme information and therefore not greatly similar to Ceefax
and Oracle; pilot projects in cable broadcasting
planned to start in the near future in four centres
(Berlin, Dortmund, Ludwigshafen and Munich) for
which the federal States are responsible; the expansion of and experimentation with local and regional
radio services (particularly in north Germany and
Baden-Württemberg); and, finally, first steps on the
road to new legislation to accommodate the proliferation of broadcasting services and particularly
private broadcasting companies (in Baden-Württemberg
and Lower Saxony). These latter may seem premature,
given that the pilot projects in cable television
have still to start, but they are best seen as part
of the same search for the way forward. The two
States involved have been able to introduce draft
legislation at this stage because a foundation of
fundamental principles has been created in the past,
most relevantly perhaps in the very recent past,
that makes current and future legislation essentially a matter of adjustment and adaptation to new
circumstances.

THE WEST GERMAN CONSTITUTION

To understand this process fully, one must be aware
of the essential elements in the West German constitution and their origins - it is an easy and mis-
taken assumption that West German institutions, because they were apparently drafted on a *tabula rasa*
after 1945, have only shallow roots and are somehow
'culturally neutral', even easily transferred to
other countries (e.g. the view that the West German
models of industrial democracy and proportional
representation might be emulated in Britain). The
West German political system involves a very complex
set of finely gauged checks and balances; it rests
on long traditions of political thought, has been
tempered by the experience of history and was honed
under the guiding hand of the powers of occupation
after the war.
    The present discussion is concerned less with
the daily politicking that affects the media than
with the importance of constitutional infrastructures for the shaping of the political and institutional superstructure: the institutions are shaped
by and embody the principles of the constitution, in
turn transmitting them and nurturing the values that
are characteristic of the West German political
culture. It is an organic process and just as one
can better understand the development of an institution if one is aware of the principles of the
constitution, so one can better appreciate the
workings of the constitution through the study of an
institution (here broadcasting).
    It is, perhaps, worth making the preliminary
remark that the West German constitution acts essentially as a force for stability and that this is
reflected in the shaping of the broadcasting system.
The founding fathers sought, above all, to ensure
that history did not repeat itself. The salient
features of German history of relevance here - a
detailed analysis is unnecessary - are the lack of
legal means to prevent the all-embracing National-
Socialist *gleichschaltung* of state and society and
the weaknesses of the Weimar constitution which, together with factors relating to the state of the
economy and the international situation, opened the
way for Hitler's rise to power. The Bonn *Basic Law*
(*Grundgesetz* - with the attendant complementary legislation, effectively the constitution) has pronounced federal characteristics to encourage a decentra-

lisation of decision-making in crucial areas, is
underpinned by a codex of basic rights which emanate
from and seek to guarantee a concept of the inviolable dignity of man and envisages an important role
for organisations representing the public in various
ways, particularly the trade unions and the political parties. The power of the latter is related to
a sophisticated system of proportional representation designed to promote a fair balance of representation and at the same time to avoid excessive fragmentation (parties must win 5% of the vote before
they are entitled to any parliamentary seats, making
it very difficult for the proliferation of small parties that undermined Weimar democracy to recur). The
fear of instability also explains the limited powers
of the President to dissolve the federal parliament
before a legislature has run full term.

The two essential relationships the Bonn constitution seeks to regulate - both rooted in German traditions - are that of the central authorities *(Bund)*
to the federal States *(Länder)*, where the latter have
extensive powers and are sovereign in the crucial
area of culture (which includes both education and
broadcasting), and that between the state (all levels
of state administration) and the title *Bundesstaat*
(federal state), the latter forms the substance of
the much more difficult concept *socialer Rechtsstaat*.
[12]. In the *Rechtsstaat*, the law rules supreme; no aspect of life, including government, is above the law
- and since the foundation stone of the West German
Rechsstaat is the codex of the inalienable rights of
the individual[13], the freedom of the individual is
protected by the law (and by specific legislation)
against all influences that might curtail or undermine it.

The potential inequalities of the *Rechtsstaat*,
where the weaker members of society might be unable
to exercise their rights on an equal footing with
its stronger members, are offset by the duties
assumed by the state as a *Sozialstaat* to ensure that
all citizens have an equal chance in life. However,
the state in the *Socialstaat* performs only a subsidiary function as a provider of welfare (subsidiary
to the individual, his family and the local authorities who, as free agents, are directly responsible
for the provision of welfare); this differs from the
welfare state where the state has a primary role to
play - with possible negative implications for the
freedom of the individual.

The system is complex and there are clearly
many points at which conflicts of interest can (and

do) arise in it. Since these have ultimately to be
resolved in such a way that the basic principles of
a written constitution amplified in specific laws
are upheld, the courts have an important role to
play in shaping political and social relationships
in the federal Republic. The federal Constitutional
Court (*Bundesverfassungsgericht*), in particular, as
the supreme interpreter of the *Basic Law* and the
final arbiter on the compatibility of any piece of
legislation, any administrative act or any court
ruling with the constitution, holds a position of
paramount importance in the West German system. No
organ of the state is above it and its decisions
have the force of law, requiring the appropriate
legislation as a necessary consequence; it plays a
crucial role in the resolution of conflicts between
the various organs and levels of government, between
the States and the central authorities and in regulating the relationship of the state to the individual citizen in all its manifestations.[14]

West Germany has become a model of stability
because its constitution provides a firm framework
and clear point of orientation for the resolution of
conflict situations by negotiation, compromise and,
particularly, judicial mediation. It allows creative tension around a system of values on which all
the principal actors are agreed; the problems that
do arise do not call into question the validity of
fundamental principles, rather do they relate to
their interpretation as conditions change and the
understanding of the system and its values deepens
and develops.

THE BROADCASTING SYSTEM

All of these features of the West German political
system are reflected in the broadcasting system as
it has developed since the early postwar years.
There are ten broadcasting organisations ('houses')
broadcasting to the native public; two others provide external services and there are also networks
for the foreign military personnel stationed in the
country. The number of houses reflects the cultural
sovereignty of the federal States: six have their
own broadcasting house (Berlin - *Sender Freies
Berlin* (SFB); Bremen - *Radio Bremen* (RB); North
Rhine-Westphalia - *Westdeutscher Rundfunk* (WDR);
Hessen - *Hessischer Rundfunk* (HR); Saarland -
Saarländischer Rundfunk (SR); Bavaria - *Bayerischer
Rundfunk* (BR); one State Baden-Württemberg, has
effectively two: *Süddeutscher Rundfunk* (SDR) serves

the southern part of the State, while the northern
part shares *Südwestfunk* (SWF) with the neighbouring
Rhineland-Palatinate; the three north German States
(Hamburg, Lower Saxony and Schleswig-Holstein) share
Norddeutscher Rundfunk (NDR); and all of the eleven
States together founded the second television
channel, *Zweites Deutsches Fernsehen* (ZDF).[15] The
fact that three broadcasting houses (NDR, SWF and
SDR) serve areas that are not coterminous with the
political and administrative boundaries of any
single State reflects, on the one hand, the reorganisation of the State boundaries in south-west Germany,
(notably the creation of Baden-Württemberg in 1951)
and, on the other, the influence of the powers of
occupation: the British founded only one broadcasting house for the whole of their zone (*Nordwest-
deutscher Rundfunk*, NWDR) and this later split into
three as Berlin (in 1953) and North Rhine-Westphalia
(in 1954) felt the need for broadcasting houses of
their own. The three north German States continued
to share a broadcasting house because further sub-
division of the region seemed undesirable at the
time; recently, given the demographic and political
changes in the region, the bonds between these three
States have been severely tested.

The federal States have developed various
patterns of cooperation in order to give themselves
greater corporate strength and also to ensure the
equal treatment of all citizens irrespective of
whether they live in a small and fairly isolated
State such as Saarland or a large and well-inhabited
one such as Bavaria. This system of cooperative
federalism finds expression in broadcasting in agreements both between the broadcasting houses and between the States (usually represented by their Prime
Ministers). The broadcasting houses established a
loose corporate identity when, in 1950, they founded
their joint working group, the *Arbeitsgemeinschaft
der öffentlich-rechtlichen Rundfunkanstalten der
Bundesrepublik Deutschland* (ARD) through which they
manage various levels of cooperation; the most
obvious example of this is the first television
channel, *Deutsches Fernsehen* (DFS) which they produce jointly on a proportional basis and which they
all receive. A system of financial equalisation is
operated by which the larger corporations subsidise
the smaller; this requires the endorsement of the
States. ARD and ZDF also cooperate at a number of
levels (for example, with regard to common problems
and projects of shared interest). This pattern of
cooperation and equalisation has strengthened the

broadcasting houses as a group and reduced potential anomalies, but it has also tended to decrease the natural variety which is the life-blood of the federal system (for example, by programme-sharing). Thus, the output is not as regionally diverse as one might suppose given the decentralist structure of the system.

The relationship of the individual citizen to the state is mirrored in the patterns of control in broadcasting; these seek to guarantee the freedom of information and opinion by ensuring that an accept-able plurality of views is present in the organs of control and, most importantly, in the programme out-put. All of the broadcasting houses are public corporations; they are controlled not by the State, but by boards (broadcasting councils) representing the public and the bulk of their income is drawn from licence fees. However, no system is perfect, and the West German system has its weak points: the level of the licence fee is fixed by the Prime Ministers of the States; there is some dependence on income from advertising and this reaches worrying proportions in some broadcasting houses (SR is usually cited here, while ZDF depends for almost 40% of its total income on advertising revenue); finally, the selection of members of broadcasting councils can similarly be considered less than perfect where the system is inflexible, where it relates only to established interest groups and where it favours the main political parties at the expense of other, non-political interests.

Since each broadcasting house is governed by the broadcasting law of the relevant State (or by agreement between States), no two situations are identical; some problems, however, have over the thirty five years of the federal Republic's history confronted all of the broadcasting houses to a greater or lesser extent. Indeed, the history of broadcasting can be seen as the progressive explora-tion of these basic relationships, where each point of definition and orientation has been marked by a conflict of interests. Many of these conflicts have been resolved in the courts, with the three 'television judgements' (*Fernseh-Urteile*) of the federal Constitutional Court (1961, 1971 and 1981) being the most famous[16]; all of them, following the principles of the constitution, have been resolved in the interests of free broadcasting under plura-listic public control.[17]

What the advent of cable and the attendant technologies has brought that is new is their

potential to blur or remove two fundamental dis-
tinctions and this could have consequences for all
of the structures outlined above. Broadcasting (the
making and transmitting of programmes) has always
been seen as different and separate from telecommunications (the prerogative of the federal Post
Office) and, by dint of its technical limitations,
also from the press whose freedom is seen as guaranteed in the plurality of newspapers and magazines
available. This sort of pluralism has not hitherto
been possible in broadcasting, hence the need to
ensure a plurality of views *within* the broadcasting
councils and in each programme.[18]
     It is possible to identify four sources of
pressure on the broadcasting system which have had
to be resisted at different times; one was effectively neutralised by the 1961 judgement of the
federal Constitutional Court, the other three have
still to be resisted today - although their relative
significance has changed over time. The first, the
attempt by the central, federal authorities to become involved in broadcasting by founding the second
television service was a clear case of incipient
misconceptions about the constitutionally defined
areas of competence outlined above (see also below
for a further discussion of the 1961 ruling). The
other three sources of pressure might be considered
legitimate in a democratic system with a market
economy; here it has been a question of regulation,
of balancing interests and of defining and redefin-
ing the parameters and range of their respective
influence as the system and available technologies
have changed. The three interests are those of the
political parties, broadcasting personnel and commercial lobbies. Although the three are treated
more or less discretely here, they have been con-
current, competing and complementary by turns and to
varying degrees in different broadcasting houses.
The commercial groupings, now at the point of breakthrough, have emerged as the most potent of the
three in terms of future developments and for this
reason will be dealt with in a separate section.
     The problems with the first group, *the politi-
cal parties*, have been most publicised in relation
to NDR and, although this does not mean that the
parties have not influenced other broadcasting
houses and that these have not shown a leaning to
the Left or to the Right in their programmes, it is
certainly in the north German station that the
phenomemon known as *Proporz* has been most pronounced.
Proporz might be described as the worst side of

proportional representation: the political parties
share out seats and posts proportionally between
themselves according to their local parliamentary
(or, for example, town council) strength at the expense, often to the exclusion, of other legitimate
interests. In NDR employment of this tactic by the
parties tended in the early 1970s to go beyond the
legal limits set for their representation on the
broadcasting and administrative councils and also to
lead to deadlock situations in the latter.
   The roots of the problem in NDR can be traced
back to the preference of the British for the one,
large broadcasting house serving the whole of their
zone and to their belief that the State parliaments,
as elected representatives of the public, were emi-
nently qualified to appoint the members of the
organs of control of a public broadcasting corporation. This is the 'parliamentary' model of control,
as opposed to the 'social groups' or 'pluralistic'
model of control where the interest groups entitled
to representation nominate their own representatives
on the broadcasting council.
   There were, then, two levels of division involved in the appointment of NWDR board members and
this was retained in NDR when the larger broadcasting house was split up: each of the three north
German States had its allocation of NDR broadcasting
council seats and these, in turn, were proportionally divided between the parties in the respective
parliament. This process was taken a step further
when the States founded ZDF after the 1961 ruling;
here, the senior posts in the broadcasting house
itself became the subject of *Proporz* and the parties
sought to influence their men at meetings held outside the purview of the broadcasting house and its
controlling organs.[20]
   These developments can be seen as part of the
process of political self-definition that extended
over a period of some fifteen years from the mid-
1950s: the federal Republic became fully sovereign
in 1955 and the CDU gained a massive election victory in 1957, while the SPD, which had a number of
strongholds in the States (Berlin, Hamburg, North-
Rhine-Westphalia and Hessen) revised its platform in
order to contest the middle ground of German politics.[21] The early 1960s saw the building of the
Berlin Wall (1961), the defeat of Adenauer's plans
for the second television service *Fernseh-Urteil*
(1961) and the humiliation of his Minister of
Defence, Franz-Josef Strauss in the *Spiegel* affair
(1962). With the formation of the Grand Coalition

between CDU/CSU and SPD in 1966 (as a result of the
breakdown of the CDU-FDP coalition after a year in
office), new fora for the expression of political
views not adequately represented in the West German
parliament (*Bundestag*) had to be found - the 'extra-
parliamentary opposition' movement started, bringing
with it the swing that finally brought the SPD to
power as the senior coalition partner in 1969 and
also the onset of urban terrorism. It was also at
this time that the polarisation in broadcasting increased and the parties' drive to gain extra influence over the medium provoked responses from the
broadcasters and also from the public, resulting
ultimately in the definition of acceptable limits
for their involvement in the control of the broadcasting houses.

Limits were set for the political parties by
two events, each involving the redrafting of broadcasting legislation: the change in the Bavarian
broadcasting law in 1973 and the renegotiation of
the NDR treaty in 1980. At no time was the importance of the political parties as vehicles of public
representation challenged, indeed they have a constitutional role to play[22]; what has been altered is
the weight they are allowed to wield in the control
of broadcasting. Let us look at the two events in
turn.

In early 1972, mid-way through the SPD's first
legislature as senior partner, the CSU government in
Bavaria introduced amendments to the clearly pluralistic Bavarian broadcasting law. The amendments
implied a move towards the north German model,
giving the political parties (with the CSU dominant
in Bavaria) increased representation on the broadcasting council, and a first step towards the introduction of commercial broadcasting. This thinly-
veiled CSU government attempt to interfere in public
broadcasting aroused strong public reaction, culmina-
ting in the amendment of the Bavarian constitution.[23]

The new article (111a) guarantees the public,
pluralistic control and accountability of broadcasting; 'political' representation is limited to not
more than one third of the broadcasting council
seats, with the other 'social' groups nominating
their own representatives directly. The 'Bavarian'
model also contains the idea of representation for
all groups that can be considered significant and
lays down the public accountability of broadcasting
in such a way that all future forms are encompassed,
including any private commercial broadcasting

ventures that might be launched in Bavaria. It is
worth noting that the constitutional amendment did
not, contrary to public demand, specifically exclude
any form of broadcasting, but simply stipulated the
public accountability of *all* broadcasting.

The NDR treaty of 1980[24] follows and extends
the Bavarian model. Not only is the party-political
apportionment that had rendered the public control
of NDR virtually ineffective properly extirpated and
the one-third limit on political representation
observed, but the seats allocated to the socially
significant groups also include nine which are not
earmarked for named groups as is normally the case.
These seats can change hands at the end of each term
of office of the broadcasting council; applications
for membership of the council can be entered by any
group considering itself representative of significant public opinion in the north German area. This
is clearly a useful innovation in an age when new
interests can emerge and take on politically and
socially significant proportions with great rapidity.

With regard to the second group of interests
involved in West German broadcasting, *the broadcasting personnel*, the history of NDR and the debate
surrounding the formulation of the new treaty are
again of importance[25], as are two rulings of the
Constitutional Court: the second *Fernseh-Urteil*
(also known as the VAT ruling) of July 1971 and the
ruling of 13 January 1982, which established the
freedom of broadcasting houses to exercise flexibility in their employment of staff (broadcasting
personnel).[26]

While the broadcasters can be seen to have
acted initially in defence of their editorial freedom and in the public interest (for example, the
statutes movement), later developments tended to
focus attention both on increasing political bias in
their programmes[27] and on their demands for rights
of representation and tenure which would have made
their position similar, on the one hand, to that of
the public's representatives in the organs of control and, on the other, to civil servants. In
short, they would have enjoyed privileges greater
than those of any other group and, perhaps, become
masters rather than servants of public broadcasting.

In terms of the constitutional task set for
public broadcasting - to maintain as wide a spectrum
of information and opinion in programming as possible - the January 1982 judgement of the Constitutional Court, which overturned several Labour Court
decisions, makes good sense. The Court took the

view that to give protection against termination of
contract to broadcasters normally employed on fixed-
term contracts would tie down resources in the
broadcasting houses and thus limit their ability
(their freedom) to promote variety in programming by
drawing on a large pool of broadcasting talent and
expertise.

The 1971 ruling is interesting because the
adjudication supposedly related to the imposition of
VAT on licence income, but the judges, in reaching
their verdict (a majority decision against the fiscal authorities), also reviewed the constitutional
principles relating to public broadcasting and
commented on these, in part, in the light of problems and developments significant at that time.

As they sought to delineate the protected area
of public control, the judges differentiated, on the
one hand, between areas of administration for which
the State was responsible and public service that
occurred outside the State's administrative machin-
ery and, on the other hand, between the public
service and those who perform it. On the first
count, if the State became involved in broadcasting,
it took a public service function upon itself but
could not thereby make broadcasting a matter for
administration by the State; on the second, the
broadcasters were essentially servants and not
masters of the service:

> It follows ... that the agencies responsible
> for the fulfilment of the public task are not
> really "masters" of radio and television, and
> that even less may those professionally active
> in these agencies see themselves as masters of
> radio and television, but that the agencies are
> merely instruments by means of which the
> socially relevant forces and groups fulfill the
> public task.

The question of editorial rights (statutes) was very
much in the air in 1971. It is interesting that the
new NDR treaty brings NDR into line with the other
broadcasting houses: NDR staff had been very active
over the statutes issue and had been the only group
to emerge with a document termed a 'statute' - in
the other broadcasting houses other means were found
which stopped short of the agreement to a full
statute of editorial rights but still granted increased opportunities for the representation of
staff views.[28] The final version of the treaty
steers a middle course between the demands of the

CDU[29] for punitive clauses which would have made the
observance of programme guidelines legally binding
on broadcasters, and the proposals of the FDP[30] and
the SPD[31] which would have given the broadcasters
rights of representation at various levels in the
control structures - including seats on the administrative council and special sub-committees to review questions relating to their work.

In the treaty, broadcasters are granted no
special rights; they are subject only to the 1974
Federal Personnel Representation Act. Similarly
significant was the ban imposed by the Labour Courts
on a strike called by the media union during the
negotiations on the new treaty. The strike, in
support of the continued existence of the then
threatened NDR, was deemed political and thus illegal - German unions have the right to strike only to
promote the welfare interests of their members in
the work relationship; the future of NDR was a
matter for the legislators and the public. Thus, at
all points, a clear distinction has been drawn between the rights of the broadcasters as agents in
the articulation and formation of opinion in the
public media and the rights of the public who control these media.

The NDR crisis and its outcome can be seen, in
relation to the roles played by the political parties and the broadcasters, as a response to a
situation that had developed over the preceding
twenty-five years and in some ways actually contra-
vened existing legislation; by thus clarifying these
questions, a firm platform was created for the
future. In other ways, too, the NDR crisis led to
the proper ordering of elements of broadcasting
legislation that had previously been vague or con-
tentious. For example, it became clear when the
future of NDR seemed utterly bleak that the withdrawal of one party from a multilateral treaty did
not render the treaty void for the other parties to
it; this is of relevance to many arrangements between the States, particularly the jointly financed
broadcasting projects. Then the legal monopoly of
broadcasting in the north German region enjoyed by
NDR, a privilege unique among West German broadcasting houses which had proved a point of strength
in the past, was removed and the path opened for
greater diversity in the region. It had been a
perhaps inevitable complaint against a service embracing three States in which there had been considerable demographic and political change that
large areas in the region had been neglected. In

particular Ernst Albrecht, CDU Prime Minister of Lower Saxony, had wanted to found a broadcasting house in his own State, offering local services and opportunities for private companies; he failed, mainly for legal reasons associated with the termination of the old treaty, but gained undertakings in the new treaty that local services would be improved and the door opened to new enterprises as from 1983. In the event, the decision to reinstate NDR with an improved treaty while allowing future diversification must be seen as felicitous.

THE ATTACK FROM COMMERCIAL INTERESTS

Just as the NDR house was at last being put in order the Constitutional Court was finally setting straight the record on private broadcasting companies, resolving problems raised by the amendment of the Saarland broadcasting law in 1967. With this, the last uncertainties left by the first *Fernseh-Urteil* of 1961 were removed and the role of the third group of interests involved in West German broadcasting, *the commercial lobbies*, clarified.

In the mid-1950s, as it became clear that a second television channel could soon be opened, the federal government (after the success of the 1957 election) emerged as the strongest contender to found the new broadcasting service. The intention was to create a company to operate a service drawing, in part, on commercially produced programmes and a company, *Deutschland Fernsehen GmbH*, was founded. CDU interests in the second channel can be interpreted as part of the polarisation which was steadily developing in West German politics; in broadcasting, because the bigger corporations served SPD (north German) areas, any joint services appeared in an oppositional role - a tendency most apparent in the first television channel (DFS).

When the action of the central government was challenged in the Constitutional Court by the States, led by Hamburg, the resultant ruling set decisive points of orientation for all future developments in West German broadcasting. All doubts about the sole competence of the federal States to legislate in the field of broadcasting were removed, with the federal Post Office and the central authorities (*Bund*) being excluded. Pluralistic organs of control and balanced programmes were laid down as essential in public broadcasting, protecting it from domination by one group or individual, particularly the state; the freedom from monopolisation by one body of opinion

had to be guaranteed in a law - only specific legislation could safeguard basic rights. The balance of
interests thus envisaged was related by the Court to
the programme as a whole, and it was the Court's
guarded formulation here ('minimum balance of content') that underlay the ensuing altercations about
programme bias between the south and north German
broadcasting authorities, between politicians and
broadcasters.[32]

A further broadly drawn feature of the ruling
related to the legal form of the broadcasting companies, for while the Court insisted on legislation
to guarantee pluralism, it did not prescribe any
particular vehicle for that pluralism. The fact
that the central government's plans for the second
channel, which involved a private company, had been
declared unconstitutional did not mean that private
companies *per se* could not be involved in broadcasting - the state (in any form) could not. The Court
went further, stating that, while the forms of control practised in the existing public broadcasting
corporations met the requirements of the constitution, this did not mean that they represented the
only acceptable form; however, any other forms of
control introduced would have to show comparable
guarantees of public representation and pluralism.

Thus this ruling, which is acknowledged as the
cornerstone of broadcasting democracy in West
Germany, specifically left open the door to private
broadcasting companies, some of which were already
in existence, with others soon to be founded. Since
1961 their problem had been to find ways to realise
in practice the opportunities made for them. Several
groups have tried to enter the system, notably in
Berlin and the Saar, and the legal terrain explored
from time to time. It was 1981, however, before the
fundamental position of 1961 was taken a step further when the Constitutional Court, commenting on
the parts of the 1967 Saarland broadcasting law concerned with private broadcasting companies, defined
more precisely the nature and location of pluralism
in broadcasting: an unequivocal distinction was made
between internal pluralism (in the organs of control) and external pluralism (in the programme output). In 1981 the Court made what can be considered
the definitive statement about the relationship between the three main pillars of support for democracy in West German broadcasting: guarantees in law,
public accountability and pluralism in programming.

It is easy, when the two rulings of 1961 and
1981 are juxtaposed, to see the latter as a natural

and obvious complement to the former. The fact that
it took twenty years to arrive at the new position
in itself indicates that the additional insight was
not easily gained; it came only after a number of
false starts and legal battles - and when the potential of the new technologies had taken on distinct
contours. The Berlin company (*Fernsehgesellschaft
Berliner Tageszeitungen mbH*), for example, founded
in 1960 by seven Berlin newspaper publishers, was
finally denied access to broadcasting by the federal
Administrative Court in December 1971 on the grounds
that the technical limitations on broadcasting were
such that a freedom of broadcasting similar to that
of the press was still not possible.[33] The Bavarian
and the NDR cases both showed that the issue had not
died, but the fact that private broadcasting continued to feature on the political agenda from the mid-
1960s onwards was due above all to the persistence
of the Saarland conundrum.

In 1967, the Saarland parliament, acting as it
thought in keeping with the 1961 judgement, amended
its law on broadcasting, in particular including a
section on private broadcasting companies. A private company was then founded (the *Freie Rundfunk AG*
or FRAG) by a group made up of Saarland newspaper
publishers and French broadcasting interests involved with *Europe 1*, the French commercial broadcasting company based in the Saarland. An application
was placed for the appropriate franchise. In the
first instance, the Saarland government failed to
react to the application; when forced by the courts
to do so, its verdict was negative - however, the
reasons it gave were felt by FRAG to be not material
to the granting or otherwise of a franchise. At
this point, after cases in various administrative
courts and one reference to the Constitutional Court,
the case was referred again by the Administrative
Court to the latter on the grounds that the actual
legislation was unconstitutional. If the law was
unconstitutional, the whole question of a franchise
would be nul and void; on the other hand, if the law
was constitutional, then the franchise, which had
been refused on grounds outside the terms of the law,
had to be granted. The question was one of substance; the Constitutional Court accepted that a
ruling was necessary.

The articles in question were found to be unconstitutional; the judges' analysis of and commentary on the points of law mark the step forward from
1961. The Saar law was in conflict with the Basic
Law not because it allowed the possibility of

private broadcasting, but because no unassailable guarantees of pluralism were provided in the actual law (as had been required by the 1961 judgement). This is the key to the FRAG ruling of June 12 1981 (the third *Fernseh-Urteil*) which is the signpost for future legislation; and many of the supplementary explanations are directly relevant to the detailed shaping of broadcasting structures. In particular, sections CII and CIII, in which the judges set out their basic principles and then point out the weaknesses in the Saar law, deserve a full summary and comment here.

The argument of the Court can be summed up as follows. If the freedom of individuals and of the public to form and express opinion is to be guaranteed, then the freedom of broadcasting, which constitutes a necessary complement to and amplification of the freedom of opinion under the conditions of modern mass communication, must also be guaranteed; the basic freedom (of opinion) is realised in laws which guarantee the constituent freedom (of broadcasting). The system of broadcasting and the legislation that supports it are therefore both shaped by their function of implementing basic rights. There is a negatory aspect to this, the freedom from state control, as well as a positive act of organisation and regulation to guarantee the greatest possible variety and completeness of information and opinion.

There are limitations to the latter, not only in the areas normally protected by law (for example protection of young people and children), but also in areas where different interests might conflict - the right to full information on the part of the public and the right to express opinion on the part of the broadcasters. In all such instances, it is the task of the legislator to make the rules; this must not be left to either the executive or any eventual organiser of the broadcasting service. Similarly, it is the legislator who must provide adequate guarantees for the basic pluralism of broadcasting and such rules will *still* be necessary even when the technical limitations on broadcasting are finally removed.

Here the Court included the interesting observation that the freeing of broadcasting from technical limitations would not guarantee broadcasting freedom because of the peculiar nature of the laws of competition governing the market. A limited variety, as in the supraregional press, might be possible, but cannot be guaranteed. The press, in

any case, grew historically into its present position; with the new possibilities in broadcasting an
'opinion market' would be created which might be
prey to concentration and the legislator must
guarantee that the overall supply represents sufficient variety of opinion to be constitutive of a
free democratic order. The Court admitted that
there can be no absolute guarantee of this, but the
law must provide sufficient probability of a balanced variety and not just leave it to the free play of
market forces.

It is interesting that the Court did not men-
tion the local press nor did it make the point that
technological innovation may well take broadcasting
away from supraregional programmes towards local
services. However, one principle can be related to
this: the Court made the point that the continued
existence of the public broadcasting corporations
does not relieve the legislator of his duty to
ensure that the total programme output is balanced
and varied: private broadcasting companies with
distinct individual messages would disturb, if not
destroy, the essential balance in the total programme output reaching the public.

The Court also referred to experiments using
the new technologies. Although the legislator does
have greater flexibility here in the interests of
gathering wider information and experience, the
basic principles remain the same: the State legislature and no other body must set up the system, must
protect it from the control of one group and must do
so in detail in a law.

Here the Court spelled out the possibilities
that are crucial for the future development of West
German broadcasting. If the legislator opts for the
familiar *internally* pluralistic model (*binnen-
pluralistisch*), then due guarantees must be given
that the existing variety of opinion in society is
represented in the organs of control and that these
organs have an effective influence on the broadcasting service. However, other forms are possible.
Provided that guarantees are given that the programmes *in their totality* do actually reflect the
existing variety of opinion, then there is no need
for each individual broadcasting group to provide a
'balanced' programme output. This model is *externally* pluralistic (*aussenpluralistisch*). In this
latter case, the freedom of broadcasting must be
protected by legislation ensuring that access to
available frequencies is governed by proper criteria
for the granting or refusal of franchises, for the

selection of franchise-holders where applications
exceed facilities and even for the sharing of frequencies to alleviate the latter problem, particularly where a shortage of frequencies would not
encourage an acceptable balance. Finally, the
legislator must provide for a limited supervision by
the State of the observance by all involved in
broadcasting of the laws that thus guarantee its
freedom.

The situation defined by the Court is one in
which nothing is left to chance or discretion and
where every material point is covered by any effective law and can be referred, if need be, to a
court of law. The requirements of the *Rechtsstaat*
would thus be met, for any court could then adjudi-
cate on the basis of clear regulations designed to
implement the basic rights as set out in the constitution.

The articles admitting private broadcasting in
the Saarland failed to meet these requirements in a
number of essential ways: too much was left to the
discretion of the government, while the advisory
committee foreseen was not necessarily representative of the range of public opinion and had no
effective power, only a right to advise, discuss and
recommend. The advisory committee was weak particularly in its potential to protect the interests of
the general public against the entrepreneurial and
other interests of a private broadcasting company.
There were no mitigating factors: the fact that
finance was to be raised from advertising did not
imply that a wide range of audience views would be
considered in the programmes; the fact that the
company took the form of a 'limited liability company' offered no guarantees for the public interest;
the board of directors (*Aufsichtsrat*), obligatory in
all such companies, could not have the legal right
to safeguard the public's interest in the programme
- it had other functions to perform; the inclusion
of two members of the advisory committee on the
Aufsichtsrat did not help, because they could be
outvoted; and controls on the sale and possession of
shares could not produce a situation where the range
of shareholders represented the full range of public
opinion. Finally, the Court noted, the provision
for supervision by the State could not redress these
inadequacies because its supervision applied to the
observance of the law as formulated - it would be
acting *ultra vires* if it went beyond this and, for
example, stepped in to exercise internal controls
reserved for the public.

In June 1981, the federal Constitutional Court
finally established the norms for private broadcasting in the federal Republic. However, since the
Court can act only when questions are referred to
it, and since any invocation of the Court must be
fully explained and documented, it is hardly surprising that much of the ground covered in the
ruling had been explored and discussed elsewhere.
Certainly, as in the earlier rulings, the questions
raised by the FRAG case were very much in the air
and, indeed, much progress had been made since the
problems had first arisen: the States had agreed in
principle to the four cable pilot projects, while
Baden-Württemberg and Lower Saxony had given full
consideration to the possibility of new legislation
- the former had even commissioned a major survey of
the media in the State[34] which contained a set of
expert recommendations where attention is drawn to
the difference between *Binnenpluralismus* and
Aussenpluralismus.[35] The Court ruling came late in
the day for FRAG, but very much on time for the next
stage in the development of West German broadcasting.

THE NEW MEDIA

While the four cable projects (in Rhineland-
Palatinate, Bavaria, North Rhine-Westphalia and
Berlin) are only now entering the final stages of
preparation for their eventual launch (Ludwigshafen
at Christmas 1983, Munich on 1 April 1984, Dortmund
and then Berlin later in 1984) and are expected to
test different aspects of programming and organisation on behalf of all the States[36] (and, of course,
are related to quite different local circumstances),
they do have a number of points in common. These
features, perhaps, offer some indication as to
future organisational forms; and the fact that all
the projects, while officially of limited duration,
aim to test the scope for and actually to introduce
new technologies as they become available, must be
taken as a sign of a potential for permanence at
least in the technical infrastructures to be created.
Longer term perspectives are also apparent in the
fact that the organisational structures are designed
to accommodate the new technologies without the need
for further legislation, as well as in the fact that
all of the projects build to some extent on existing
cable, with the additional new cables intended to
further improve local poor reception conditions.
    In all of the projects, channels are reserved
for the existing broadcasting services, i.e. the

regional television and radio services, ZDF and any
other programmes normally received locally over the
air. Additional services are to be grafted on to
this foundation, with the existing broadcasting
house offering extra facilities including more local
broadcasting, open channels, a wider range of programmes from other broadcasting services and some
form of service involving the individual retrieval
of programmes. In addition to these *broadcasting*
services, since all of the projects are conceived as
cable communication projects, individual information
and communication services will be added in varying
degrees depending on availability.

All of the broadcasting services envisaged are
required to conform to the strictures imposed on the
public broadcasting corporations, but clearly the
linking in of services which go beyond what is normally associated with the existing broadcasting
houses (teletext forms, access channels and services
provided by groups outside broadcasting - including
the press and business interests) allows a series of
interesting propositions, some of which could blur
the existing separation of broadcasting and its control structures from other institutions. The three
projects with confirmed outlines (Berlin is still
involved in preliminary tests) display a gradation
from a clear public bias (Dortmund) to a clear
private one (Ludwigshafen).

As far as the Dortmund project is concerned,
the North Rhine-Westphalia law[37] effectively channels all responsibility for broadcasting through WDR
and ZDF; it prohibits private companies and advertising in the experimental programmes, but requires
WDR to offer one access channel on each of radio and
television. Teletext services are offered in
accordance with the appropriate law of March 1980
which was enacted to facilitate the teletext experiment in Düsseldorf.[38] Clearly, the emphasis is on an
extension of the public service, resistance to
commercial pressures (in keeping with WDR traditions) and creating no more than a technical link to
the teletext services. A project advisory committee
representing a pluralistic selection of groups
similar to those found on broadcasting councils will
monitor and advise the project.

With regard to the Ludwigshafen scheme, the
Rhineland-Palatinate, which as already stated shares
its broadcasting house, *Südwestfunk* (SWF), with part
of Baden-Württemberg and originally envisaged a
joint project with its neighbour, set out to break
new ground in broadcasting structures. The legis-

lation, *Landesgesetz über einen Versuch mit Breit-bandkabel* (State Act on an Experiment with Broadband Cable)[39], has all the attributes of a State broadcasting law and could easily be the blueprint for permanent legislation to follow. The crucial feature of the law is the 'public institution' it establishes to coordinate and control the experiment, the *Anstalt für Kabelkommunikation* (AKK).

The AKK, which is reminscent of the Independent Broadcasting Authority in Britain, is very similar to the public broadcasting corporations in structure with an assembly of 40 representing a wide cross-section of groups with interests in the project (though not direct involvement); this assembly appoints a board of management (virtually an administrative committee) and has powers to monitor the programme and make recommendations about franchises. The *Vorstand* (the board) appoints a (managing) director who is more like a company secretary (Geschäftsführer) than an *Intendant* (the title given to the director general of the existing broadcasting houses).

The AKK does not make programmes, but rather coordinates and controls what is broadcast. Thus, legal responsibility for what is broadcast, which must conform to the normal regulations, lies with the individual broadcasting group, while the AKK determines the general shape of the different channels (*Aussenpluralismus*) within loosely set rules: at least one channel is to offer a variety of content; there has to be at least one access channel; SWF and ZDF broadcast their normal services plus one additional channel each and then compete for any further time with other users - they may not offer local radio programmes and no local advertising; local advertising is permitted only in local programmes; all advertising is to be clearly distinguished from the rest of the programme output.

The Munich project is not anchored in a State law but in a *Grundvertrag*, a basic treaty or contract[40], which amounts to a contract of association to found a consortium for the 'Cable Pilot Project Munich' (KPM) involving the state (Bavaria), the city of Munich, BR, ZDF and three newly formed companies representing newspaper publishers, periodicals publishers and film and audio-visual interests. These have agreed to found a limited liability company called the *Münchner Pilot-Gesellschaft für Kabelkommunikation mit beschränkter Haftung* (interestingly enough: the Munich pilot company for cable communication with limited liability) which is

to install, maintain and manage the technical equipment necessary for the experiment in as far as this
does not infringe the competence of the federal Post
Office. The company is the *Technische Zentrale*
(technical headquarters), but it also organises the
experiment and allocates cable capacity in accordance with the terms of the contract to third parties. This seems an alarming departure from established practice; however, the terms of the contract
bind all broadcasting to article 111a of the
Bavarian constitution and give special responsibilities to BR and ZDF. This is reminiscent of the
role of WDR in Dortmund, but there is no exclusion
of private groups. The press groups and the film and
audio-visual groups are expected to participate in
appropriate ways and to experiment with innovatory
material.

What is perhaps unnerving about the Munich
project, apart from the actual name of the company
and the vagueness about all groups except those involved financially in the technical headquarters
(the consortium members plus the local chambers of
trade and industry), is the apparent lack of public
control and the ultimate scope of the services anticipated: there is no advisory board, although the
project commission, convened in December 1980 to
advise on the design and to monitor the project,
will continue to function; the target is 50 broad-
band channels, a corresponding number of narrowband
channels and one interactive channel (Rückkanal).
There is no provision for an access channel,
although the idea is not excluded. Advertising is
allowed on the same terms as in Ludwigshafen.

Of the above three projects, Munich poses the
most problems. There are safeguards in the principles outlined, but there are also clear indications
of a desire to stretch the interpretation of article
111a (§4.1 of the *Grundvertrag* specifically calls
for this). Furthermore, there are hints of a new
role for the public broadcasting corporations, which
are tied in financially to the consortium and also
serve as umbrellas for one branch of its activities
(broadcasting). Given the ultimate range of services envisaged, BR and ZDF could find themselves
making only a minor contribution to the overall
programme, while their major function could, in
practice, be to act as a buffer between the public
organs controlling them and the private entrepreneurs using them - there would be public control,
but it would be indirect, transmitted through the
two public broadcasting corporations; it might be

face-saving rather than effective. On the other hand, in as much as BR or ZDF assume responsibility under broadcasting law (§4.3) for the various programmes, the makers of these programmes could become subject to the scrutiny of the BR broadcasting council or the ZDF television council - the former would seem more appropriate. The project may well serve to test this point for the West German public as it may test the proper classification of some of the media (the innovatory forms to be produced by the press, film and audio-visual groups) which seem to lie at the fringe (or beyond) of the normal understanding of broadcasting (§5.2 foresees this).

Other 'grey' areas may well be explored in Berlin where, although the shape of the project is not yet clear, it is hoped to involve control groups in different parts of the city as well as to link in the various other experiments the city is host to: the teletext tests (cf. Dortmund), the fibre optics tests and interactive tests based on the Heinrich Hertz Institute. It should be noted that local conditions in Berlin are much more complex than those elsewhere: apart from SFB and ZDF, local stations include RIAS (Radio in the American Sector), AFN television and, of course, East German programmes as well. All of the projects allow for the eventual introduction of international material via satellite, and many parts of the federal Republic normally enjoy good reception of at least one foreign television programme; in the case of Berlin this is a matter of fundamental importance.

The two draft laws, which seek to anticipate the results of the projects, reflect many of the features already discussed. Lower Saxony has been eager to establish its own broadcasting service for some time in order to admit local private broadcasting; it is hardly surprising that the door left open deliberately in the new NDR treaty has been entered so promptly. The fact that Schleswig-Holstein is about to follow suit is, perhaps, inevitable. These events should not be detached from the north German political situation. However, it would be wrong to view them in isolation from events in Baden-Württemberg; indeed, the accompanying notes to the Lower Saxony draft[41] acknowledge that account has been taken of a wide spectrum of developments both in the federal Republic and elsewhere, particularly of expert investigations such as the one into the new media in Baden-Württemberg.

This fact alone provokes a comparison of the two drafts, both of which are, in any case,

conceived as documents for wide discussion -
although this seems more applicable to the Baden-
Württemberg draft[42] which is much less a final version than the Lower Saxony one (the former is called
a 'draft for a law on the new media', the latter
'draft for the Lower Saxony State broadcasting law').
In spite of the broader application implied in the
Baden-Württemberg title, the draft as it exists is
concerned exclusively with broadcasting; the Lower
Saxony draft, while it relates ostensibly to broadcasting, is virtually open-ended and can be seen as
adaptable to the same range of information and
communications services as the four pilot projects.

The link to the pilot projects is closest in
the case of Baden-Württemberg. The original plan
for Ludwigshafen included Mannheim and proposed a
joint project by Rhineland-Palatinate and Baden-
Württemberg. The latter was not prepared to commit
itself until the Prime Ministers of the States had
agreed full details of how the four projects were
to be financed; Rhineland-Palatinate pushed ahead
with legislation for its own project and Baden-
Württemberg chose instead to set up its expert
commission into the new media. The findings of the
commission were to be Baden-Württemberg's contribution to the debate.

The two drafts differ in detail and also fundamentally in their approach to the introduction of
the new media, but both proceed from the same
assumption that any increase in broadcasting services to the level where the 'external pluralism'
model would become a practical proposition still
lies some way in the future and, even when technically possible, is still subject to a number of
uncertain factors relating to programme demand and
supply. The responses of the two States to this
same proposition could not have been more different.

The Baden-Württemberg scheme sets out to define
a minimum pluralism in programme output and effectively suspends the implementation of all the
measures envisaged in the draft until this minimum
pluralism becomes feasible in practice. The Lower
Saxony scheme is designed for immediate implementation and seeks to facilitate a gradual progression
from a model of private broadcasting based on one or
two full programmes (channels) controlled by an
internally pluralistic committee to a large number
of channels eventually offering in their totality a
viable pluralism. The Baden-Württemberg scheme
seeks simply to prepare the ground for the new
technologies and the results of the projects; the

Lower Saxony scheme proceeds alongside them, sharing
some of their characteristics and yet potentially
preempting one crucial outcome: further discussion
among all the States about appropriate legislation
- Lower Saxony would already have its new broadcasting act. The positive argument for the Lower
Saxony procedure is that it seeks to avoid stagnation while controlling the transition from the old
to the new.

How the transition would in fact be controlled
is, however, open to debate, for the Lower Saxony
draft, while it foresees an interesting State broadcasting committee (*Landesrundfunkausschuss*) with all
the positive qualities of the new NDR broadcasting
council, is distinctly reluctant to invest real
power in the committee rather than the State government. The latter is not given the powers of discretion that the Saarland law allowed the Saar
government, but it does have the power to issue and
withdraw franchises and also exercises final legal
supervision over the committee and over the bodies
involved in broadcasting (though not over programming). The committee must be consulted in matters
relating to franchises and it has the right of
appeal if its advice to withdraw a franchise is
ignored - hardly the guarantees the Constitutional
Court called for in 1981. The weighting in favour
of the State government would become critical in the
ultimate situation when, with external pluralism
established, the committee might become superfluous.

The draft is perhaps also lacking in circum-
spection in its totally open view of potential forms
- it sets no limits here, except the normal, legal
restrictions; it is less cautious, too, about advertising: there are stipulations about the separation
of commercials from the programmes, interruptions to
programmes, influence on the programme output and
local advertising, but the upper limit of 20% of
total broadcasting time seems very high. However,
the document is a draft, which does allow for
change, and has been drawn up with all the present
technical uncertainties in mind. It is undoubtedly
too early to discount the draft and, as part of the
general debate, it represents an interesting
approach to the problem of the transition.

The Baden-Württemberg draft, by comparison
almost pernickety in the detail it sets down - particularly in relation to the quantitative and quali-
tative control of commercial advertising, contains a
number of ideas that are quite innovatory and far-
sighted. For example, in addition to the normal

strictures giving protection to children and young
people, the draft calls for a scientific advisory
committee (*Wissenschaftlicher Beirat*) (§63) to support the controlling body by monitoring the content
of programmes and seeking to strengthen the pedago-
gical potential of the media. However, the major
innovations relate to the control of private broadcasting, the controlling authority and the positive
attempt to create and define adequate external
pluralism.

The authority is a remarkable conception
(§§29-38). The *Landesanstalt für Kommunikation*
(State institution for communication) is a public
law institution with a board of five elected by the
State parliament (proportionally). These cannot be
members of a parliament or government, members of a
controlling body of a public broadcasting corporation or civil servants, judges or other officials at
State or government level. Their office is honorary
and they have complete power over the private broadcasting sector - the State government exercises only
final legal supervision. It is the *Landesanstalt*
which decides when the situation is ripe for external pluralism to function, which allocates and with-
draws franchises, allocates channels and transmission times and monitors the observance of the
regulations by the broadcasting bodies. The boldness
of this concept, when set against the backcloth of
decades of conflict about the control of public
broadcasting in West Germany, is quite staggering;
it meets a new situation with a new (almost British)
structure which seems to match up to all the requirements of the Constitutional Court - except one: the
board does not represent a wide range of public
interests. However, it is easy to see that such a
board could be impartial in a way new to Germany -
had it not been for the proportional rule: one must
fear that the appointments could easily fall prey to
the problems of *Proporz* so familiar in West German
broadcasting (see above).

The draft is equally bold in its attempt to
mark the threshold of minimal external pluralism.
It includes a number of measures relating to the
allocation of channels and time which are calculated
to increase the chances of a viable pluralism in the
private sector (for example giving preference to
private broadcasting where there is a shortage of
channels and channel-sharing coupled with time
quotas to increase access) and the critical threshold is strikingly unambiguous: at least half of the
private households in the State must be linked to a

cable network capable of offering a minimum of 30
private programmes (of at least half-an-hour duration each) between 17.00 and 23.00 daily before any
franchises can be issued (§§14 and 74). The rule
applies separately to radio and television; it is
clearly more demanding than Lower Saxony's 'one or
two full programmes' initially.

The definition of minimal external pluralism is
interesting in the apparently technical nature of
the targets it sets, yet the human factor is also
vital to their realisation: there must also be
sufficient public demand for these 30 programmes.
It is quite clear that the new technologies will
soon be available and that the cables will be laid
(the economy demands this); however, there is so far
nothing to indicate that the West German population
is any more ready for the brave new world of un-
limited broadcasting than any other.[43]

Ultimately, a plurality of programmes on the
scale envisaged depends for its success on the corresponding demand for these programmes on the part
of the public, and there is no guarantee that the
simple availability of cable will generate that
demand. Nor is pluralism in the programme a necessary consequence of the opening up of broadcasting
to private enterprise - the groups that have so far
registered an interest are predominantly from one
field, the press[44], with some interest shown by
business circles and a dutiful interest indicated by
the churches. So far other groups, notably the
trade unions, have shown no inclination to become
involved, while the public response to the idea of
an open channel has so far been minimal.

The above four pilot projects are intended to
discover who is prepared to participate in cable
broadcasting, how this can be achieved and what the
possible effects of their involvement might be;
similarly, they are seeking to establish the extent
and the quality of the public response, the demand
for more services and the effect of increased exposure to television on the public (particularly the
family). The fact that two States have pushed
ahead with draft legislation is, in part, a sign of
little confidence that the projects will find out
much that is new.

On the demand side, since participation is
voluntary and involves expense (the actual costs of
equipment and fees are not yet clear), there is some
fear that households joining in the experiment will
be pre-selected by interest in the media and ability
to pay - hardly making for a valid cross-section of

society. On the supply side, there are doubts
whether a gradually developing three-year project
will reveal much of relevance to the long-term situation, to such questions as: does what the press
produce remain 'press' or does it become 'broadcasting'; will their participation provoke reaction in
the shape of 'counter-programmes' - thus promoting
pluralism in programme output, or will other groups
hold back and thus reduce the value of the experiment; what will be the effect of participation on
the press itself?

     There can be no answer to questions of this
kind at this stage, but it does seem clear that the
next crucial decision on the West German media could
revolve around a redefinition of the role of the
press. (Private) cable broadcasting is much less a
problem for (public) 'cableless' broadcasting than
it is for the press. The technology that 'cable'
most effectively supersedes is the printing press.
German newspaper publishers seem to have realised
this; indeed, for them the situation is likely to be
particularly difficult because, with cable, broadcasting will for the first time become a local
phenomenon - breaking into a field so far reserved
for the press. To survive the press must become
involved and since the local press (often a local
monopoly) will probably also provide the local cable
coverage, problems of opinion monopolisation of a
new and particularly insidious kind could soon
arise.

     If this happens, before this happens, there
will have to be discussions at many levels. It is
here, since the press has never been subjected to
the close scrutiny often brought to bear on the
broadcasting media, that the real debate about the
new age of the West German media could and should
begin.

     However, this is for the future; in terms of
the present situation and condition of West German
broadcasting, in spite of the apparently confusing
level of activity, the general assessment must be
that clarity prevails on most points; and clarity
is strength. There is now final certainty in
matters which have long been problematical: the role
of the parties, the status of the broadcasters and
the acceptability of private broadcasting. In
addition, there would seem to be little room now for
new questions relating to established structures in
the traditional field of broadcasting: the federal
government is still excluded - Helmut Kohl's idea
of a dialogue with the States will probably prove

abortive[45]; the independence of the States will not
be reduced and could be increased as they enter a
new round of legislation, with each State introducing its own 'cable communication' act and the
States corporately drafting guidelines on standards
and cooperation; the particularist tendency could be
underpinned by an increase in local and regional
broadcasting: the public corporations will continue
to operate, perhaps with increased responsibilities
(Dortmund, Munich); public accountability will have
to be demonstrated, perhaps more clearly than it has
been in the past and at more levels in the system
(Rhineland-Palatinate, Baden-Württemberg); commercial exploitation will, in all probability, continue
to be subject to the strictest limitations. The
increase in broadcasting services could, in effect,
bring more power to the federal States and to the
public, to whom ultimately account will have to be
made - it will be for them to exercise it wisely.
     Given this framework, in which liberty is
coupled with accountability in a way fully consonant
with the ideals of the *sozialer Rechtsstaat*, it
seems reasonable to assume that 'public' broadcasting will continue to be of crucial importance for
the realisation of basic rights. Beyond this, since
broadcasting occupies a key position in the 'new
media', it could provide a model for the exploitation and control of many of the new facilities
provided by the new technologies.
     In all of this it is difficult to find anything
new for Helmut Kohl and his Minister of Posts, Dr.
Schwarz-Schilling, to do.[46] As West Germany pro-
gresses steadily and somewhat slowly along a path
towards the new technologies marked by many continuities and considerable renewal of basic values,
the central authorities cannot even make the pace,
for the States and the municipalities must decide
when cable for broadcasting is to be laid. And it
will be the task of the States, if the old problems
of party competition to manipulate the broadcasting
companies raise their heads in a new guise, to
bring these to order; the structures of public
accountability are such that the proper guardians of
pluralism in the broadcasting media, the public themselves, will have the means at their disposal to ensure that the media are exploited with fairness and
responsibility - if they are prepared to use them;
and there is evidence (Bavaria is but one example)
that the West German public is increasingly prepared to stand up for its rights.[47]

114

References

1. *Konstruktives Misstrauensvotum.* The West
German parliament can express its lack of confidence
in a Chancellor only by electing a successor (Basic
Law 67.1).
2. The West German parties are: CDU/CSU -
Christian Democratic Union/Christian Social Union,
the latter is the Bavarian sister party of the former; FDP - Free Democratic Party; *Die Grünen* - the
Greens; SPD - Social-Democratic Party of Germany.
3. By the contrived loss of a vote of confidence. If the Chancellor asks for a vote of confidence (*Vertrauensvotum*) and fails to get one, the
federal President may dissolve parliament and call
new elections at the request of the federal
Chancellor (Basic Law 66). This is one of only two
ways in which the West German parliament can be
dissolved before the end of a legislature.
4. October 28 1969 (*Bulletin* 39/69, published
by the *Presse und Informationsamt der Bundes-
regierung*).
5. October 13 1982 (*Bulletin* 93/82).
6. May 4 1983 (*Bulletin* 43/83).
7. Something of this is explored in A.Williams,
'West German Social Policy since 1969: a discussion
of perspectives', *Quinquereme,* vol.6 no.2, July
1983, pp.167-187.
8. As early as November 1982 both the Minister
of the Interior (Friedrich Zimmermann) and his
secretary of state (Horst Waffenschmidt) were at
pains to set the government's policy in perspective
(*Bulletin* 109 and 115/82).
9. Peter Ziller in *Frankfurter Rundschau*,
January 22 and 28 1983.
10. Schmidt called for one 'television-free'
day each week and, for example, in his 1980 statement of government policy (November 24 1980,
Bulletin 124/80) went out of his way to express his
personal worries about the increasing exposure of
young people to television and the effect of the
electronic media on family life.
11. The nationwide introduction of Btx on a
standard European system planned for autumn 1983 has
had to be postponed until mid 1984 because IBM has
failed to produce the necessary equipment on time.
12. *Basic Law,* article 20 (which cannot be
altered) describes the Federal Republic as 'a democratic and social federal state', and article 28
refers to the principles of 'republican, democratic
and social government based on the rule of law,

within the meaning of this Basic Law'.
13. *Basic Law*, articles 1-19 set out the basic
rights and the terms under which they might be
withdrawn. Article 1 (which cannot be altered)
proclaims the dignity of man to be inviolable.
14. D. Kommers, *Judicial politics in West
Germany: a study of the Federal Constitutional
Court*, London, Sage, 1976, is a useful study of the
Constitutional Court.
15. The States involved in shared broadcasting
services agree a treaty between themselves
(Staatsvertrag) which each of the State parliaments
endorses as the law of the respective State.
16. The texts of these can be found as follows:
(1961) E.W. Fuhr, *ZDF-Staatsvertrag*, Mainz, 1972,
pp.228-259; W. Lehr and K. Berg, *Rundfunk und Presse
in Deutschland*, Mainz, 1971, pp.221-256; (1971)
Fuhr, *ZDF-Staatsvertrag*, pp.260-283 and *ARD Jahrbuch
1971*, pp.238-250; (1981) *ARD Jahrbuch 1981*, pp.330-
343 and *Media Perspektiven*, June 1981, pp.421-443.
17. A number of works provide more detail on
the sections that follow. H. Flottau, *Hörfunk und
Fernsehen heute*, Munich, 1978; J. Sandford, *The Mass
Media of the German-Speaking Countries*, London,
1976; and A. Williams, *Broadcasting and Democracy in
West Germany*, Bradford UP, 1976.
18. What the freedom of the press amounts to in
practice in West Germany if one considers the actual
variety of opinion readily available to the individual citizen is, unfortunately, a question that can
be noted here only in passing.
19. See Williams, *Broadcasting and Democracy in
West Germany*, pp.122-124 and 130-133.
20. These were called *Freundeskreise* (circles
of friends). See Williams, *Broadcasting and Democracy in West Germany*, pp.124-127 and 134-137.
21. With its *Godesberger Programm* of 1959.
22. *Basic Law*, article 21; Law on Political
Parties, July 24 1967.
23. Williams, *Broadcasting and Democracy in
West Germany*, pp.113-119.
24. Text in *ARD Jahrbuch 1980*, pp.331-338 and
Media Perspektiven, September 1980, pp.633-644.
25. A discussion of the NDR situation forms a
major part of A. Williams, 'West German Broadcasting
in the Eighties - plus ca change ...?', *ASGP Journal*, forthcoming.
26. Text in *ARD Jahrbuch 1982*, pp.350-364 and
Media Perspektiven, April 1982, pp.293-299.
27. Williams, *Broadcasting and Democracy in
West Germany*, pp.138-157.

28. *Ibid.*, pp.139-148.
29. Prime Minister Stoltenberg's first draft, *Media Perspektiven*, September 1978, pp.654-666.
30. Draft of the North German Liberals, *Media Perspektiven*, February 1979, pp.96-106.
31. Hamburg Senate draft, *Media Perspektiven*, November 1978, pp.805-816.
32. Williams, *Broadcasting and Democracy in West Germany*, pp.83-92.
33. Text in *ARD Jahrbuch 1972*, pp.295-304.
34. *The Expertenkommission 'Neue Medien'* (EKM) was set up in 1980 and presented a three-volume report in 1981. *Media Perspektiven*, February 1981, pp.124-139 reproduces the basic principles on which the report proceeds.
35. The two ideas are sometimes termed *Integrationsrundfunk* and *Kooperationsrundfunk*.
36. This is, in itself, an example of cooperative federalism; the difficulties encountered in agreeing terms, in particular finance, indicate the complexity inherent in the federal system.
37. Text in *Media Perspektiven*, June 1982, pp. 409-417.
38. *Media Perspektiven*, May 1980 contains the text of this *Bildschirmtextversuchsgesetz* (pp.335-336), the text of the Berlin law (pp.330-334) and also the text of the videotext agreements between the broadcasting houses and between the broadcasting houses and the association of newspaper publishers (pp.337-340).
39. Text in *Media Perspektiven*, December 1980, pp.836-843.
40. The term is unusual, being reminiscent of the *Grundvertrag* between the two German states (1972), the proper title of which is 'Treaty on the fundamental principles of the relations between ...' *(Vertrag über die Grundlagen der Beziehungen zwischen ...).* The text of the Munich document, dated July 16 1982, is in *Media Perspektiven*, August 1982, pp.531-533.
41. Text in *Media Perspektiven*, November 1982, pp.723-733.
42. Text in *Media Perspektiven*, March 1982, pp. 202-213.
43. The evidence is well-known. Reports in the West German press, quite varied opinion polls, participation to date in the Btx projects, reports from the United States, the *Financial Times* conference of January 1983, the response to the fourth channel and breakfast television - all of these give reason for serious doubts about the size of the

potential demand.

44. There has been a steady growth in the number of associations and companies formed by local newspaper publishers (i.e. within their respective States) to give them a basis for involvement in cable. An investigation of the pattern of these foundations and their interconnections (if any) would form a very interesting research topic.

45. The SPD-FDP coalition set up a commission of enquiry into the *Neue Informations - und Kommunkationstechniken* in May 1981 which failed to produce any significant results because it ran up against the limits on federal government involvement in broadcasting; there is no reason to believe that the new government can do any better.

46. The projects dropped by the SPD (to cable 11 cities) have not been reinstated in spite of Schwarz-Schilling's criticism of the SPD; all cabling which is being sanctioned at present as part of the new drive is for small communities (at their request) to improve poor reception and is exclusively of coaxial cable - in effect, continuing the existing programme but speeding it up (potentially, it could be argued, moving these communities to the bottom of the waiting list once large-scale cabling with optical fibre commences). While it condemns the SPD for blocking the progress of the new technologies, the CDU's actions to date can be construed as a tacit endorsement of SPD thinking.

47. Citizens' action groups *(Bürgerinitiativen)* are rife; the extent of the anti-nuclear demonstrations in West Germany is well-known. The leaders of such movements will not be slow to see the potential and dangers of the new technologies in broadcasting.

Chapter Four

ITALY: THE ADVENT OF PRIVATE BROADCASTING

Donald Sassoon

The broadcasting institutions of Italy, like those
of virtually every Western European country, are
in a process of transition, the features of which
are shaped by a combination of developments in
the national and international political, economic
and media systems. For example, within Italy
recent years have witnessed changes in the composition of the governing coalition and a reduction
in the power of the principal coalition force, the
Christian Democratic party (DC). This political
evolution has had important consequences for Italian
broadcasting. Furthermore, Constitutional Court
rulings in the late 1970s significantly altered the
face of broadcasting by allowing the establishment
of local and regional radio and television stations
outside the previously secure state monopoly exercised by the Italian national broadcasting company,
the RAI (Radiotelevisione Italiana-Societa per
Azioni). The ramifications of these judicial decisions continue to have a profound effect on the
Italian broadcasting system in the 1980s.
     At the same time, the field of mass communi-
cations is one of the main terrains on which a
radical restructuring of the world economy has been
taking place. This restructuring has two essential
characteristics, which are particularly evident in
the case of the most important medium, television:
a very pronounced centralisation of production in
the hands of a few (mainly American) transnational
companies on the one hand and a widespread decentralisation of distribution on the other. Italian
broadcasting has certainly not been immune from
the effects of this restructuring in the international media economy.
     The case of Italian broadcasting is of great

interest because it presents a number of similarities with broadcasting systems in other Western European states while also displaying one important difference. The similarities are obvious and can be quickly enumerated. First, Italian broadcasting, both radio and television, has until recently been a state-controlled monopoly. Secondly, Italian television became in the 1960s the chief organiser of culture and principal producer of cultural artefacts for the mass of Italian society. Thirdly, Italy is now well on the way to becoming an information society. The MacBride report for UNESCO calculated that 65% of the American population would soon be involved in some form or other with the transmission of information or with the manufacturing of equipment required for this task.[1] Though Italy is probably still far from this level, the 1981 census showed that the tertiary sector of the Italian economy has now reached over 50% of the employed population as against 37% in industry and 13% in agriculture. Italy, then, like other developed countries, is already a 'post-industrial' society. Fourthly, all the indicators point to the consistent growth of the information sector of the Italian economy. For example, in 1982 the go-ahead was given for the construction of a nationally integrated telecommunication network whose principal objective would be the extension and modernisation of the telephone system. The project envisages the gradual substitution of the existing coaxial network by the more advanced fibre optic cables which would permit the development of an integrated, interactive ('two-way') system.[2] Fifthly, Italian broadcasting will become an integral part of the international communication system when the five-year 'space plan' has been completed. This plan includes the launching of a telecommunication satellite for Italy which would permit the average Italian to receive up to sixty television channels from all over the world once the appropriate paraboloid microwave antenna ('the dish') has been purchased. Finally, the electronic and telecommunications industry has become an important pressure-group in Italian politics.[3] Until ten years ago the most powerful industrial lobby was the car industry which had been the main force behind Italy's sustained economic growth in the 1950s and early 1960s. In the 1970s the crisis of the traditional industries led the industrial elites to shift resources towards the electronic and telecommunications sectors of the economy. The growth in consumption in these sectors contribu-

ted to their profitability: programme production
and distribution, components, video records, video
cameras, cables, etc. Television in Italy is,
therefore, not just of political significance. It
is now part of the fastest growing sector of the
economy.

All the above features are common in some form
or other to most Western European countries. What
differentiates Italy is that it is the only country
in Western Europe with a multichannel private radio
and television system *not subject to any form of
regulation whatsoever*. According to figures obtained from the RAI's documentation centre in September
1983, Italy has at present between 700 and 800
private television stations with well over 5,000
transmitters and between 6,000 and 8,000 private
radio stations (including a large number of a transmission capacity of only a few miles). Only about
half of the private television stations transmit
regular programmes. Of these, 125 are connected to
four semi-national networks: *Retequattro* (24 stations), *Italia Uno* (31), *Canal Cinque* (38) and *Euro
TV* (32). These four networks alone can reach over 70%
of the population. If one then includes the three
state television channels managed by the RAI, 32
million Italians enjoy a multichannel television
system which gives them on average between seven and
eleven channels for approximately 13 hours a day,
just like Los Angeles. In some cities it is possible
to select from eighteen to twenty channels. In
Venice, Milan or Turin, for example, the well-equip-
ped Italian household can receive programmes from a
variety of foreign stations transmitting from France,
Monaco, Switzerland, Austria and so on, as well as
the native Italian output. The recent growth of
private radio and television has been so spectacular
that by 1981 Italy had reached the highest density
of radio and television stations per capita in the
world: one radio station for every 16,000 inhabitants (1:25,000 in the USA) and one television
station for every 93,000 inhabitants (1:274,000 in
the USA).[4]

An unregulated private broadcasting system
means that there is no limit on advertising, no restriction on sex or violence, no enforceable code
of values relating to good taste or offensive
material, no obligation towards fair reporting or
political balance, no limits on imported material
and no necessity to broadcast a minimum of educational or cultural programmes. Sparsely populated
or 'unprofitable' sections of the national territory

do not receive any of the four main private networks. For all intents and purposes Italy is already in the situation envisaged by some as being the inevitable result of the introduction of unrestricted cable television. But before one can appreciate the consequences of this and other changes in the Italian broadcasting system over the past few years, it is first of all necessary to sketch out the history of the traditional system: a state monopoly officially run by the RAI and unofficially controlled by the leading political force in post-war Italy, the DC.

THE TRADITIONAL SYSTEM: THE DC-CONTROLLED STATE MONOPOLY

The Italian broadcasting corporation was a part of the state sector from its very inception.[5] Strictly speaking the RAI is a public company whose shares are entirely owned by the IRI (Istituto per la Ricostruzione Industriale), the state holding company set up by the Fascist government in the 1930s. When the RAI began television transmissions in 1954, these were received by about half the Italian population, though only two years later the potential audience was an impressive 90% of the population. At first both radio and television were financed by licence-fee. However, with the escalation of production costs it was decided in 1957 to introduce commercial advertising on the state services. There was no serious opposition to this measure, with the main restriction, still in force today, being that it should be 'block' advertising at the beginning and end (but not in the middle) of programmes. Initially, advertising was also confined to no more than 5% of total broadcasting time so as not to upset unduly the press lobby.[6]

From the very beginning television in Italy came under the tight political control of the DC, the party which has been at the centre of all Italian governments since 1945 and which until 1981 provided the Italian Republic with all its Prime Ministers. From 1954 to the mid-60s DC control of the RAI meant essentially a politicisation of radio and television news content. This was carried out in a fairly blatant propagandistic manner. The voice of the opposition, in particular that of the Communists, was virtually ignored. Apart from the news sections the rest of broadcasting output was in the hands of cautious producers who were left fairly free provided their programmes did not offend Catholic values.[7] This meant that language was strictly controlled, political or religious jokes banned and showgirls had their legs covered in woolly socks.

The DC faction which in the early 1950s sought to colonise the RAI was led by Amintore Fanfani, who in 1954 became party leader. He began to modernise the party, which until then had been relying on the Catholic Church's political machine, by increasing its penetration of the public sector. In June 1954 a Fanfani supporter, Filiberto Guala, was appointed chief executive *(amministratore delegato)* at the RAI. In his first speech to broadcasting management in Turin he declared, 'I have come here to get rid of homosexuals and Communists.'[8] Guala proceeded to appoint a number of close supporters to key positions in the RAI, nominating, for example, Luigi Beretta as deputy general secretary. Beretta had previously been the DC nominee on the commission of Italian experts involved with the Marshall plan.

Guala, however, was extremely unpopular with the staff and exhausted his political resources in a long struggle with the head of radio news, the right-wing Christian Democrat, Antonio Picone-Stella. In 1956 Guala was forced to resign and a few years later he joined (quite appropriately) the religious order of the Trappists, known for their vow of silence.[9] A new chairman of the board was appointed, again on political grounds: Marcello Rodino, the son of one of the founders of the *Partito popolare*, the Catholic predecessor of the DC.

The DC was keen not only to maintain control over the RAI's output, but also to prevent the development of any competition in the shape of private television. In the late 1950s a private group, *Il Tempo-TV*, began to exert pressure for the creation of a commercial television channel. However, the Constitutional Court in an important decision in 1960 argued that the state monopoly over broadcasting was justified because of the shortage of frequency bands available. On the other hand, the Court also expressed the view that some competition was necessary. The RAI moved quickly: a second television channel, which had been in the planning stages since 1958, began regular broadcasting in November 1961, reaching 52% of the population. By 1967 channel two could be received by 86% of the population, a figure well ahead of BBC2 which in the same year could reach only 56% of British viewers. Television was thus going through a period of rapid expansion in the early 60s, with domestic production

of television sets rising to 900,000 units in
1962.[10] The second channel did not modify the extent of political control, but it did provide at
least some competition among broadcasters, even
though programming policies tended to concentrate
the bulk of the audience on the first channel.

Throughout the 1960s the RAI was dominated by
Ettore Bernabei, its director general. Bernabei,
who had previously been editor of the DC daily newspaper *Il Popolo*, owed his appointment and his powerful position within the broadcasting corporation to
Fanfani. However, at the same time as Bernabei was
seeking to impose himself at the RAI, changes in the
national political environment were weakening the
previously entrenched rule of the DC.

During the early 1950s the DC had still largely
relied on the Church to legitimise its rule. Ideologically the party was committed to the upholding
of traditional values, while also in this cold war
period portraying its virulent anti-Communism. The
latter part of the decade and the early years of
the 1960s saw a massive expansion of industry and a
formidable modernisation of the Italian economy: the
so-called 'economic miracle' which reached its
climax in 1962-63. The more traditional terrain of
DC support, the agricultural sector, was shrinking
fast as the northern industrial regions achieved a
substantial export-led growth on the basis of cheap
southern labour.

The end of the 'economic miracle' led to a
general re-thinking on the question of economic
growth. The DC could no longer allow the private
sector to establish the priorities of development.
At the same time the Church, under John XXIII's
aggiornamento policies of modernisation, could no
longer be relied upon to provide the legitimacy the
DC required. Church attendance was declining as the
effects of the consumer society pushed more and more
Italians towards a secularisation of daily life.

The DC re-directed its strategy both politically and economically. Politically it had to abandon
the 'centrist' form of rule characteristic of the
1947-63 period: a succession of coalition governments with the minor parties of the centre (Liberals,
Social Democrats and Republicans). By 1963 that
basis of power was not sufficient to repair the
damage the anarchic growth of the 50s had caused and
to face up to the problems resulting from the end of
the economic boom. It was necessary to open up the
coalition to another force from the Left, the
Socialist party (PSI), which would also achieve the

effect, or so it was thought, of isolating the Communists (PCI) and marginalising them in a self-contained ghetto. The entry of the Socialists into the governing coalition (the 'centre-left') would also allow the DC to engage in a series of structural reforms which would considerably expand the public sector. This expansion, directed as it would be by the DC dominated government, would in turn provide a political network of clienteles which would be more efficient politically than the traditional system of party bosses.11 The 1960s would thus be defined as a reforming decade: Italy would modernise itself.

The centre-left coalition formula, which within the DC had been actively pursued by Fanfani and Aldo Moro, by bringing the Socialist party into government meant that the DC could no longer hope to have an unchallenged monopoly over the public sector after 1963. It managed to maintain the lion's share of appointments and consolidate its virtual complete control over the banking system, but it had now to negotiate with the PSI. This negotiating process occurred within the RAI as well. As a result, more posts were created to accommodate the Socialists: in 1963, for example, a Socialist, Giorgio Vechietti, was given the post of deputy director of television news, while a year later the distinguished novelist Giorgio Bassani, a PSI supporter, became vice-chairman of the RAI board.12 In so doing, Bernabei revealed his undoubted skills at increasing rapidly the numbers of RAI staff whilst still retaining ultimate control.13

Until the early 60s the DC had taken an interest in the RAI only to control particular messages, especially news content. Now the RAI had also become an integral part of a massive patronage system which could be used to obtain the support and consent of the intellectual strata. Many intellectuals became freelance contributors and consultants for the RAI. These included journalists, writers and academics, who would receive a retainer every year and special compensation when their help was required. In this way the RAI organised Italian intellectuals and contributed to their growing politicisation. The Bernabei system depended on the ability to control this growing number of people. By the late 1960s there was an increased ferment among the intellectual elites, a reflection of the student and labour struggles of 1968-69 - the famous 'hot autumn'. As the Italian crisis deepened and social

unrest grew, the pressures for internal reform within the broadcasting establishment increased remarkably.

By 1970 the centre-left experiment had demonstrably failed. The structural reforms which had
been promised in the early 60s never materialised.
The central problem for the DC consisted in devising
a way whereby unrest could be coopted and absorbed.
This strategy was only partly successful. The early
1970s witnessed the promulgation of new regional
legislation which devolved considerable powers to
Italy's twenty regions and a new law called the
'Workers' Charter' which enshrined new rights for
factory workers. But in 1970 for the first time in
postwar Italy a major piece of legislation was enacted in the face of DC opposition: the divorce act.
Fanfani, Bernabei's main protector, attempted to
reverse it by a popular referendum in 1974, but lost
miserably. In 1975 the Communist party made sweeping gains at local elections and obtained control
(with the Socialist party) of most major cities.
Fanfani resigned the leadership of the DC. The
Bernabei era was coming to an end and with it any
chance of the DC retaining its privileged control
over the RAI. The age of the traditional system,
the DC-controlled state monopoly, was coming to a
close.

THE REFORM OF THE RAI

Any reform of the RAI had to take into account the
relative strength of the parties in the Italian
political system. In a country as politicised as
Italy in which the presence of political parties can
be felt throughout society there could be no question of transforming the RAI into an Italian
version of the BBC. The ethics of being 'above
parties' is quite foreign to Italian intellectuals
and state functionaries alike. There is no 'Establishment' which ensures continuity as governments
come and go. In Italy governments do come and go,
but they are all dominated by the DC. It is the DC
and its power bloc which ensure continuity.

The broadcasting reform which took place in the
mid-1970s did not aim to offer the Italians a better
television system, but rather to break the DC
stranglehold. The ensuing battle for control was
waged between the DC and the PSI, the principal ally
and rival of the Christian Democrats. This battle
allowed other political forces to enter the fray:
the PCI in the first place, followed by other groups

such as RAI journalists, technical staff, the cinema industry and media trade unions among others. The result of this conflict was the end of the DC domination and the formation of a power duopoly: the DC and the PSI now carved up the RAI. While the DC still maintained a strong position, it could no longer rule unchallenged.

In the course of this struggle the PCI had become the leading representative of those professional groups in broadcasting who had hoped to see their skills and professionalism guaranteed and upheld. This posed a dilemma for the PCI:

- it could choose to fight the battle on behalf of professionalism and quality. In that case it would have had to fight against both the DC and the PSI. If it had done that it would have probably lost and would have had to content itself with the role of a 'protest party' condemned to continued isolation. Furthermore it could not ignore that it shared one of the main objectives of the PSI: the end of DC dominance.

- the other strategy available was to join the PSI in the carve-up operation. This would have considerably damaged the PCI's prestige as the one party which had always fought against the patronage system and which had sought to defend professionalism and competence against the systematic use of political criteria for appointments.

The PCI could not avoid a clear condemnation of the PSI's attempt to play the same game as the DC. In so doing it remained confined to an oppositional ghetto. What happened to the PCI in the struggle for the RAI is but an illustration of the fate of the party since 1947 when it was excluded from the post-war coalition along with the Socialists: to be excluded *a priori* from government. It has been the DC which has played the role of the 'legitimising party', that is, a party which may not be able to rule without partners but has the power to define *de facto* the limits and the framework of 'legitimate' political participation, i.e. which parties can have access to power. Between 1948 and 1963 the 'legitimate' area of government was constituted by the DC and the smaller parties of the centre. After 1963 the PSI was legitimised and brought into the new centre-left coalition. By 1973 the PCI had openly accepted that the DC had the power of legitimising any other party at both the national and

international level. It thus developed the strategy
of the 'historic compromise' which recognised that
Communist access to power would have to be negotiated with the DC.[14]
    The PCI lost the battle for the RAI not only
because the rules of the game were not in its
favour but also because it did not possess a modern
theory of mass communication.[15] The PCI conceived
of the television system purely in terms of a
'public service' which as such had to remain under
the control of the state, with the only problem
being how to democratise it.[16] The PCI did not
appreciate that television had also become an industry which would soon have to face competition from
the private sector and be subjected not only to
political and professional demands, but also to the
laws of the market. Finally, even though the PCI
was, at least for a time, the principal point of
reference for professional groups and even though
it had long sought to go beyond obsolete concepts of
simple class analysis by cultivating the new middle
classes, it has never really been able to involve
large groups of professional and technical cadres in
the formulation of its policies.
    As the PCI could not alter the rules of the
game, the DC and PSI proceeded to carve up the RAI
in the process known as *lottizzazzione*. This carve-
up occurred immediately after the promulgation of
Law 103 (July 1975) which reformed the RAI in the
direction of parliamentary accountability and away
from the control of the executive branch. A
'secret' agreement was reached at the Camilluccia
just outside Rome by the mass media 'specialists',
all of them politicians, of the DC (Bubbico, later
chairman of the Parliamentary Commission on Broadcasting), the PSI (Manca), the Republican party
(Bogi) and the Social Democrats (Orsello).[17] This
agreement stated that the DC would be the dominant
voice at Channel 1 (TV) and Radio 2, whilst the PSI
would get Channel 2 (TV) and Radios 1 and 3.[18]
    The significance of this carve-up lay in the
control established over the news programme of the
two channels, since the evening news had the highest
rating on Italian television. The DC-dominated
Channel 1 evening news (TG1) was organised in direct
competition with the PSI-run TG2 in a successful
attempt to maximise the audience. Both news programmes partly overlapped, but as TG1 occupied the
most favourable time spot it achieved a far greater
rating than its Socialist rival. Journalists could
choose which channel they wanted to work for. The

results showed not only the political colour of the
two news and current affairs sections, but also that
political affiliation was virtually universal among
journalists: e.g. of the 95 journalists opting for
TG1 there were only 4 Communists, 1 Socialist (most
of the other Socialists having opted for 'their'
TG2), 2 Social Democrats, 1 Republican, 2 Liberals
and 5 'independent' of left-wing orientation, while
the remaining 80 were all DC or DC-leaning. As for
the senior executive positions at the RAI, such as
channel director or departmental head, there were 8
DC, 2 Social Democrats, 4 Socialists, 1 Republican,
1 left-wing independent and no Communists.[19]
      Control over the message generally took the
form of giving far more time to the ruling parties
than to the opposition; only the news programme of
Radio 2 was unashamedly the mouthpiece of one of the
factions of the DC (Fanfani's faction). According
to the Radical Party, from March 1 1981 to January 31
1982 the leaders of the five government parties were
interviewed for a total of over ten hours, whilst
all opposition leaders together were interviewed for
only two hours.
      A study conducted by Mario Morcellini of the
University of Rome showed that the time devoted to
the political parties on the evening news programme
of the two channels could be divided as follows:[20]

Period: 15 November - 15 December 1981

	TG1	TG2	1979 elections (Lower Chamber)
DC	50%	44%	38.3%
PSI	12%	20%	9.8%
PCI	17%	21%	30.4%
all others	21%	14%	21.5%

Official RAI figures confirm the imbalance:

Time spent interviewing political representatives during the same period:

	TG1	TG2
Members of the government	50%	31.2%
Members of government parties	34.4%	40.3%
Members of opposition parties	10.9%	20.3%
Others	4.7%	8.2%

It should be stressed that there is no evidence

that, in electoral terms, the media are able to influence the results to any significant degree.
However, there may be some influence exerted over a
small percentage of the population which may contribute to small electoral swings. With a system of
proportional representation as exists in Italy these
small swings do not affect the overall result, but
they have great symbolic value and do affect the
composition of the ruling majorities and the
strength of the opposition, as was clearly shown in
1983.[21]

The push for a reform of the RAI in 1975 came
from a variety of sources: many personalities in the
fields of journalism, culture and, no least,
politics had been opposed to the state monopoly for
some time. Moreover, this opposition was not necessarily linked with a neo-liberal political outlook
in general: many left-wing intellectuals adopted it.
The dislike of the state monopoly was due to the
fact that in Italy, as we have seen, in practice
this meant DC monopoly. Left-wing groups also
wanted greater access and hoped to obtain this if
control of broadcasting shifted to Parliament. The
defeat of the DC in the 1974 divorce referendum had
been a personal defeat for Fanfani and hence for his
protege, Bernabei, who left the RAI in 1975.[22] Moreover, the Constitutional Court in its verdict of
July 10 1974 which allowed the installation of
transmitters for foreign broadcasts had come out
against executive control of the RAI. As a result,
the pressures were such that all the parties of the
centre-left coalition (the DC, the PSI and the smaller parties of the centre) supported the reform
legislation. The PCI abstained, not because it
opposed the new law in principle, but as a gesture
of protest against the allegedly biased television
coverage of its thirteenth party congress.[23]

Under the provisions of Law 103 control of the
RAI shifted from government to Parliament. A
Parliamentary Committee on Broadcasting composed of
40 members in proportion to the strength of the
parties in Parliament was established to ensure that
the RAI was managed as a pluralistic organisation
representing all shades of opinion. The Committee,
however, precisely because it reflected the political composition of Parliament, was dominated by a
majority which in turn reflected the importance of
the parties of the governing coalition.

Control of the RAI thus passed to an oligopoly
of political parties dominated by the DC-PSI duopoly. The law also required that the board of

governors be composed of 16 members, of whom 10 would be nominated by the Parliamentary Committee (i.e. by the political parties) and 6 by the 'shareholders of the RAI' (i.e. the stateholding company IRI, or in practice the minister in charge of the public sector). In other words the RAI board of governors also had an in-built governmental majority.

Neither the board nor the Parliamentary Committee had power over planning, the level of the licence or resources generally (except on the amount of advertising permitted), with the licence remaining under the control of the Minister of Posts and Telecommunications. However, the board was made responsible for all appointments at the executive level. It followed that most of the staff continued to be made up of people politically trusted by the ruling majority. This personnel also possessed the technical skills with which to run a modern broadcasting system, a knowledge which enabled them to play a significant role in the elaboration of a media policy at the political level.[24] Thus, even though the board is on paper an all-powerful body, in practice it tried to obtain 'correct' political messages by appointing the 'right' personnel. Party political control was therefore limited by the fact that the apparatus of the RAI, like all apparatuses, has a life of its own.

There is another important limitation to the exercise of political control over programming. While mass behaviour may not be unduly influenced by the degree of bias in news programmes alone, it may be by the whole range of television messages and by what these messages define as 'normal', 'acceptable' or 'reasonable'. However, political control cannot be established over the totality of television output because this depends on the entire cultural industry, including the cinema, the theatre, the press, the educational system and all other producers and disseminators of information inside and outside the nation-state. Thus, the colonisation of the RAI by the governing political parties could not prevent the growing autonomy of the broadcasting media from the political level, while at the same time these media were becoming increasingly subordinate to the world (i.e. American) communication and cultural industries. In any case the entire efforts of both the DC and PSI were directed towards establishing control over public broadcasting just as the Constitutional Court was about to emit a sentence which would revolutionise the structure of broadcasting in Italy by allowing for the development of private radio and television stations.

THE ADVENT OF PRIVATE BROADCASTING

The 1975 reform had defined the status of the RAI as a public sector monopoly. A year later, on July 15 1976, the Constitutional Court declared that status to be unconstitutional: the state broadcasting monopoly was now considered valid at the *national* level only. In a series of judgements the Court decided that local cable television services would be legal and that transmitters for foreign television stations and for local Italian radio and television could be set up. In another decision the Court explained that a state monopoly over broadcasting would have been justified only if it could offer a full range of programmes, if it could be impartial in news output and open to all cultural developments, if it could guarantee the 'right of access' and 'right of reply' subject to parliamentary control and, finally, if it could ensure that journalists could fulfill their professional duties.[25]
     Even before the Court's decision some transmitters for foreign television stations had been installed and a few cable networks had begun to operate. The government was preparing to legislate against these developments and would have done so but for the Court's intervention. By dismantling the RAI monopoly, the Court also indirectly destroyed cable television. Direct broadcasting is cheaper and does not require any new expenditure on the part of the viewers. Thus, the way was wide open for an unrestricted multiplication of private television and radio stations.
     At first the new private sector was widely welcolmed by public opinion. It was hoped that it would offer a broader variety of broadcasting material and that the competition would force the RAI to improve its programmes. This belief reflects the long-term crisis in the legitimacy of the RAI. It was assumed that the unexciting and cautious programmes the RAI was broadcasting were due to the control exercised by the governing political parties. The RAI could not be seen as a public service broadcasting organisation because it had become the servant of politicians. With the RAI's lack of legitimacy strengthening the case for private television companies, the very concept of public service broadcasting came under threat.
     The advent of private radio and television was

welcomed by business groups, in particular those
operating in the publishing sector such as Rizzoli
and Mondadori, and in the advertising industry. The
possibility of starting a private radio station also
appealed to left-wing fringe groups and to the small
Radical party. As the capital required for this
kind of operation was minimal, it was hoped to start
an 'alternative' network of highly politicised radio
stations. Some of these, such as *Radio Alice* in
Bologna, even became a support system for the violent activities of leftist organisations connected
to the *Autonomia operaia* and were eventually closed
by the police. Eventually even the Communist party
established its own radio stations in some main
cities. The bulk of private radio stations, however,
offered a large dose of pop music and little else
but an amateurish type of news reporting. Unlike
the private television sector, private radio has remained fragmented because it could not provide a
sufficiently high rate of advertising revenues. In
most localities a private radio station can reach
only a specific neighbourhood and the kind of advertising it can attract consists of local businesses.

The RAI obviously opposed the privatisation of
mass communications but, being controlled by the
political parties, it could not express its own independent position. While the Communist party was
distinctly cool towards the new private sector, it
eventually accepted the principle of a mixed public-
private system and fought for its regulation. The
Christian Democrats were ambivalent and split. Those
factions which were still strong at the RAI were un-
happy about the developments, but some leaders, such
as the then Minister of Posts and Telecommunications,
Vittorino Colombo, were enthusiastic.[26]

To this day the government has not been able or
willing to regulate the private sector. This is
substantially a reflection of the continuing weak-
ness of Italian governments and the growing inability of the DC to resolve its own crisis and run
the country. The loss of monopoly control by the
DC over the RAI was not an isolated case. Since
1969 the DC has been unable to reconstruct its own
hegemony over the rest of Italian society. While it
tried to absorb conflict using all its mediating
skills and its control over public spending, after
1969 the state, i.e. the DC, was faced with demands
from a variety of groups and social forces. Yet the
capacity of the productive system to provide the
necessary resources to absorb these new demands was
clearly limited, particularly as the crisis was not

confined to Italy but involved the whole industria-
lised world. A weakened DC with fewer resources had
to negotiate with a greater number of socio-political
actors.

Though weakened, however, the DC could not be
replaced. Between 1976 and 1979 it tried to involve
the PCI in its own power bloc and successfully
sapped some of the Communists' strength. In 1979
the PCI stopped supporting the Christian Democratic
government and the DC was forced to return to the
negotiating table with an aggressive and less timid
PSI. The carve-up of the RAI reached new heights.
In September 1980 the board of the RAI agreed to a
reshuffle of senior appointments, thus implementing
a decision which had been reached behind closed
doors by the leaderships of the PSI and the DC. As
a protest the PCI representatives on the board refused to be present at the crucial meeting. A number of senior journalists and broadcasters (including members of the Socialist party not loyal to
the PSI leader, Bettino Craxi) were fired. The
overall intention was to move from a situation in
which the composition of the senior staff reflected
the governing majority to one in which the senior
staff would be directly connected to the leading
factions of the governing parties. The RAI was no
longer an organisation which the ruling elite considered necessary for the mass reproduction of its
policies. It had now clearly become a locus for the
production and reproduction of its own political
personnel.[27]

The intensity of the battle within the governing parties over the RAI precluded a proper legislative framework for the control of the private
broadcasting sector. This, however, was not the
only reason for the non-regulation of private broadcasting. Having lost considerable power in the RAI
carve-up, the DC was trying to re-establish its
hegemony in the private sector. It could use the
banking system, which it largely controls, to
favour certain broadcasting organisations at the
expense of others. The strategy seems to be not to
regulate private television until the establishment
of an oligopoly situation which would succeed in
unifying the private sector and driving the smaller
independent companies out of the market altogether.
Thus it is unlikely that any regulation will be
attempted until the development of the private
sector has reached some degree of stability. It is
equally possible that there will never be any regulation, partly because it is unlikely that any order

can emerge in an industry which is only at the dawn
of a massive technological transformation and partly
because new satellite developments such as direct
broadcasting by satellite will make regulation ex-
ceedingly difficult.

CONSEQUENCES OF THE GROWTH OF PRIVATE BROADCASTING

The introduction and expansion of private broadcasting, especially television has had profound consequences for the Italian media, politics and society.
The RAI, the press, the advertising industry and the
cinema have all been affected by the new developments. For example, so far as the state broadcasting organisation is concerned private television
has destroyed the chances of RAI developing a decentralised third channel, has had a negative impact on
the quality of RAI programme output and has adver-
sely affected RAI's financial base.
    In the 1970s decentralisation became a keyword
in Italy. The decade had opened with the institution of a system of regional government and had
continued with the growth of a new system of local
government. Following the students' unrest of 1968
and the workers' protests of 1969 the DC had realised that it could no longer contain popular pressures
purely from the centre. Consequently the DC sought
to facilitate the formation of decentralised areas
of decision-making by accepting the Left's demands
for new forms of local democracy: school councils
elected by parents and teachers, university councils
with student participation, health authorities subject to local control and neighbourhood committees
following the pattern first experimented with in the
Communist stronghold of Bologna. Decentralisation
within the RAI was to be achieved by the creation of
a third channel which would be regionally oriented
and therefore more in tune with local needs and
demands. The PCI and the PSI were also in favour of
a decentralised third channel but for reasons
different from those of the DC.
    The PCI, having abandoned the 'Jacobinism'
characteristic of its tradition, had become the most
outspoken advocate of decentralisation. Furthermore, after the success of the local elections of
1975, the PCI had become a very powerful force in
local government: 60% of the population now lived in
areas partly controlled by the Communists, while
within the PCI the weight of the lobby of local
government representatives had become very strong.
The latter demanded greater influence not only

within the party but also within society as a whole.
Finally, the decentralised third channel was seen by
the PCI as a way of acquiring a stake in television
without facing a head-on clash against both the PSI
and the DC.

The PSI too supported decentralisation, although
it conceived of it not so much as an extension of
popular access but as a development which might lead
to the establishment of Socialist control over the
Milan centre of the RAI. This could then be built
up as a PSI fortress against the main Rome centre of
the RAI 'owned' by the DC.[28]

The expansion of private television broadcasting at the local level, however, meant that from its
very inception the Third Channel (conceived of as a
'cultural' channel) was faced with formidable competition. It might have been able to survive if the
RAI had poured in massive resources. The opposite
happened: the two leading channels tried, successfully, to monopolise as many resources as possible
to maintain their audience against the private sector. Had the RAI monopoly been preserved, then the
Third Channel (which is not allowed to carry advertising) could have had adequate financing. Instead
Channels One and Two of the RAI began to compete
with the private companies in the international
market, purchasing more and more American material.

The Third Channel's experimental output and
community programmes were no match for *Dallas, Happy
Days, Streets of San Francisco, Starsky and Hutch*
from the USA and programmes such as *George and
Mildred* and *The Professionals* from the UK. Furthermore the two main RAI channels intensified the use
and productivity of their studio space. This meant
shifting from quality production (such as serials)
to low cost production such as games, debates, etc.
Whilst the average TV studio can produce only about
15 episodes of a high quality serial a year, it can
dish out up to 150 hours a year of 'talking heads'
programmes. This permitted the RAI to save considerable sums which could be used for the purchase
of foreign television material thus competing with
the private sector in the same market.[29] While
Channel Three continues its broadcasts, the regional
element is much diminished and its audience is tiny.
Privatisation has thus damaged the chances of
success of the decentralised channel and lowered the
quality of RAI programmes on Channels One and Two.

The growth of the new private sector has also
had consequences for RAI's finances. Traditionally
the RAI has been financed in two ways: by a

television licence-fee which every owner of a set
has to pay and by advertising. The law regulating
the RAI (Law 103) empowers the Parliamentary Committee on Broadcasting to establish the proportion of
total advertising which the RAI can obtain. This
was a way of protecting the press, because it was
assumed that the bulk of what was left would go to
the printed media. Now, however, after the RAI has
obtained its share of advertising, the rest is
further carved up between the press and the private
television companies.[30] Unable to compete with
public and private television, the press is facing a
severe financial crisis.

The Italian press has never been able to
establish a mass readership as in the UK and probably never will. The most obvious explanation for
the low level of readership is that Italy is a
latecomer in the fields of mass literacy and mass
education. When these were achieved the age of
television had already come. Italian daily papers
are read by an elite, with total readership around
the 5 million mark for nearly fifty years[31], thus
exceeding in Europe only countries such as Spain,
Portugal and Turkey. The highest circulation paper,
the *Corriere della Sera*, is also the most presti-
gious.

The financial crisis of the daily press (the
weekly press is much more diffuse than in the UK and
fulfills the functions of the British popular
dailies and of the Sunday papers) has forced many
papers to resort to banks and these are controlled
by the DC. This dependency has led publishing
groups to become deeply involved in the shady world
of Italian finance: the Rizzoli group, which owned
the *Corriere della Sera*, had to turn to the Banco
Ambrosiano for huge loans, while its chairman
Angelo Rizzoli joined the secret freemason group P2
and has been subsequently arrested and charged with
illegally exporting 25 million dollars. The head
of the Ambrosiano group, Roberto Calvi, was later
found hanging under a London bridge.

Some publishing groups, however, have successfully diversified in the private broadcasting
system. What is taking place is a process of verti-
cal integration which connects banks, publishing
groups, advertising companies and television and
radio stations. There have been two alternative
developments: either various radio and television
stations come under the direct ownership of a single
group or a 'concessionary agency' is created which
in turn gathers advertising revenues and directs

them towards specific radio and television companies.

Let us take as an example the most successful private radio and television network: *Canale Cinque*. Its owner is Silvio Berlusconi who made his money in the building industry. The system he created includes a finance company, Cofint-Finanziaria; a company for the purchasing and distribution of videotape programmes, Rete Italia; a production centre, Videoprograms; a technical centre concerned with high and low frequency bands; a television broadcasting station, *Tele Milano*, the original element in the network; an advertising company, Publitalia; and the network itself, *Canale Cinque*. Berlusconi is also a shareholder in *Il Giornale Nuovo*, a conservative daily based in Milan. In 1979 he bought a huge amount of films from two film companies, Fida and Titanus. *Canale Cinque* is a network which broadcasts daily the entire programme schedule of *Tele Milano* in ten regions. Programmes are not beamed directly via transmitters. Videotapes are sent every day to each station in the network. In this way the verdict of the Constitutional Court which had established that only non-national broadcasting was permitted in the private sector is respected.[32]

This type of integration not only leads to a formidable concentration of power and the eventual creation of oligopolistic 'networks', but also facilitates the planning of television-related products. For example, small locally based television stations purchase the same US-made television series from a distributor. The distributor is also an advertising company (or a purchaser of advertising material) and will provide the advertising revenue which the local stations will use to pay for the series. The distributor will then organise the production and distribution of comic books, novels, T-shirts, toys and other goods which relate to the films sold. Thus the local television companies, far from being examples of a new dynamic entrepreneurship, are but the agents of a few oligopolies which dominate the market: they are mere terminals for distribution. This model of financing has a clear origin: it is the American model which had been hitherto excluded from Western Europe in favour of public service television.[33]

The private broadcasting companies have been the main beneficiaries of the growth of advertising expenditure (see table 1). This, however, has benefited only the largest among them. 80% of private

television advertising revenue goes to the top three
companies. Of these *Canale Cinque* has emerged as
the largest and is now set to overtake the RAI itself. It has recently bought out one of its competitors, *Italia Uno*, and now controls 75% of advertising revenue in the private sector and has a 60%
share of its audience.[34]

Table 4.1: Growth of advertising expenditure
(excluding production costs) on selected media,
1977-1981 (1977=100)

	1977	1978	1979	1980	1981
Daily Press	100	117	142	184	220
RAI-TV	100	130	150	204	301
Private TV	100	192	435	1028	1357
Total expenditure on advertising	100	119	151	206	251

Table 4.2: Percentage distribution of total advertising revenue in each year

	1970 %	1977 %	1978 %	1979 %	1980 %	1981 %
Daily Press	30	32.2	31.5	30.2	28.9	28.3
RAI-TV	12.4	12.5	13.6	12.4	12.4	15
Private TV	n/a	2.4	3.9	6.9	11.9	13
Others (e.g. other press, cinema, radio, billboards, etc.)	57.6	52.8	51	50.5	46.7	43.7

Author's calculation on the basis of data in Roberto
Albano 'Mille miliardi ... in ritardo' in *Il milli-
metro*, N.68 cited in Balassone and Guglielmi, *RAI-TV
L'autarchia impossibile*, p.81 and p.85 (See reference 3).

The figures show that even allowing for inflation
there was a remarkable growth in advertising

spending between 1977 and 1981 (table 4.1). Table
4.2 shows that advertising expenditure in the daily
press decreased as a proportion of total spending,
that it has taken five years for the private sector
to catch up with the RAI and that between 1978 and
1980 the RAI-TV's share of advertising revenue decreased. Table 4.1 shows that the growth of advertising expenditure on the RAI-TV was not keeping up
with the general growth of expenditure in the same
period. 1981 changed the trend: the RAI-TV increased its share from 12.4% to 15% and its lead on
the private sector by attracting advertising revenue
at a faster rate than the rise in total advertising
expenditure. Why? There are two main reasons for
this post-1980 improvement, one political, the other
technical. In the long-run the technical reason
will have more important effects and represents a
warning for the unrestricted expansion of multi-
channel reception in other countries.

a. The political reason: The fall in revenue coincided with the period immediately following the
reform (i.e. 1975-79). During the DC-PSI battle for
control which was then taking place the RAI had
succeeded in acquiring some independence and the PCI
had obtained representation on the board of governors. The political elite and the DC in particular
was losing its grip over the RAI. The loss of
revenue was a warning to the RAI that it could not
do without political protection. Political intervention on the level of expenditure was achieved
through the Parliamentary Committee which - as we
have explained - is empowered by Law 103 (the Reform
Act) to fix the amount of advertising revenue. At
the same time the real value of the licence-fee was
allowed to deteriorate.[35] Thus the RAI lost revenue
on both the advertising and the licensing front. In
1980 when many independent-minded functionaries and
broadcasters were sacked political protection returned: advertising revenue *and* the licence-fee went
up.[36]

b. The technical reason: The amount of advertising
broadcast in the private sector is reaching saturation point, whilst the RAI-TV, which broadcasts
more hours, has still some way to go. In fact it is
widely held that the private companies have now
reached what is considered the natural limit of advertising per hour, namely 14% or 8½ minutes.

The consequences for viewers of this authentic

onslaught of advertising can be far reaching. The
enormous growth of channels available to the viewer
has entailed a rapid diffusion of remote control.
According to the RAI one third of the Italian television audience now has a remote control instrument.[37] The ability to change channel without
moving from one's armchair, the existence in main
cities of up to 20 channels and the weight of advertising has radically changed the pattern of consumption of television output. Thanks to remote control
many viewers now follow two or three programmes at
the same time by switching back and forth taking
advantage of advertising breaks and of any pause in
the action. Psychologically it may amount to a
desperate search for something worth watching while
at the same time the viewer's subconscious is perfectly aware that the 'perfect' programme will never
appear. The frequent changes and the real possibility to follow two or three films at the same time is
also helped by the repetitive nature of much television production. The viewer is by now fairly
familiar with the main genres, can predict what is
going to happen with accuracy ... and can switch
channel.
     The frequent use of remote control means that
viewers are now constructing their own television
programmes made up of fragments of broadcast programmes.[38] The advertising break is now not only
the universal sign that one can go to the toilet or
make a cup of tea (or, given this context, mix a
Campari) but also that the search for alternatives
can start. To obviate this popular threat against
the advertising break it is quite possible that an
agreement will be reached among the private companies to broadcast their advertising material at
the same time. The other possibility is that the
Italian companies will follow the pioneering example
of their American equivalent: the gradual merger of
the broadcast image with the advertising break so
that there is no clear break between films and commercials: as our hero on horseback disappears in the
sunset an almost identical horseman extracts a well-
known brand of cigarette from his breast-pocket and,
before even the fastest viewer can reach the remote
control switch, utters the advertising slogan. No
doubt when videorecorders will have reached in Italy
the diffusion they have in the UK, the speed-up
button too will be used to cut off commercial breaks.
It is too early to tell what this will do to the
economics of advertising and broadcasting.
     The expansion of private television has there-

fore had dramatic effects on the RAI, on advertising, on viewers and on the press. As one would expect it has also accelerated the crisis of the Italian cinema. Consumption of films has increased, but it now takes place at home in front of the television screen, not in the cinema. In 1978 there were 11,560 cinemas in operation, by 1980 there were only 8,440 and two years later only 6,500.[39] This is, of course, a staggering figure compared to the UK: 1,500 cinema *screens* in 1981[40], but then Italy traditionally has had a very high density of cinema screens. The pattern of ticket sales demonstrates that the crisis has intensified since the introduction of private television.[41] The only way out of this crisis is for further integration between the cinema and television. Cinecitta, the Italian Hollywood, should produce more and more for the mass television market. This could generate sufficient revenue to enable it to continue the production of films for the cinema and would provide both the RAI and the private companies with much needed nationally made programmes. In the long run this development would also go some way towards limiting the growing americanisation of Italian culture.

Audience ratings indicate that the overwhelming majority of viewers want to watch films. The ratings for the main types of programmes are as follows: 75% for films, 74% for news, 68% for made-for-TV films and serials and 55% for pop music.[42] The high ratings for the news programme reflects partly the low level of press readership and partly the well-established habit of eating dinner between eight and nine in the evening and watching the RAI main news during or after dinner. At 8.30 p.m. the news is over and the average viewer begins the search for a film. This is when private television audience reaches its peak: 13 million viewers between 9.00 and 10.00 p.m.

To illustrate the extent of the change resulting from the introduction of private television, let us take a day in May 1981 in an area of Rome.[43] Our viewer can receive fairly well thirteen private channels plus the three RAI channels for a total of 196.2 hours of programmes. The total supply is apportioned as shown in figure 4.1. Anyone sitting in front of the set at 9.00 pm can choose between sixteen channels, but thirteen of these will offer films. Most cartoons and made-for-TV films have been purchased from abroad and dubbed in Italian, with nearly all imported films made in the USA.

Thus the bulk of the material from which an

Figure 4.1: Private Television in the Rome Area, May 1981

TOTAL HOURS SUPPLIED
196.2 hours

HOME-BASED PRODUCTION
45.1 hours

PURCHASED MATERIAL
151.1 hours

SPORTS:
9.15 hours

NEWS:
12.62 hours

GAMES,
POP MUSIC, etc.:
23.33 hours

FILMS:
120.9 hours

CARTOONS:
30.2 hours

increasingly fragmented and differentiated audience
(as modern audiences are in advanced industrial
countries) must choose tends to be homogeneous and
repetitive. A country with a major artistic and
cultural tradition which has made a significant contribution to the cinema has a broadcasting system
which is increasingly like a huge network of terminals transmitting programmes produced in and
around Los Angeles.

The television audience, of course, turns to
films of its own free will. The increase in the
supply of films has not been forced on the Italian
audience, nor has the americanisation of Italian
culture been imposed by some evil force. Nevertheless the audience is clearly bored. The frantic use
of remote control as well as various surveys demonstrate that whilst it is true that the public want
films, it does not follow that they get the films
they want or might want if they had a wider choice.
Television viewing is now an established activity of
a large part of the Italian population and the
principal though not exclusive focus of their
leisure time. There are no other leisure activities
to which people can turn so easily and so frequently
(unless one envisages as a *realistic* alternative a
population of bookworms reading novels for 25 hours
a week - the number of hours the average person
spends in front of the television screen).

The success of American films does not depend
on their aesthetic or cultural content but on the
fact that they fill a popular demand. The way had
been paved by the American film industry which has
dominated the cinema since the 1920s. The consequences for Italy's cultural balance of payments
have been severe.

In 1981 Italian television companies (public
and private) imported 2,369 films plus 2,043 made-
for-TV films and episodes of TV serials. Of these
4,412 units of production the RAI accounted for the
purchase of 786 units. If we include also the 796
films to be shown in cinemas which were imported in
the same period the total expenditure was 102.16
billion lire, three times as much as during 1980. In
1981 Italy also exported 2,484 units of television
fiction and films and received in payment 29 billion
lire. Thus the deficit was 73.16 billion lire.
These data show that the resources Italy can command
for the production of television fiction are not invested internally, but are directed towards the USA.
Thus private television stations (and to a much
lesser extent the RAI) act, *de facto*, as agents for

the distribution of products manufactured by the great multinational companies. As was stated in our opening remarks, centralisation of production and decentralisation of distribution go hand in hand.

The international structure of the information system and the subordinate role Italy plays within it are mirrored within Italy itself in the unevenness between North and South. If we look at 'traditional' or written information we will notice a persistent gap.[44] The South has 34% of the total population but published only 400 out of 12,200 titles of books a year (1975 figures), prints only 16 out of 87 daily papers (each selling less than 100,000 copies) and buys only 10% of daily papers and 17% of periodicals. If we examine the figures for television we see that there is virtually no 'consumption' gap between North and South: 94% of the southern population own a television set against a national average of 96%. The closing of this particular gap is relatively recent.

In all cases, however, there is a production gap: most of the programmes broadcast in Italy come from abroad, but most of the *Italian* programmes broadcast come from the North or the Centre. Southern culture has no outlet. The cultural unification of the South with the North thus proceeds essentially through the americanisation of the national culture. The role of the South in this domain is, even more than that of the rest of Italy, its traditional one: a market for goods made elsewhere.

CONCLUSION

Many of the problems facing Italian television are similar to those faced by other national, and particularly West European, television systems: the question of a national culture, the expansion of leisure time, the challenge of new technologies, etc. There are also two major problems which are more or less specific to Italy. In the first place Italy is a 'late comer' which has jumped a stage: it is already experiencing unrestricted multi-channel television. It has seen the future and it does not work. A sense of history tells us that the past does not work either (and anyway it is the *past*) and that the demand for a return to the purity of 'public service television', particularly public service in the image of the DC, is not only unrealistic but undesirable. In the second place Italian state television, like the French broadcasting system, has traditionally been under excessive

political influence and party interference. This is
neither particularly democratic nor has it managed
to produce especially good television. Clearly
these are two problems on the agenda of any Italian
reformer. Are there any solutions?

Let us take an aspect of the first problem: the
'cultural balance of payments' deficit caused by the
growth of private television and the imitative
effects this has had on the RAI in terms of programme purchasing policy. Some have argued that as
the international market is already dominated by
American products, Italy has no possibility of ob-
taining a decent share of it. What is needed is a
severe regulation of private television with a limit
on imported material. The effect of this cultural
protectionism would be the rapid bankruptcy of many
private television companies and the further development of the existing monopolies, the only ones
with the resources for producing their own programmes. What might well happen, however, is that
they will produce national versions of American products. It is not impossible that these might obtain
international recognition. After all the 'sphag-
hetti westerns' have been very successful elsewhere
including the USA and are seen by many as a new art-
form. What the protectionists fail to see is that
in the near future it will become nearly impossible
to regulate the supply of television on the basis of
the nation-state because of the development of
satellite broadcasting. This development will spell
the beginning of the end for any form of national
control over the whole range of broadcasting.

A modified 'free trade' version of this would
be for Italy to try to enter the international
broadcasting market with a range of products similar
to that of the US: either 'straight' imitations like
the 'spaghetti westerns' or Italianised versions of
American material. Mafia stories would provide an
internationally familiar theme which would more than
match Texan oil tycoons and their families.

This solution may well enable the Italian
broadcasting industry to recoup some of its losses
and to finance some of its internal consumption.
However, it may not be realistic for Italian industry to compete on the home ground of the United
States. The kind of series which are devised in
Hollywood and which can find the appropriate networking agreement and the required level of sponsorship
go through a formidable selection. It has been estimated that the leading 20-25 serials which do eventually appear on US television screens and are sold

throughout the world (e.g. *Dallas* or *Streets of San Francisco*) are but the end result of a process which starts with tens of thousands of ideas, then proceeds with thousands of so-called 'treatments', then down to 1,500 projects and, eventually, 150 pilot programmes.[45] It is difficult to imagine Italy (or any other country) being able to enter this kind of system and compete effectively on a long term basis.

The RAI seems to have attempted another strategy: the production of major serials based on an internationally well-known historical figure, usually connected with Italy: Leonardo Da Vinci, Marco Polo, Guiseppe Verdi, but also Jesus Christ (a Zeffirelli film co-produced with Britain's ATV) on whom Italy, historically, has had some claims. Many of these have been successful and it could well be that this strategy will pay off in the long run, particularly if it is combined with the production of television serials which can offer the international audience something which is both familiar (i.e. American) and yet different (i.e. Italian).

This strategy, however, means that the system of producing fiction will have to change considerably. Until now Italy has relied on flair and improvisation. As long as production was in the hands of directors like Visconti, Antonioni, Fellini, De Sica and others, as well as more commercial people like Sergio Leone of 'spaghetti western' fame, Italy could hold her own in the international cinema industry. The point now is to compete in the mass market. This requires a proper production system with adequate funds, an infrastructure, schools for training the technical staff, and so on. Private television has so far not made any significant contribution in this field and the RAI has done far too little. This development clearly cannot be left to the private sector which, in its shortsightedness, will always prefer the policy of buying from abroad, even though they may take the first timid steps on the road to internal production (a road which *Canale Cinque*, the largest private television company, has already begun to travel). A way will have to be found for the state, through RAI, to establish some framework within which a system of mass production can be set up and in which the private sector can play a part. There is already an example for this: the system whereby RAI commissions films from an outside director. Here the RAI acts as a producing company and is also the distributor for the film both on television and in the cinemas. Well-known directors such as Olmi, Bertolucci and the Taviani

brothers have produced important work through this
system. The point is to expand it on a wider and
more commercial basis.

Italy is not the only country in the world
which is increasingly worried by the excessive number of American made programmes which are appearing
on its screens. It might be possible to take advantage of this fact through co-production at the
European level which would be marketed not only in
Europe, but also in Third World countries seeking to
diversify the cultural origin of their imported
broadcasting material. This, of course, would be
the development of a process which has already begun.
West Germany, France, the UK, Italy and other European countries regularly co-operate on a number of
arts programmes. The *South Bank Show* - one of the
most successful British arts programmes - is co-
financed by various European sources. Serials like
The Borgias and *Marco Polo* are co-produced and the
latter was sponsored by Procter and Gamble and the
advertising giant Denzu-Japan among others.

The strengthening of the RAI, however, is only
one aspect of the solution to the problem. The
other must be the regulation of private broadcasting.
So far the only existing regulation is represented
by the Constitutional Court's decision which limits
private broadcasting to the 'local' area. There is
as yet no definition of 'local' television and
nothing has been done to stop private companies from
swapping videotapes of their programmes and transmitting them at the same time. Furthermore no one
has, so far, enforced existing laws regulating frequency bands. If this were done private companies
could be forced to stop operating altogether.[46] The
reason why no-one, including the PCI, has demanded
the enforcement of this law is that everyone
realises only too well that the existing level of
demand for broadcast television is such that no
state monopoly would have the capacity to satisfy
it. There is thus total agreement among all the
political forces as to the 'mixed' nature of the
system: private television is here to stay. At the
same time virtually all political forces also agree
that private television should be regulated.

The PSI had been the first party to examine
seriously the entire question of the mass media and
had been very active in opening the debate through
its own press, round table discussions and conferences. The ideas which were emerging pointed in
the direction of liberalisation of the system and
were, therefore, strongly aimed against the public

sector.[47]   However, since the PSI managed to
strengthen its controlling interests in the RAI and
appoint its own people, it has been spectacularly
quiet.

On the whole the governing parties are, at
least officially, opposed to the present unregulated
state of the private sector. The leaderships have
privileged access to the RAI and obtain the 'right'
sort of messages in the news programmes. Individual
parliamentarians (deputies and senators) have a
different attitude: they need private radio and
television stations because they can obtain from
them what they cannot obtain from the RAI: publicity
for their own activity at the local level. Before
the development of mass media they could keep in
touch with their electorate through public meetings.
Now they can no longer obtain a large audience:
everyone stays at home watching television. Local
notables can only enter private homes through small
television stations which beam their message for a
radius of 10-20 miles.[48] During an election this
can make a significant difference particularly as in
Italy the voter must vote for a political party, but
can then write in the name of his favourite three or
four candidates from within that party's list: the
so-called preferential vote.

Only the PCI has presented a comprehensive proposal for reform during the life of the last parliament (1979-1983). In the first place it has insisted that private companies be allowed to operate
only within the local dimension thus upholding the
Constitutional Court's decision. Realising that
this dimension cannot be excessively restricted it
has suggested that the twenty Italian regions can
provide the framework for roughly as many private
companies. This would not prevent the growth of
networking to which the PCI has no objection provided that ownership is not concentrated in a few hands.
Hence the PCI advocates anti-trust legislation along
the US pattern. Furthermore private companies would
be required to produce and transmit their own programmes for at least 30% of their total weekly
broadcast time. There would be a public body which
would specify when and how much of these internally
produced programmes would have to be shown in order
to ensure that they would not all be broadcast at,
say, 4.00 a.m. Finally the PCI has declared its
willingness to reform the existing law 103 which
regulates the RAI provided that the principles embodied in it of parliamentary control and managerial
independence are not infringed.[49]

This proposal has encountered some objections even within the PCI's own ranks. It has been objected that the acceptance of networking would go against the principle of a regional dimension. One could produce as an example the British ITV system: it is undoubtedly a network with a regional dimension, but the latter is not much in evidence. Furthermore, the emphasis on the regulation of private companies keeps this question separate from the overall question of the connection between the public and the private sectors. It may be necessary to rethink the role of the RAI. Like the BBC it still has the structure it had when it had a monopoly of broadcasting: it both produces and distributes its own programmes - apart, of course, from the films it commissions and the programmes it purchases. It might be possible to separate the production and distribution functions and to envisage a system whereby the public sector would produce programmes which could be purchased by private companies on the basis of agreements with respect to broadcasting times.[50] Alternatively the RAI could enter into 'networking' agreements with some private companies for specific programmes. This issue is of great importance because it deals with the complex problem of regulating a mixed system of ownership in a developed country.

A modern mixed system cannot depend on a simplistic division between the public and the private spheres, i.e. between state-owned and privately owned. The public sector is increasingly subjected to the laws of the market and to commercial criteria, whilst the private sector faces, sooner or later, the existence of state legislation and public pressures. The mixed system is therefore a system of different forms of ownership which are deeply intertwined. Those who reject both central planning (Soviet-style) and unregulated free enterprise and who, therefore, accept the principle of the mixed system must face the question of its overall regulation.

Any regulation of the existing system, to the extent to which this is possible, cannot deal exclusively with broadcast television, but must concern itself with the whole of the information field and in particular with the development of new technologies. No regulation and restructuring of Italian media can be lasting and satisfactory if it fails to do that.

Let us take the question of cable television. It is obvious that the unrestricted expansion of over-the-air private television has dealt a blow to the possibility of cable expansion in Italy. The viewers who now have access to twenty channels will not even envisage further expenditure in order to be able to receive thirty more, particularly if these show the same kind of programmes currently being broadcast. Yet without a cable network there can be no development of a modern and competitive information society. After all the political and commercial pressures behind cable television do not aim to show thirty *Dallas* a day, but rather to rewire an entire nation so as to provide an interactive system (two-way) of information: no longer the passive reception by many of messages from a few senders, but an active intervention into a network of data which will permit shopping, learning, working and communicating, all by cable. At this stage there is no great popular demand for this. It has therefore been assumed that it is possible to 'sell' cable lines with interactive capability only by offering the possibility of more television programmes by assuming there is a mass demand for further such programmes. In the present Italian situation this is clearly not the case. Thus market forces on their own would not be able to generate sufficient demand for an interactive information system and without this the chances of Italy's transition to the information society would be seriously diminished. Given the growing weight that information technology will have, it is no longer possible to envisage a reform of the telecommunication system which separates the public sector from the private one.

Let us now turn to the second specific Italian problem to be solved: the undue influence exercised by the ruling political parties, the so-called *lottizzazzione*. In discussing this question we have tried to explain that the carve-up of the RAI by the government parties is not something peculiar to television. Unlike the UK the whole of the Italian political and economic system is subject to this form of control. In the United Kingdom political parties are essentially electoral mechanisms whose main function is to enable a particular parliamentary group to obtain a majority. The organisation of political and civil society does not depend on political parties but on a complex network of formal and informal institutions: trade unions, employers' associations, the press and pressure groups, as well as the actual apparatuses of the state and the civil service.

In Italy the fundamental task of organising
political and civil society is in the hands of
political parties which are present and active not
only in a clearly defined parliamentary arena but
also throughout society. The Italian elections of
1983 may have considerably weakened the Christian
Democratic Party and, in so doing, have increased
the difficulty this party faces in attempting to
mediate conflict and negotiate with other political
forces. However, while a weakened DC may entail a
more feeble Christian Democratic grip on the public
sector, it does not follow from this that the system
of *lottizzazzione* will be in crisis. On the contrary, the PSI and the other smaller parties in the
governing coalition may be able to impose on the DC
political deals which will be more favourable to
themselves. As long as the conditions are not ripe
for an entirely different form of government which
will exclude the DC, or which, at least, will break
up its system of rule, its power bloc - and this *may*
(but *may* only) occur with an alternative coalition
led by the PCI - it is difficult to imagine the RAI
and the rest of the public sector free from the
colonising grip of the ruling political parties.

This difficulty is compounded by the quasi-
total politicisation of technical and intellectual
cadres. One cannot find many authentically independent, i.e. 'non-political', experts in Italy. In
countries such as the UK 'independent experts' are
all those who are politically committed to the
general consensus within which - at least until re-
cemently - most political decisions were taken.
Within this consensus it has been possible to have
an alternance of political parties at the helm of
the state. This kind of consensus does not exist in
Italy. There is instead a narrower terrain which is
the 'area of government' dominated by the DC and by
those parties which the DC accepts as possible
government partners. This area is now supported by
less than two thirds of the electorate and the complexity of mediation has reached such a stage that
it is difficult to imagine any of these forces
being willing to give up any share they possess in
the intricate web of clientele and patronage.

If the practice of *lottizzazzione* were little
more than a deviant phenomenon in an otherwise
healthy system then a vigorous political campaign
might well eradicate it. If it were merely the
expression of political backwardness then one could
simply wait for or accelerate the modernisation of
Italy until it 'caught up' with the rest of Europe.

If it is, as we believe, a moralistic description of a major feature of the Italian system of government, then there can be no simple and, certainly, no partial solution.

This, of course, does not mean that nothing can be done until the system of power of the DC is destroyed, an event which is unlikely to occur in the foreseeable future in spite of its serious electoral losses in the elections of 1983. A coherent battle for the modernisation of Italian telecommunications, a concerted European entry into the technological software market, the development of information technology, the professional training of competent cadres, an intelligent system of regulation which recognizes, at least formally, the need for some demarcation between technical competence and professionalism on the one hand and political control on the other might well produce a situation in which at least the worst aspects of *lottizzazzione* will appear increasingly irrelevant and counter-productive.

It is unlikely that, short of a historical crisis, party political control will be totally eliminated. Nor is there any reason why it should. Political parties still have popular legitimacy and are subject to a regular electoral verdict. On the other hand there is no reason why a party like the DC which has little more than one third of the vote should have four fifths of political power and control. Moreover, control should not be exercised *only* by political parties. There are other actors on the political stage, namely social forces which claim some sort of access to political resources: trade unions, women's organisations, professional groups, cooperatives, etc. Conflicts and compromises are good for democracy and Italy has had its share of both. It is time now to expand the framework of conflicts and compromises so as to include as many social forces as possible. It will not be easy. Some will say that excessive pluralism is a recipe for disaster. However, in this case, the disaster is already happening. The bottom of the well may not have been reached but the situation is desperate and, before desperate remedies are applied, a bold and radical break is urgently needed.

References

1. S.MacBride (ed.), *Multiple Voices One World*, Paris, UNESCO, 1980.
2. See G. Vacca, 'L'Italia verso la società dell'informazione. Quale?', paper presented at the conference *Telematica e Mezzogiorno*, Bari, December 1982, mimeo, p.1.
3. S. Balassone and A. Guglielmi, *RAI-TV L'autarchia impossibile*, Rome, Riuniti, 1983, pp. 29-30.
4. Figures in Carlo Gagliardi, 'La Televisione in Italia: Tendenze del sistema misto', in *Sociologia e ricerca sociale*, no. 9, 1982.
5. For a history of the RAI during Fascism see A. Papa, *Storia politica della radio in Italia 1924-1943*, Naples, Guida, 1978; for the post-fascist period see F. Monteleone, *Storia della Rai dagli Alleati alla Dc*, Rome-Bari, Laterza, 1979.
6. Franco Chiarenza, *Il cavallo morente*, Milano, Bompiani, 1978, p.91.
7. G. Cesareo, 'Il "politico" nell'alba del quarternario' in *Problemi del Socialismo*, vol.22 no.22, 1981, pp.22-23.
8. Giovanni Cesareo, *Anatomia del potere televisivo*, Milan, Franco Angeli, 1970, p.35.
9. Chiarenza, *Il cavallo morente*, p.73.
10. Cesareo, *Anatomia del potere televisivo*, p.80.
11. For an analysis of this transition in Naples see P.A. Allum, *Politics and Society in postwar Naples*, Cambridge, CUP, 1973.
12. Fabio Luca Cavazza, 'Italy: From Party Occupation to Party Partition', in A. Smith (ed.), *Television and Political Life*, London, Macmillan, 1979, p.95. For an analysis of Bernabei's management see F. Pinto, *Il modello televisivo*, Milan, Feltrinelli, 1980.
13. Cesareo, *Anatomia del potere televisivo*, pp.45-46.
14. For a history of the PCI in the postwar period see D. Sassoon, *The Strategy of the Italian Communist Party: From the Resistance to the Historic Compromise*, London, Frances Pinter, 1981.
15. In the 1950s Communist intellectuals - in spite of Gramsci's influence - tended to despise television and other forms of mass culture. See F. Pinto, *Intellettuali e Tv negli anni '50*, Rome, Savelli, 1977.
16. The idea of television as a 'public service' dominated most thinking about television

in Europe.   The concept pervaded British thinking on
the subject as early as the Sykes Report (1923).
This principle began to be disregarded only in the
late 1970s.   The Annan Report (1977) broke with this
tradition; see James Curran and Jean Seaton, *Power
without Responsibility. The Press and Broadcasting
in Britain*, London, Fontana, 1981, ch.16.

17. The Camilluccia agreement is discussed in
Chiarenza, *Il cavallo morente*, p.22.   The entire
background of the operation was leaked to the press
and has been authoritatively confirmed in an auto-
biographical book written by a Socialist nominee to
the RAI Board.   See Massimo Pini, *Memorie di un
lottizzatore*, Milan, Feltrinelli, 1978, esp. pp.63-
72.

18. Stefano Gentiloni, 'L'informazione dopo la
riforma' in G. Vacca (ed.), *Communicazioni di massa
e democrazia*, Rome, Ruiniti, 1980, p.149.

19. C. Fracassi, 'Poltrona per poltrona tutto
il potere lottizzato alla RAI-TV', *Paese Sera*,
March 1982.

20. *Ibid.*

21. This point is made in F. Rositi, *Mercati di
cultura*, Bari, De Donato, 1982, pp.100-1.   If this
is valid then it would be even more so in the U.K.
where a small swing is transformed by the electoral
system into a disproportionate number of seats
gained.

22. See Chiarenza, *Il cavallo morente*, pp.185,
192, 194-5 and 200.

23. Pinto, *Intellettuali e Tv negli anni '50*,
pp.161-173.

24. Gentiloni, 'L'informazione dopo la riforma',
p.149.

25. Cavazza, 'Italy: From Party Occupation to
Party Partition', p.104.

26. See interview with Vittorino Colombo in
Aldo Biscardi and Luca Liguori (eds.), *L'impero di
vetro*, Turin, SEI, 1978, p.101.

27. Rositi, *Mercati di cultura*, pp.53-57.

28. Balassone and Guglielmi, *RAI - TV
L'autarchia impossibile*, p.41.

29. *Ibid.*, p.52.

30. Vacca, 'L'Italia verso la società
dell'informazione. Quale?', p.17.

31. Alberto Asor Rosa, 'Il giornalista: appunti
sulla fisiologia di un mestiere difficile', in
Storia d'Italia. Annali, vol.4, (*Intellettuali e
potere*) edited by C. Vivanti, Turin, Einaudi, 1981,
p.1235.   In the last few years the increase in the
number of dailies has pushed circulation to just

Italy: The Advent of Private Broadcasting

over five million copies.

32. See Renato Venturini, 'Verso un sistema misto', in *Studi sociali*, no.1-2, 1983, pp.111-112.

33. *Ibid*.

34. Vacca, 'L'Italia verso la società dell'informazione. Quale?', p.17.

35. Balassone and Guglielmi, *RAI-TV L'autarchia impossibile*, pp.87-88.

36, The revenue from the licencing-fee in real terms (1974=100) was the following:

1974	1975	1976	1977	1978	1979	1980	1981
100	87	79.3	92	89.5	84	89	100.2

Revenue from the licence-fee is, on average, more than two and a half times the size of the advertising revenue.

37. The study on remote control was conducted by the audience research services of the RAI. See Vacca, 'L'Italia verso la società dell'informazione. Quale?', p.7 and Balassone and Guglielmi, *RAI-TV L'autarchia impossibile*, pp.70-71.

38. Raymond Williams has argued that broadcast television is organized like a 'flow ... of differently related units ... in which the real internal organization is something other than the declared organization'. (*Television*, London, Fontana, 1974, p.93) Remote control enables the viewer to organise his/her own 'flow' of fragments.

39. Official government figures quoted in Vacca, 'L'Italia verso la società dell'informazione. Quale?', p.11.

40. John Ellis, 'What's one Odeon less anyway?' in *Marxism Today*, October 1981, p.39.

41. F. Pinto, 'Cinema e TV: una integrazione auspicabile' in G. Vacca (ed.), *Communicazioni di massa e democrazia*, Rome, Riuniti, 1980, p.96.

42. Data in Vacca, 'L'Italia verso la società dell'informazione. Quale?', p.6.

42. The following data are in Balassone and Guglielmi, *RAI-TV L'autarchia impossibile*, pp.64-8. For comparison, a London-based viewer on a Saturday in July 1983 would be supplied with 63.5 hours of broadcasting including Open University programmes (on a weekday fewer hours would be broadcast).

44. The data that follow are in Vacca, 'L'informazione negli anni '80', paper prepared for the Conference of the FNSL (the press trade union), April-May 1981, mimeo, pp.1-6.

45. C. Sartori, *L'occhio universale*, Milan, 1981, pp.30-50, quoted in Balassone and Guglielmi, *RAI-TV L'autarchia impossibile*, p.158.

46. G. Vacca, 'Perche misto' in *Rinascita*,

156

No. 7, February 1983.
  47. See the proceedings of the PSI conference *Informazione potere*, Rome, November 14-16 1978.
  48. Venturini, 'Verso un sistema misto', pp. 98-99.
  49. L. Pavolini, 'Tv, la legge bloccata' in *Rinascita*, No. 1, January 1983.
  50. Vacca, 'Perche misto'.

Chapter 5

UNITED STATES: A SYSTEM OF MINIMAL REGULATION

Muriel and Joel Cantor*

Although communication and social science studies
of the mass media in general and broadcasting in
particular are well established in the United States,
few have investigated the topic being considered
here. Rather than focusing on the politics of
broadcasting, American social scientists have spent
more time on how broadcasting has influenced politics. The presentation of candidates, the conduct
of election campaigns, presidential and other debates, Congressional hearings and political conven-
tions have all been investigated and critically
appraised through both scholarly and journalistic
accounts. The basic question raised in such discussions is whether and to what extent broadcasting
(first national radio and later television) has
changed the political process. In other words,
focus has been on the *effects* of media presentation
and not on who *controls* broadcasting and how groups,
individuals, and organisations gain access to the
airwaves.[1] In contrast, the politics of broadcasting includes technical, programming and, most importantly, commercial concerns. The political
actors are mass media industries, politicians and
office holders such as the President and members of
Congress, the Courts, citizen groups, the Federal
Communications Commission (FCC) and at times other
agencies such as the Department of Justice and the
Federal Trade Commission.[2]
    A long-standing and recurring debate revolves
around the issues of free speech and censorship on
the one hand and oligarchic-monopolistic control
from industrial and corporate interests on the other.

*The authors would like to thank Raymond Kuhn and
Jeremy Tunstall for their careful reading of the
manuscript and helpful criticisms.

The United States is a capitalistic, constitutional democracy and free speech is guaranteed in its formal Constitution. In 1791, shortly after the original thirteen States ratified the Constitution, ten amendments, known as the Bill of Rights were adopted. The First Amendment reads in part as follows: 'Congress shall make no law ... abridging the freedom of speech or of the press.'[3] That amendment has never been applied absolutely to all forms of communication, though verbal and print material have been freer from government control than broadcasting. The law, especially the Communications Law of 1934 supported by judicial decisions, has treated broadcasting differently from books, newspapers and magazines. In addition to the major regulatory legislation, the 19th century anti-trust laws are used to limit the authority of media organisations (film, print, as well as broadcasting).[4] Thus, the First Amendment, the 1934 Communications Act (with its amendments, regulations and rules) and the anti-trust acts together form the body of law which governs the politics of broadcasting. Various participants try through legislative, judicial, and regulatory processes to change or maintain the broadcasting system. This struggle over access and control has been going on since before the beginning of broadcasting for home consumption, starting shortly after World War I.

Although commercial interests remain the most powerful influence in determining programme content and related matters, at various times the public (through public interest and lobbying groups), the judicial system through its power to interpret and police the law and the FCC through its power to establish and rescind regulations have had differential impacts on content and programming decisions. Certain facts remain constant: first, although primarily a commercial, profit-making enterprise, broadcasting exists at the pleasure of the United States government; secondly, the US broadcasting industry has always been an oligopoly; thirdly, it is supported primarily from advertising revenues and other corporate funds[5]; and finally even though broadcasters are required to programme in the 'public interest', there is no satisfactory definition of that term, agreeable to all parties involved in the politics of broadcasting.

American broadcasting as it now exists has its critics, and certain lawmakers and several different groups representing all points on the political spectrum would prefer a different kind of broad-

casting system. Critics on the Left, found primarily in academia, contend that American media
in general reflect capitalist concerns and policies.
To simplify the message from the Left: American
media reflect the capitalist system and can change
only if the politico-economic system were itself to
change.[6] Most critics, on the other hand, whether
liberal, moderate, or of the Right, have sought to
work through the existing institutions to try to
change public policy towards broadcasting. As will
be elaborated later, some of these groups, such as
the United Church of Christ, have been effective,
while others, in fact the majority, have not. For
example, Action for Children's Television (ACT), a
nationwide group which is concerned with the effects
of broadcasting on children, has advocated that
commercial advertising should be eliminated from
children's programmes and that programme content
itself should be more educational and less sensa-
tional. This organisation petitioned the FCC in
1970 to demand that the broadcasting industry provide 14 hours of commercial-free programmes each
week, a petition which failed. However, the ACT
continues to pressure for less commercialism, through
regulation. Along with other interest and citizen
groups, it recognises that capitalism is entrenched
and that the basic structure of commercialism in the
media is unlikely to alter unless competing market
forces were to change. Some groups, such as ACT,
look to the government for more regulation. Others,
such as the Christian Coalition for Better Television, try to change programmes through advocating
consumer boycotts. Still others, especially civil
libertarians and broadcasting decision-makers,
believe that regulation usually interferes with the
rights of free speech and is an unwarranted intrusion of government into the business of broadcasting.
The on-going debate concerning broadcasting is not
whether the system of free enterprise should change,
but rather to what extent broadcasting should be
regulated in a capitalistic society and whose interests should such regulation protect.[7]
   This chapter examines the history and application of regulation in US broadcasting, and in particular how the various segments of the broadcasting
industry influence the regulatory process. The
chapter is divided as follows: after a short introductory overview of the contemporary American broadcasting system, the first section describes the rise
of commercial broadcasting and governmental regulation in the United States. The second section

discusses the changes in regulation from the mid-1960s to the present. In this section, several specific examples (the Family Viewing controversy and the Financial Interest and Syndication Rules) will be presented to show how the policy-making process operates at the national level. These rules, their adoption and their political consequences show how social and economic forces influence the politics of broadcasting. In the final section, the future of regulation will be discussed in terms of transnational operations.

THE AMERICAN BROADCASTING SYSTEM

Broadcasting in the United States has for the last 50 years been considered by some as synonymous with the three major networks: the National Broadcasting Company (NBC), the American Broadcasting Company (ABC) and the Columbia Broadcasting System (CBS). These broadcasting organisations are formal, complex bureaucracies, organised for profit. They are also segments of large, corporate conglomerates. Although they had their roots in broadcasting, they are organised and managed like most other large American corporations. Each is required like all divisions of the parent corporation to try to increase its profits over previous years'. Therefore, unlike the traditional West European model, the emphasis is not on public service or on presenting artistic, informational or educational programmes, but rather on profit, return on investments, asset management and price-earnings ratio. The power to decide what will be shown over the air rests with a very few. For example, the prime-time schedule for the three networks is made by top officials who usually put commercial and competitive concerns before concerns about access and diversity.[8]

   In addition, there has developed in the USA a number of bureaucratically controlled organisations which together as conglomerates make up the broadcasting and film industries. Since 1970 it has been difficult to separate film-making from broadcasting because the major Hollywood studios are heavily involved in television, while the television networks often finance films which are first distributed in the cinema. It is particularly difficult to distinguish between production of prime-time drama and motion pictures, both for cinema distribution and for pay-TV. The production companies making programmes for television can be divided into three types: major film studios, major independent producers and minor independent producers. The most important of these are the major film studios because they make television shows, cinema films and other cultural products. They also rent space and facilities to the independent producers when necessary. These film studios include Universal, 20th Century-Fox, Paramount, Columbia, MGM, Warner Bros and Walt Disney. Each of these is large and to varying degrees diversified. With so many studios now producing both cinema films and teleplays, the demarcation between the television industry and the film industry, which was already fading in the 1950s, has now become completely blurred.[9]

Even with the growth of cable television in the last 15 years, the basic unit of the broadcasting system remains the over-the-air station. There are approximately 8,000 radio stations and about 1,100 television stations. Approximately 900 of the latter are commercial stations, while the others are public/educational. (See table 5.1 for the actual numbers.)[10] The emphasis in this chapter will be on television, because although radio provides news and remains important to citizens for emergency information as well as for entertainment, it is television broadcasting which has been the focus of political debate and controversy since it became a national medium in the early 1950s.

Table 5.1: Number of Broadcasting Stations (April 1983)

AM radio	4710
FM radio	3427
FM educational radio	1089
UHF commercial television	308
VHF commercial television	527
UHF educational television	175
VHF educational television	112

Official FCC figures

Television stations are dependent on varied kinds of professionals and outside organisations to supply the bulk of their information and entertainment programmes. These programmes, especially those broadcast in peak viewing hours (or prime-time), must also attract large audiences to be supported by commercial advertisers. If a television station is affiliated or owned by one of the three major networks (as are 77% of all commercial stations), then

a large percentage of entertainment, news and information programmes are provided by the networks. It
should be noted here that by law, no one can own
more than five VHF or seven UHF stations. However,
through rental agreements, the networks contract
with local stations to broadcast the programmes they
select and sell to advertisers. Network affiliated
(and, of course, owned) stations are more prosperous
than 'independent' stations because network programmes usually bring large audiences and the stations can sell more advertising time in the station
breaks between programmes. Both networks and the
pay-TV film channels depend on Hollywood production
companies for drama programmes (series, serials and
films). Other production companies provide quiz and
variety shows, while the wire services and sometimes
local stations provide the news items to the networks.[11] Each network also produces programmes, in
particular nightly news shows and current affairs
programmes, but also some entertainment, especially
daytime drama - the so-called soap operas.[12]
     The independent commercial stations must buy
programmes from distributors or syndication companies, and most programmes seen on these stations
are re-runs, that is programmes first broadcast over
network affiliates. It is possible to see old network shows or old films nightly, but only rarely are
programmes made for direct (first-run) syndication.
Because of satellite transmission, the independent
stations are more likely to form buying cooperatives
for new programming.[13]
     As of now, however, the three networks and the
Hollywood production companies have a virtual monopoly over programming in the US. Some believe the
networks are the most powerful because no shows can
be syndicated (which brings greater profits) without
first being on network television for at least three
or four years. The networks act as gatekeepers,
financing all pilot films for series and all films
made especially for television, many of which are
never broadcast. They select what is finally aired
and decide the time-slot when a show will be seen.
     All over-the-air broadcasting is regulated by
the United States government through the FCC. A
commonly held belief among media scholars in the
United States is that entertainment programming is
relatively free from these regulations while news
and current affairs are not. As will be explained,
there is some truth in this belief because two
major rules, the Fairness Doctrine and the Equal
Time Rule are applied more frequently to news and

current affairs broadcasting. However, entertainment programmes can also be political, although less
so in the traditional sense than news and current
affairs.14 Part of the purpose of this chapter is
to show how many *political* battles have been (and
are now) being fought over *entertainment* television.
The outcome of these political battles has worldwide
consequences because the programmes most likely to
be broadcast internationally are drama series and
films.15

US BROADCASTING HISTORY: THE RISE OF COMMERCIAL BROADCASTING AND LIMITED GOVERNMENT REGULATION16

Although broadcasting (wireless) is international in
origin, its historical development in the US has
been completely American in philosophy. Four
American companies, American Telephone and Telegraph
(AT&T), General Electric (GE), Westinghouse and
their offspring, the Radio Corporation of America
(RCA), hold the key to understanding the direction
broadcasting took in the US. AT&T controlled the
long-distance lines necessary to link the stations,
with the result that without AT&T the networks would
not have been possible. Also, all four manufactured
radios or the component parts necessary for radio
receivers or transmitters. Together with the support of the United States government, they were all-
powerful in the fields of communication and electri-
cal manufacturing at the end of World War I and set
the pattern of industrial control and favourable
governmental actions which have prevailed since.
There was a time when US radio could have been
a federal government monopoly as in Western Europe.
In April 1917 the US Navy was given control of all
private broadcast facilities as a security measure.
When World War I ended in November 1918, the government did not relinquish its control. The Navy believed that radio was too vital to the security of
the US to be entrusted to private industry, especially American Marconi which was essentially a subsidiary of British Marconi. A bill introduced in
Congress late in 1918 proposed that radio be made a
government monopoly, but the bill was poorly drafted
and ineptly defended by the Navy. However, the Navy
remained concerned that British Marconi would gain a
monopoly over US broadcasting if it was allowed to
buy the rights, then held by General Electric, to
the Alexanderson alternator, important to over-the-
air broadcasting. When the Navy failed in its
attempt to monopolise radio, the Director of Naval

Communications proposed that an all-American radio
communication company be created as a depository for
patents necessary for producing a broadcasting
system. GE in cooperation with the US Navy began
planning for the creation of such a company, while
British Marconi was persuaded to sell GE its interest in its American subsidiary. On October 17 1919
RCA under the sponsorship of GE was incorporated.
Westinghouse and AT&T, as well as GE, both held
patents, but none held enough patents to make a complete system. Consequently, all three agreed to
utilise RCA as the basis to establish a consortium
among themselves that would enable the manufacture
of profitable radio receivers and allocate responsibility for the various aspects of commercial broadcasting. (The military did not relinquish all its
control immediately. Admiral Bullard of the United
States Navy sat on the original RCA board.)
    Early in the 1920s, initial conflict over the
use of long-distance lines and commercial advertising was not a governmental matter but rather a
private industry one fought out among the large corporations themselves. AT&T and its subsidiary
Western Electric (known as the telephone group) sold
their stock in RCA in 1923 and opposed RCA, GE and
Westinghouse (known as the radio group). The controversy between the groups was over differential
access to equipment and facilities, and in 1926 an
agreement was reached. AT&T agreed to sell its toll
broadcasting network (see below) to RCA, which was
still jointly controlled by GE and Westinghouse. In
turn, AT&T and the newly created RCA subsidiary,
NBC, entered into a long term service contract to
use AT&T's long lines to interconnect network
stations.
    The industrial structure of American broadcas-
ting was set by this agreement. NBC was the first
company organised to function solely and specifically as a broadcast network. A four and a half
hour inaugural coast-to-coast broadcast took place
on November 15 1926 and it is estimated that 25
stations in the network reached five million listeners on that occasion. Regular coast-to-coast broadcasts began in 1927 and by that time RCA had organised NBC into two semi-autonomous networks, the Blue
and the Red.[17] The Red network was to become ABC
when the Supreme Court ordered NBC to divest itself
of those stations. With the establishment of ABC,
there were four major radio networks: besides NBC
and ABC, there was CBS, established in 1927, and the
Mutual Broadcasting System.[18] (Mutual and other

competitors, such as Dumont, were not able to compete successfully in television).

Looking ahead, although ABC was the weakest of the three television networks during the 1950s and 1960s, by the beginning of 1970 its place was well established. For several years during the 1970s, ABC commanded the largest proportion of the television audience and NBC, still part of the larger RCA corporation, fell to third place.[19] However, as an oligopoly the three networks remain in secure control of American television and from early in 1950s to the present, in spite of technological advances, the networks remain extremely powerful, possibly the most important corporations involved in broadcasting in the United States.

The first commercial radio station (KDKA in Pittsburgh, Pennsylvania) was opened in 1920 by Westinghouse.[20] Eighteen months after it started, radio broadcasting had become a national pastime. Receivers became a popular consumer item and many different kinds of business enterprises acquired federal licences and many colleges and universities also opened stations. Thus, from its very origin, broadcasting in the United States divided, albeit unevenly, between what became known as educational broadcasting (later public broadcasting) and the commercial sector. By the time RCA was established, however, there was no question but that broadcasting was to become primarily a profit making endeavour. At first only those who sold receivers and transmitters profited from broadcasting. Although many of the first stations were owned by the largest businesses in the US, there was still a question as to how the programmes would be financed and how popular and talented performers would be obtained.

According to Erik Barnouw, industry discourse on the topic of financing programmes had begun almost academically. In its first issue in 1922 the magazine, *Radio Broadcast*, mentioned several possible methods of financing. One was that philanthropists, such as steel tycoon Andrew Carnegie, supply the funds. This suggestion, rather far-fetched now, was plausible at the time because Carnegie had funded free libraries for the public throughout the United States. Another suggestion called for funding by local governments. The magazine recognised that this might be considered 'socialistic', but also noted that local governments were financing schools, museums and other institutions for culture and learning. In fact, several cities and many State governments through State-

supported universities did actually establish broadcasting stations. However, the then Secretary of
Commerce, Herbert Hoover, and other Department of
Commerce officials were unenthusiastic about public
ownership, preferring the approach to be through
free-enterprise, although uncertain of the exact
mechanism to be employed.[21]

In that article, neither a tax on equipment nor
advertising was mentioned as a possible means of
support. The magazine offered a $500 prize for the
best essay on the topic. 'Who is to pay for broadcasting and how?', with the award going to a version
of the British plan of taxing radio sets. A varia-
tion of this plan had also been proposed earlier by
an RCA employee David Sarnoff, later (in 1930) to
become its president. He suggested the creation of
a separate organisation to carry on broadcasting as
a national service, financed by a levy on the sale
of equipment. The funds would have been collected
by the industry itself for the broadcasting service.
Barnouw believes the Sarnoff plan was not accepted
because hostilities among factions in the industry
were not settled until 1926, by which time advertising had become the established method of paying for
broadcasting.[22]

This occurred although most, even those supportive of private enterprise, were opposed to such
support. Hoover said it was 'inconceivable that we
should allow so great a possibility for service (as
radio) ... (to become) ... drowned in advertising
chatter.' It was the opinion of *Printer's Ink* that
advertising would be positively offensive to a great
number of people.[23] Nonetheless in 1922, AT&T
opened WEAF in New York City as the flagship station
for a proposed nationwide chain to provide 'toll
broadcasting' or 'radiotelephone' modelled after
telephone booths. Those with the necessary fees
could broadcast messages over the air in the same
way one could place telephone calls. From that inauspicious beginning, private sponsorship of commercial radio grew despite the criticism it drew from
many government officials, intellectuals and educationalists. By the time the Radio Act was passed in
1927, the floodgates had opened and commercial
sponsorship was entrenched. The decision about how
broadcasting was to be financed had been made, not
through informed discussion by policy makers or
educationalists, but rather through default by business leaders interested in making profits, not in
pursuing 'public service' goals.

This did not mean, however, that the US broad-

casting system became a wholly unregulated free
market. The basic statute regulating the broadcasting industry in the United States is the Communications Act of 1934 which established the Federal
Communications Commission (FCC). This act is fundamentally identical to one passed earlier in 1927,
the Radio Act, which established the Federal Radio
Commission (FRC). Until 1927 Congress had passed
just two acts dealing with radio: the Wireless Ship
Act of 1910 and the Radio Act of 1912, both regulating primarily ship-to-shore and ship-to-ship mari-
time communications. These acts were not designed
to deal with broadcasting and were inadequate to
regulate the large number of stations emerging
during the 1920s. Because of the way the 1912 act
was written, Hoover, as Secretary of Commerce, was
powerless to turn down any request for a licence.
He tried several methods of allocating channels, but
when he tried to divide the spectrum and assign
stations to specific frequencies, the District Court
in 1926 ruled that he did not have that power under
the 1912 statute. Even before that decision, it was
clear that there were no adequate means to take care
of the problems arising because the number of
licence holders was increasing yearly. To solve the
problems, Hoover convened four annual radio conferences solely for broadcasters (the first in 1922)
to discuss ways to control and allocate the limited
number of frequencies available. These conferences
demonstrate that, even early on, the broadcasting
industry itself played an important role in initiating the regulatory process.

　　After two months of study, the First Radio
Conference unanimously decided that regulation by
private enterprise alone (self-regulation) would be
inadequate and recommended that legislation be
introduced to authorise government control over the
allocation, assignment and use of broadcasting
frequencies. During the next five years, until 1927
when the Radio Law was finally enacted, the industry
continued its pressure for government regulation
because the increase in stations continued unchecked.
By November 1925, 578 stations were on the air and
applications were pending for 175 more. With every
frequency filled in urban areas, most stations were
beginning to experience considerable interference
from other stations and those on the air were forced
to work out complex time-sharing schemes.

　　The situation became chaotic, and finally the
Radio Act of 1927 was passed. With the FRC established, broadcasting 'as a system' in the United

States was in place, a system including networks
linked by the telephone lines, local stations on
temporary renewable licences and a regulatory commission required by Congress to allocate frequencies
and to uphold 'the public interest, convenience and
necessity'. Broadcasting had become a commercial
enterprise supported by law. When the 1927 Act also
proved inadequate to handle all the emerging communication technologies, a new law was passed in 1934,
identical to the earlier one in the role allocated
to broadcasting, but changing the name of the regulatory commission to the FCC.

The FCC, an independent US government agency
responsible directly to Congress, is charged with
regulating interstate and international communications by radio, television, wire, satellite and
cable. Its domestic jurisdiction covers the 50
States, plus Guam, Puerto Rico and the Virgin
Islands. It is directed by five commissioners (before June 30 1983 there were seven) appointed by the
President and confirmed by the Senate for seven
year terms, except when filling unexpired terms. The
President designates one of the commissioners to
serve as Chairman. The Chairman's position is also
at the pleasure of the President, so that with
changes in administrations a new Chairman is usually
appointed to uphold the incoming administration's
views. No more than three commissioners may be members of the same political party.

The primary duties of the FCC are technical and
procedural, including the allocation of spectrum
space for AM and FM radio and VHF and UHF television
broadcasting services, assigning frequencies and
call letters to stations and generally supervising
matters relating to programming. In the international sphere, under the leadership of the Department of State, the FCC administers domestic compliance with the telecommuncation provisions of
those treaties and international agreements to which
the US is a party and participates in related international conferences. In addition, it licences
radio and cable circuits from the US to foreign
points and regulates the operating companies.[24]

The FCC is more than simply a regulatory agency,
with just power to licence stations and assign frequency allocations. A phrase was written into law
destined to cause much confusion and conflict in its
interpretation, a vague statement requiring the FCC
to uphold 'the public interest, convenience and
necessity'. That broad mandate has led to numerous
contradictions and conflicts over broadcasting

regulation. The concept had originally appeared in
an act to establish a transportation regulatory
system in 1920 and was used by Hoover in a speech
directed to the Third Annual Radio Conference in
1924.[25] Many critics and scholars believe the
phrase has provided the battleground for the general
debate surrounding broadcasting regulation in the
United States.[26]

Congress had originally included the phrase in
the 1927 Act because it believed that the courts had
interpreted the 1912 Act too narrowly and thus left
no power to the executive branch to deny licences or
to control rapidly changing technologies. The 'public interest' notion included in both the 1927 and
1934 Acts was intended to enable the regulatory
agency to create new rules, regulations and standards as needed. The meaning of the phrase, however,
continues to elude those scholars who have tried to
define 'public interest' in empirical terms, because
it is possible that the phrase can be interpreted
only on the basis of political criteria. Several
analysts have noted that the concept has been defined differently in different circumstances both by
the courts and the FCC. Although in most cases the
Courts accept the Commission's views and give the
FCC wide latitude in determining what constitutes
'public interest', they occasionally will impose
their own definition.[27]

Thus, the public interest clause was purpose-
fully made vague to enable the regulatory agency to
have leeway in licencing and rulemaking. In addition, confusions arise from inherent contradictions between various sections of the 1934 Act, for
example, between Sections 315 and 326. Section 326
states:

> Nothing in this Act shall be understood or
> construed to give the Commission the power of
> censorship over radio communications or signals
> transmitted by any radio station, and no regu-
> lation or condition shall be promulgated or
> fixed by the Commission which shall interfere
> with the right of free speech by the means of
> radio communication. (Radio is the generic
> term used for television and radio).[28]

In almost direct opposition, Congress also recognised that the uniqueness of broadcasting entitled
it to special treatment, distinct from that of the
conventional 'press'. Section 315 of the act is the
Equal Time clause specifically declaring that if a

station gives any legitimate candidate for public
office the opportunity to broadcast, then the
licencee must afford equal opportunity to all others
for that office.[29]
     In addition to the Equal Time provision written
into the law in 1934, broadcasters are limited in
what they may present by the Fairness Doctrine which
states that broadcasters must 'afford reasonable
opportunity for the discussion of conflicting views
on issues of public importance'. In fact the FCC
has divided the doctrine into two basic tenets:
first, that a reasonable amount of broadcast time
must be devoted to controversial issues and, secondly, that a reasonable amount of time must be given
to opposing viewpoints.
     The Fairness Doctrine, originally an adminis-
trative interpretation of the public interest
principle, received congressional blessing in 1959
when Section 315 was amended. After enumerating the
types of bona-fide news appearances that need not be
considered under the equal-time provision, the
amendment ended with the words in the Fairness Doctrine, making law what had previously been simply
regulation.[30] This clause is very important to a
number of groups, especially minorities and women.
For example, the National Organisation for Women,
the Congressional Black Caucus and the League of
United Latin American Citizens have publicly opposed
deregulation, especially any legislation which would
repeal Section 315, including the fairness provision.[31] In 1969 the Fairness Doctrine was upheld by
the Supreme Court which as part of a larger decision
stated that, 'The Congress and the Commission do not
violate the First Amendment when they require a
radio or television station to give reply time to
answer personal attacks and political editorials.'[32]
     Some legal experts and most broadcasters con-
tinue to argue that the First Amendment should con-
fer on them the same freedom from interference that
the traditional press itself enjoys. However, because of the scarcity of channels, the courts have
consistently ruled that broadcasting cannot be
lumped indiscriminately with other media. In the
same decision quoted above the Supreme Court also
declared, 'Although broadcasting is clearly a
medium affected by First Amendment interests ...
differences in the characters of the new media justify differences in First Amendment standards applied
to them.'[33] In other words, the older print media
can provide a wider marketplace for ideas, while
traditional broadcasting with limited channels

cannot.

In the last five years, however, there has been
a shift in views, both in the Congress and in the
FCC. Some policy makers contend that the availability of so many multiple channels has made broadcasting similar to newspapers and magazines with the
result that regulation and legislation in support of
traditional differences among the media can now be
eliminated. The FCC (under Mark Fowler, a Ronald
Reagan appointee), certain members of Congress and
the broadcasting industry have rallied around this
issue and are trying to change the laws and regulations which they believe limit the broadcasters'
freedom to choose what is broadcast.[34]

REGULATION VERSUS DEREGULATION: THE 1960s and 1970s

The relationship between the FCC and the broadcasting industry has been complicated by the fact that
the regulation of broadcasting is to a large degree
a product of its history. Because radio and television have been largely managed by private enterprise, close government control has historically
been limited. More often than not, supposedly regulated, the local stations have imposed their will
on their regulators. The National Association of
Broadcasters (NAB) as the major lobbying organisation for the industry has been extremely effective
in influencing congressional and FCC policy.
Although not always successful, over the years their
power has been formidable. Erwin G. Krasnow and his
associates have characterised regulation as a process in which the regulatory agency and those being
regulated attempt to control each other and have
argued that the pattern of industry-FCC relationships has been dynamic, shifting constantly with
varying degrees of industry control.[35]

Until the mid-1960s, the industry and Congress
dominated the regulatory process so that the FCC in
effect seemed to be working with the three networks
in partnership rather than functioning in an adver-
sary role as regulator. Almost from the beginning
of national broadcasting, the networks have defended
the interests of all broadcasters, as well as their
own, before the FCC and Congressional Committees.
The NAB, however, which comprises the three networks
and approximately 5,200 member radio and television
stations acts as the major lobbyist for the industry. The NAB is also essentially the lobbyist for
the three networks, because 90% of the member television stations are network-affiliated. (Many

independent television stations do not belong to the
NAB.)   Until 1982, there was an NAB Code of Ethics
which worked as a mechanism for self-regulation[36]
and in the early years of broadcasting the NAB was
successful in thwarting efforts to place restrictions on broadcasting that did not meet with NAB
approval.   During the late 1960s and the early part
of the 1970s, however, the NAB encountered more
difficulty than it had earlier in its efforts to
fend off Congressional and FCC regulation.   More recently the relationship between the FCC and the industry has again become more supportive.   In the
late 1970s and especially since the election of
Ronald Reagan, the movement in Congress and in the
FCC has been to 'deregulate' broadcasting.[37]
        The change in the dynamics of regulation in the
1960s was due to the more liberal political climate
and in particular to an Appeals Court decision
allowing citizen groups for the first time to participate in the regulatory process.   Until 1966, the
law permitted only those with an economic stake in
broadcasting to participate in the radio and television licencing and renewal procedures.   In 1964
the FCC had been asked by the activist Office of
Communications of the United Church of Christ to
refuse to renew the licence of a television station
(WLBT-TV) in Jackson, Mississippi, because black
viewers (who constituted 45% of Jackson's population) were ignored in its programming.   Although the
FCC essentially agreed with the church group's
charges, the Commissioners voted 4-2 to renew the
licence for just one year with extensions pending
good behaviour.   In doing so, the FCC refused to
hold public hearings as requested by the United
Church of Christ on the grounds that the FCC itself
represented the 'public interest'.   It was these
rulings that were challenged and reversed in the US
Circuit Court of Appeals.   The FCC was ordered to
withdraw its extension and to set hearings on the
licence renewal with public participation.[38]
        Public groups had long sought to influence
broadcasting, but had been restricted to indirect
methods such as boycotts and citizens' councils. The
WLBT-TV case set a new precedent because it opened
the legal process itself to citizen groups.   Since
the 1966 decision, scores of groups, especially
those representing minorities such as Black Americans, Latin Americans and women, have petitioned the
FCC to deny licence renewals.   Although few licences
have actually been denied, the significance of the
court decision lay in its opening the way to a still

legal but more sophisticated approach to broadcasting reform at the community level.[39]

Because the Communication Act was written mainly to oblige local stations to adhere to FCC rulings, the networks have always enjoyed and continue to enjoy a favoured status in the regulatory process. However, each of the five local television stations owned by the networks is, of course, subject to FCC regulations. Thus the FCC can regulate networks indirectly, by commenting on the practices of these owned-and-operated stations. Also, the FCC can use the public interest clause of the Communications Act to limit contractual agreements and time allotments that networks rent from the local stations.

Because of the power the networks have over their affiliates and over the Hollywood production companies, there was also concern expressed in the mid-1960s regarding centralised control over television. Starting around this time, there were several attempts to achieve a more equitable balance of power between the networks and the local stations and between the networks and the production companies which produce most of the prime-time television shows. Early in the 1970s, rules were adopted which limited network power. The most important rules, the Prime-Time Access Rule[40] and the Financial Interest and Syndication Rules, were imposed by the FCC. Later in the decade, to keep the FCC from further eroding their control, the networks adopted the Family Viewing Hour. Rather than an overt FCC requirement, the networks, through the NAB, offered voluntary compliance to a set of rules requiring the networks and local affiliates to keep programmes which contained 'adult' themes (sex and violence) off the air during the early evening hours. The purpose of this action was to fend off anticipated Congressional action concerning the violent content of some prime-time programmes.

These rulings and changes in television presentations were not the only rulings adopted during the 1960s and 1970s, nor were they the only rules proposed, but the Prime-Time Access and Financial Interest and Syndication Rules are considered major, because they involved *rule making which limited network power*.

The Family Viewing controversy is important as an example of the on-going struggle between the Hollywood production companies and the networks over profits from television. One subtle form of government control is the constant threat of Congressional

hearings and related investigations.[41] Although
television is a young medium compared to newspapers
or motion pictures, there have been twelve Congressional hearings on the subject of violent content in
television drama. These hearings did not result in
formal censorship (formal censorship is forbidden
under Section 326 of the Communications Act), but
informal censorship was imposed through self-regulation via the NAB Code of Ethics and the offices the
networks established to enforce the Code (Broadcast
Standards).

For example, realising that the issue of television and violence was not going away, the industry
voluntarily designated the hours between 7 and 9 pm
the Family Viewing Hours, during which dramatic content with 'adult' themes would not be shown. The
designation was not an overt requirement by the FCC,
but rather evolved as an agreement between the FCC
and the networks in response to mounting criticism
from citizen groups, some members of Congress,
social scientists and educationalists about the content of drama shows. The plan was developed during
the winter of 1974 in a meeting of network executives, FCC staff and their lawyers. Arthur E.
Taylor, then president of CBS Television, was the
chief proponent of the plan and under his leadership
the plan was adopted into the NAB code in April 1975
to become policy at the start of the 1975-76 season.

To show how the political process works in the
US, in November 1976 the Federal District Court in
Los Angeles declared the Family Viewing Hour unconstitutional. Plaintiffs in the suit were the
Writers' Guild of America, the Screen Actors' Guild,
the Directors' Guild and several Hollywood production companies who made television drama. The
defendants argued that the code revision was merely
an attempt at self-regulation, similar to codes of
ethics issued by other industries and professions
for their members. The plaintiffs argued that the
FCC had coerced the networks into establishing the
Family Viewing Hour. The result of this network
action, according to the 'Hollywood creative community', was both a loss of income and infringement of
their freedom of expression. The judge ruled that
although self-regulation may be desirable, in fact
preferable to government regulation, it must be true
self-regulation, not a kind of restriction imposed
or threatened by the government, and if the government intimidates, as the FCC did in this case, then
self-regulation in matters of expression is unconstitutional under the First Amendment clause.

Essentially, the court stated that the broadcasters'
(NAB) action in adopting the Family Viewing Hour
violated the First Amendment Rights of those who
were creating the shows.

The networks and the FCC appealed against that
decision and their cause was successful when in 1979
the ruling was overturned. Then in 1980 the Supreme
Court denied a petition for review, upholding the
reversal. Thus the Family Hour remained as part of
the NAB Code until 1982 when the Code was dismantled.
In fact, however, it was not enforced except for the
first year or two. On paper, the 'public interest'
was served although the adult content continued to
be broadcast because network decision-makers believed it brought higher audience ratings.

During the 1960s, the FCC was also considering
rules and regulations which would assure an equitable balance of power among the networks, the
stations and the Hollywood production companies. For
several years, producers had complained that their
network shows were unlikely to show a profit. To
protect the rights of the production companies and
in battle with the monopolistic practices, the FCC
adopted the financial interest and syndication rules,
thereby initiating another political struggle over
profits. The rules barred the three networks from
domestic syndication of the programmes they lease
from producers; in addition, the networks cannot own
any portion of a programme which they lease from
producers. In most cases the contractual agreement
between a network and a production company, whether
for a series or a film, allows the network to show
a film or video-tape twice. The show then reverts
to the producer who can licence it to other broadcasters or even a different network. Thus, although
the networks finance most shows and decide if and
when they are to be seen, from 1970 to 1983 they
have not been able to retain syndication rights for
the shows.[42]

Until 1970, the networks could have financial
interests in the programmes they aired. After that
time the sole profit from the programmes came
through their sale of commercial time during the
programme's network showing. The profits through
advertising are, of course, substantial, but the
networks argue that the explosion of the new technologies will result in increased competition from
other programme distributors, particularly pay-TV
film channels, and that therefore the rulings have
become obsolete.

The FCC's 1970 Report and Order on the finan-

cial interest controversy documented the networks'
stranglehold on national television broadcasting.
According to the FCC, network economic and creative
control during the prime-time hours had increased
steadily from the mid-1950s through the 1960s; between 1957 and 1968, the share of evening programme
hours either produced or under direct control of the
networks rose from 67% to 97%. The report stated,
'Whereas in 1957 independents provided approximately
one-third of the evening network schedules, their
share in 1968 had declined to below four per cent.'
In the five year period studied, the networks
accepted almost no entertainment programmes for network screening in which they did not have a financial interest. The FCC concluded that it was clear
that the existence of subsidiary interests did pose
a significant conflict of interest in the selection
of programming by the networks and that the public
interest would be served by the elimination of conflict because there was a direct relationship between new programmes chosen for prime-time schedules
and network acquisition of subsidiary (usually
syndication) rights.[43]
   According to the FCC, the networks had a
formidable hold on national television and this hold
produced unfair marketplace conditions for the independent producers. Networks did not normally accept
new untried packager-licenced programmes for network
screening unless the producer (programme supplier)
was willing to give up to the networks a large part
of the valuable rights and interests in subsidiary
rights to the programme. The FCC further decreed
that there was an undue concentration of control in
the three network corporations over television programmes available to the public.
   The rulings, adopted after more than ten years
of discussion, became regulation (and therefore law)
in 1970. These rules barred the networks from
domestic syndication and prohibited them from acquiring ownership participation in independently produced programming. The rules also prompted the
Department of Justice to investigate monopolistic
practices in network programming, and in 1972 the
Department brought an anti-trust suit against the
three networks, claiming that each network indivi-
dually constrained trade because programme suppliers
had no other market for their product. The networks
eventually signed consent decrees, which essentially
replicated the syndication and financial interest
rules.[44] The networks, of course, were never
pleased with the rulings and still wanted shares in

the enormous profits from syndication. (For example, 20th Century-Fox Television expects to make over $200 million from *M*A*S*H* through domestic syndication, and although the *Dukes of Hazzard* is syndicated internationally, it is expected to be far more profitable when it is syndicated in the US market starting in 1984, because Warner Brothers Television Distribution Inc will be paid as much as $90,000 per one-hour episode by some local stations).

The networks have proposed that the rules be abolished, arguing that the explosion of cable and pay-TV in the video marketplace in the last decade made the rules obsolete. The battlelines in this struggle became fixed: the networks and their affiliates on the one hand versus the independent producers, independent television stations, advertisers, programme distributors and the 'Hollywood creative community' on the other. Both sides argue, of course, that the 'public interest' would be better served if their side won. The networks argue that as they represent the only system available for national distribution, if they are to compete with cable, pay-TV, video cassette recorders and the other new technologies, they must be unrestrained and allowed to play under the same ground rules as the largely unregulated new media. Also, because their competitors in pay-TV (primarily *Home Box Office* and *Showtime*, both entertainment cable channels) are free to share in syndication rights and revenues, they can afford to pay more up-front for programming. Therefore the networks contend that if they are not allowed to remain competitive by sharing in syndication revenues, the public will be the real loser. Only the networks, they argue, can provide the public, free of charge, new programmes, sports and entertainment programmes, while pay-TV goes only to those who can afford to pay.[45]

Opponents of the repeal argue that the networks are not being hurt financially and that although the audience for network television has declined in the last decade, the networks still command over 80% of the audience. Others point out that although the new technologies do give some viewers additional choice, their effect on network profits has been negligible. The networks themselves seem to have two scenarios, one for the FCC and the other for their stockholders. To the FCC, the new technologies are a threat to free television; to advertisers and stockholders, they are merely minor irritations. The networks' monopoly on prime-time viewing may have diminished, but according to

Nielsen Co, which conducts the major surveys of audience viewing patterns, the raw number of network viewers is holding steady even though the proportion of network viewers has gone down. Most analysts attribute this phenomenon to two factors: there are about 10 million more homes equipped with television in the US than there were in 1970 and people spend more time watching television.[46]
   In August 1983, the FCC tentatively approved a plan that would allow ABC, CBS and NBC to hold larger financial shares in all the programmes they broadcast. By a 3 to 1 vote the 13 year old rules, barring the networks from controlling the lucrative syndication rights to rerun network shows or from holding any other financial interest in the future use of the programming, were tentatively removed.[47] The change was approved by the FCC despite strong opposition from the Hollywood production industry and some members of Congress. The FCC concluded that the financial interest rules were not achieving their goals of increasing competition and diversity in the television programme industry and it was time to permit the networks to share in the $800 million a year syndication market.
   This particular ruling and the controversy surrounding it, although somewhat more glamorous than others, provides an excellent example of how the process for control over broadcasting content is negotiated and renegotiated through the FCC, the Executive Departments and the Congress. Rarely does the struggle spill out of that framework to involve the political parties as such. Positions over issues concerning the broadcasting industry have never formed according to party divisions in the United States, and the current trend toward deregulation in all industries is actively supported by factions in *both* the Republican and Democratic parties. (For example, the airline industry was deregulated during the Democratic Carter administration when both the Senate and the House of Representatives had Democratic majorities). However, possibly because of the glamour associated with Hollywood, legislators who might normally have taken the more conservative approach associated with deregulation, in this particular controversy have sided with the 'Hollywood creative community' in their fight to keep the Financial and Syndication Rules intact. On the other hand, the executive branch, including the Departments of Commerce and Justice, have supported the NAB position and the August FCC decision to deregulate which both the

Democratic House of Representatives and the Republican Senate appear to oppose.

The 'Hollywood creative community', usually divided politically, has been united on this particular issue. Often controversies among Hollywood personalities become public issues. For example, when Ed Asner, President of the Screen Actors Guild, attacked the Reagan administration's recent actions in El Salvador, a former Guild president and staunch supporter of Ronald Reagan, Charlton Heston, protested, declaring it was inappropriate for union leaders in the entertainment industry to take positions on controversial issues. Both Heston and Asner are now united against the FCC and the executive branch, and both, along with other Hollywood personalities, have lobbied Congress for legislation to stop the FCC from deregulating the syndication market. Moreover, Heston has taken his campaign into the Oval Office, taking advantage of his long-standing friendship with Reagan who, coincidentally, is also a past president of the Guild.[48]

As this piece is being written, the Congress is considering legislation to bar the FCC from changing its rules for at least five years with more than 100 members (of both parties) in the House of Representatives as co-sponsors of the bill. The sponsors include 10 of the 14 members of the House Sub-committee on Telecommunications, thereby presaging a favourable vote. The Senate Appropriations Committee, with the support of Republican Ted Stevens, the majority whip, has also voted to protect the Hollywood production companies for six months. The Committee by a 16-13 vote added an amendment that temporarily would bar the FCC from using its funds to implement its August ruling.[49]

The push for legislation is being led by a Hollywood group called the Committee for Prudent Deregulation, a committee made up of producers, directors, writers, actors and independent television station owners. Among the members are stars such as Alan Alda (*M*A*S*H*), Larry Hagman (*Dallas*) and Henry Winkler (*Happy Days*), as well as Asner, Heston and many other stars. The committee argues that these rulings are needed to restrain network domination of the programme-production industry. The networks and the NAB are trying to prevent the legislation from being passed by their own lobbying efforts.[50]

The battle over these rulings was heated. For example, after Heston's visit, Reagan called FCC Chairman Mark Fowler to his office to be 'briefed' on the matter. *The Washington Post* reported that

the President intended to review personally the
executive branch's long standing support of deregulation in favour of the television networks. Heston
was quoted in that article as saying that although
he disclaimed to be an expert on the President's
views, given 'the unanimity of the creative community' one could infer that the President would support
the Hollywood position. According to Heston, 'his
views could be inferred given his background'. It
would be unprecedented for a President to directly
influence an FCC decision as an 'independent' regulatory agency, but nothing could stop him from influencing the other departmental agencies involved.[51]

The August decision was tentative to allow time
for the public to comment before making the rule
final. Whether it does become final or not, it can
be predicted with some certainty that battles will
still be fought in Congress and possibly in the
Courts again over this issue. Once more in the
guise of 'public interest' it is clear to everyone
that all participants are motivated by the profits
involved.

The years from 1965 to 1975 were a decade
therefore when many regulations and laws were adopted, some in the interest of citizen groups, but
most in the interests of one or another segment of
the entertainment industries which either produce or
distribute the programmes. In addition to the rules
and legal changes mentioned earlier, two other significant changes influenced the politics of broadcasting. First, after several decades of pressure
by educationalists and interested citizen groups,
Congress passed the Public Broadcasting Act in 1967,
establishing both the Corporation for Public Broadcasting and the Public Broadcasting Service, essentially a fourth network.[52] Secondly, in 1972 the
FCC also issued for the first time detailed regulations governing cable franchise operations opening
the way to controlled urban cable development.[53]

Following on this latter decision, during the
same decade (1965-75) there was an increase in the
number of communities served by cable television
systems. Many media analysts predict that traditional over-the-air broadcasting in the US is dying,
to be replaced by cable systems which will provide a
broader range of programming as well as the other
(interactive) types of services available through
television, eg banking services. However, at present, while cable has approximately 30 million subscribers, the three networks reach more than 80

million homes, attracting as many as 25 million
viewers (often more) to network programmes. In
comparison, *Home Box Office* reaches just 15 million
homes. It should be noted that the fact that over-
the-air broadcasting is advertiser-supported and
'free' remains an important consideration because
although in many markets cable service is available,
many potential subscribers are unwilling or unable
to pay the extra costs involved.

Even though it remains to be seen whether cable
will pose a major threat to network profits, it
might still be possible for the networks to secure
deregulation on their terms by arguing that cable
and other new technologies threaten significant
competition because they can offer both a wider
diversity of programming and airing of opinion. However, Congress is aware, even with the multiplication of available channels, both through the growth
of independent UHF stations and cable, of a remaining need for *some* regulation. Thus, the consensus
is that any deregulation bill would focus primarily
on the financial aspects of the industry, with
elimination of the Equal Time requirements or the
Fairness Doctrine only a remote possibility.
Although parties in power of course flirt with the
possibility of curtailing access to the public of
those with contrary views, neither party wishes to
risk a permanent change which would impair *their*
campaigning![54] Some limited regulation of broadcasting seems destined to continue.

THE REGULATION OF TRANSNATIONAL BROADCASTING

Until now our discussion has wholly focused on
domestic politics. However, because of concern in
other nations over American domination of the media,
it is important also to discuss the political issues
surrounding distribution of programmes made in the
US to audiences abroad. What differentiates the
styles and agenda of domestic and international
politics is that the rather permissive protection
for growth and concentration enjoyed by private
enterprise in the USA will probably not extend to
marketing activities beyond American borders. Among
the constraints that US negotiators encounter at
international conferences on communications, eg
those sponsored by the International Telecommunications Union (ITU), are not only the technically
limited broadcasting spectrum, but also the continuing fear felt by many countries of being culturally
dominated by the more powerful developed nations and

in particular the US. Thus, even if the problems of
finance and technical access could be worked out,
there remain legal and political obstacles to be
acknowledged and resolved. In the case of the US
this can be especially difficult, because with its
financial resourcefulness and technological advantages it is an obvious target.

The problems facing the US in this respect were
apparent at the Regional Administrative Radio Conference for the planning of the Broadcasting-Satel-
lite Service in Region 2 which met in Geneva in
June-July 1983. The US team side-stepped the ideological issues inserted into the agenda (for example,
Argentina's insistence that the Falklands-Malvinas
be included in its planning) and sticking to its
goals, left with eight orbital slots and 256 channels, more than sufficient to meet US needs for
domestic broadcasting in this century. However, it
was not difficult for the US to avoid conflict at
this meeting because as many as 2,000 slots were
available for assignment. Fears of the developing
nations that they would be 'crowded out' were not
realised.[55] The real tests for the US, however,
will come at those meetings where the agenda is more
ideological than technical. That will be when the
US ethos of free enterprise will finally collide
with the cultural heritage and integrity of other
nations and their need to control their own sources
of information - the free flow controversy. As
pointed out in an Interim Report by the UNESCO
Commission for the Study of Communications Problems:

> The concept of free flow of information as it
> has been invoked for the past thirty or so
> years, and as it is applied today, can serve
> to justify a doctrine serving the interest of
> the powerful countries or groups which all too
> frequently enables them to ensure or to per-
> petuate cultural domination under the cloak of
> generous ideas.[56]

The concerns and tensions over free flow were made
explicit in the Declaration adopted by the UNESCO
General Conference on November 22 1978 and again in
the Final Report submitted to UNESCO by the MacBride
Commission in February 1980. Article X of the
Declaration of Fundamental Principles Concerning the
Contribution of the Mass Media, etc, states that it
is important to encourage free flow to achieve
'wider and better balanced dissemination of information' among all states.[57] The MacBride Report, more

forthright about the adverse economic, social and
political effects that the 'communication rich'
could produce, questions whether 'more powerful
countries and bigger organisations' might use the
doctrine of free flow to the detriment of those less
well endowed.[58]

As an alternative, the Commission called for a
'New World Information and Communication Order' to
achieve reciprocity in information exchange and less
dependence on existing communication flows.[59] The
Commission was also blunt in its views about the
'industrialisation' of communication which resulted
in the control of information resting in the hands
of just a few large media enterprises:

> ... there is a small number of predominant cor-
> porations which integrate all aspects of pro-
> duction and distribution, which are based in
> the leading developed countries and which have
> become transnational in their operations. [60]

There are numerous examples of the type of media
conglomerates that the MacBride Commission decries.
One is the Gulf and Western Corporation which earned
$1.4 billion in the fiscal year 1982 from motion
pictures, publishing books and music, sports programmes and video games. Gulf and Western controls
Paramount Pictures Corp, Simon & Shuster (one of the
largest publishers of paper and hardback books in
the US), the Madison Square Garden Corp (owner of
the Garden centre, a basketball and a hockey team, a
raceway and cable TV), Famous Players Ltd (operator
of cinemas in Canada and France), Famous Music Corp
(music publisher) and Sega Enterprises (designer and
distributor of software for electronic video games
in Japan and the US).[61]

Because of the ability of powerful firms such
as these to target any market, the Commission believes the owners and managers bear 'special responsibility' to safeguard the values and life-styles of
the societies they penetrate. Consequently, 'norms,
guide-lines or codes of conduct' should be developed
for transnational corporations, who would also be
expected to supply the authorities of the local
jurisdictions in which they intend to function the
information required so that their performance could
be evaluated. The Commission further recommended
that the UN Commission on transnational corporations
also give attention to their activities in the field
of communications.[62]

Will US-based corporations respect such injunc-

tions and would Congress or US regulatory bodies
seek their compliance? As put by Clippinger, such
demands 'strike at the core' of the differences in
how information is viewed in the US and elsewhere.
Whereas the government of other nations might think
it *their* responsibility to see that information is
dispensed as a 'public good', the history of regulation in the US demonstrates that the government
has essentially taken a hands-off-approach, trusting
that the 'public good' function will be adequately
satisfied in the private sector. As the American
ethos sees broadcasting as largely (if not wholly)
another commodity in the marketplace, consumers, not
the government, should be the final judge whether
their public interest is being served. Thus, the
argument continues, the responsibility of government
is merely to guarantee that information will flow
freely.[63]

Consequently, just as some would argue that
historically the FCC has been unable to improve the
range and quality of programming because it favoured
the needs of the industry over the demands of consumer groups, it is doubtful whether Congress or one
of its Commissions would impose constraints that
would limit US profit-making activities in other
countries. Just as the opponents of domestic regulation have argued that all need for statutes and
regulatory actions would disappear if private enterprise were set free to respond to market forces, one
can anticipate that permissiveness extended to
foreign markets as well. The National Association
of Broadcasters, in its role as lobbyist for the
industry, has gone on record opposing the establishment of a 'New World Information and Communications
Order' as contrary to the interests of American
broadcasters, publishers and reporters, and recom-
mends that the US withhold all or part of its financial support to UNESCO so long as this threat to
'world press freedom or freedom of communication'
continues.[66] Also, the National Telecommunications
and Information Administration (NTIA), successor to
the shortlived Office of Telecommunications Policy,
Executive Office of the President, and now in the
Department of Commerce, was equally blunt in a report submitted to the American Senate in March 1983:

> United States economic, defense, and political
> interests in international telecommunications
> and information services have become increas-
> ingly vulnerable to adverse foreign actions as
> a consequence of events over the past decade.

Steps have been taken by both developed and
developing nations to restrict the free flow of
information across their borders ... Decision-
making within the International Telecommunications Union (ITU) and other specialized UN
agencies has also begun to be needlessly poli-
ticized due to block voting by lesser developed
countries ... Projected into the future, a
gradual erosion of the United States position
in the telecommunications, information flow,
and associated high-technology markets may result, absent prompt remedial action. [65]

This theme was echoed by the Chairman of the FCC,
Mark Fowler, in his remarks to the World Communications Conference in Tokyo in October 1983:

... the freedom of individuals to receive and
transmit ideas in a free marketplace should be
undistorted by government control over content
... (and) ... make imperative a re-examination
of national and international barriers to the
free flow of ideas, whether by terrestrial
systems, satellite systems or otherwise.[66]

Thus, the doctrinal lines seem to have been drawn
and the stage set for an ideological and economic
struggle to promote, on the one hand, and restrict,
on the other, the free flow of information across
borders. It is doubtful whether the media conglomerates in the US who have prospered in partnership
with the FCC and Congress will fare as well under
the regulatory scrutiny and actions of international
bodies or foreign governments.

The issue of control has already been put to
the test. By a vote of 107 to 13 (the 13 votes
against and the 13 abstentions came chiefly from
Western and developed nations) the UN General
Assembly in December 1982 adopted a set of new principles, including one which affirms that states
bear international responsibility for direct television broadcasting by satellite carried out under
their jurisdiction and that they must notify other
recipient states of such intention and promptly
enter into consultation with those states who so
request. However, the adoption of 'principles' does
not, of course, have the force of an ITU regulation,
such as, for example, the statement agreed to in
1977 that 'all technical means available shall be
used to reduce, to the maximum extent practicable,
the radiation over the territory of other countries'

(Regulation 428A).[67] Will the US ever become party
to treaties or agreements that would have the effect
of restraining the growth of its communications industry? Given the history of domestic regulation
and the concentration of economic and political
power that has already developed, that possibility
would seem to be doubtful.

CONCLUSION: THE FUTURE OF REGULATION

Returning to domestic politics, however, one can
predict that, in spite of the urgings of its opponents, minimal regulation as such will *never* completely disappear. The principal reason is that
those already entrenched and in protected positions,
ie the networks and other media conglomerates, would
not wish to lose the advantages and special status
they have attained over years of close collaboration
with the FCC. The special interests pushing for
total 'deregulation' are now among the 'ins' and,
given the opportunity, would also try to influence
the appointments of FCC Commissioners who would make
rulings in their favour. All of this raw struggle
over profits is cloaked, of course, in the guise of
'public interest'.

In any case, to abolish the prerogative at the
Federal level through the FCC might merely shift
the arena of power-play deeper into the Congress, a
possibility perhaps too unwieldy for the networks
and other media power-brokers to consider dealing
with. That trend has already emerged. In June 1983,
by an overwhelming vote of 87-9, the Senate approved
and sent on to the House for its consideration (despite continuing opposition from AT&T and some of the
larger cities) S.66, a bill to create a uniform
nationwide structure for the cable television industry which would curtail the authority of local
governments to regulate cable operators. An earlier
bill with the same objective had died in a previous
Congress, stymied by two years of opposition and
disagreement between the National Cable Television
Association (NCTA) and the National League of Cities
(NLC). NCTA contended that when, in the 1970s, the
FCC relaxed regulation of cable operations at the
Federal level, local governments began to tighten
their controls to the point of making the enterprise
unprofitable. The League's position was that Congressional intrusion into the freedom of local
government to regulate what they considered to be
common carriers was unwarranted. The two provisions
they were especially opposed to would restrict the

rights of local authorities to regulate the fees
charged the public and allow existing cable franchises to be renewed automatically without hearings
to determine whether the public was being adequately
served. Essentially, the cities were satisfied with
the *status quo* because they welcomed the income obtained from cable operations to offset declines in
Federal subsidies and tax revenues. The cable
operators, still burdened with the debt of their
start-up costs, wanted to improve their profitability by reducing the franchise fees demanded by
the cities as well as improve their competitive
positions by dropping the non-revenue producing,
public service channels they had promised in order
to obtain their initial franchises.[68] AT&T lobbied
strongly against the bill because it might enable
cities to set the rates charged by telephone companies using their lines for services other than
telephone calls. At stake was (and is) the profitability of AT&T's (and their affiliates') venture
into the burgeoning market in data-transmission,
residential as well as commercial. The rates charged
by cable systems, if unregulated, could be too competitive for telephone companies, still subject to
State and local regulation.

The legislation was re-introduced when both
NCTA and NLC, fearing that if they protracted their
struggle a bill might pass that would be unacceptable to either side, agreed on a compromise. The
cities were willing to accept a ceiling of 5% on
franchise fees that could be charged (some cities
were as high as 20%) if no restrictions were put on
their uses of the revenue, eg municipal projects.
The cable operators agreed to continue paying franchise fees (below a 5% ceiling) if the cities were
also willing to stop regulating rates except for
'basic service' (ie retransmission of local television signals), freeing them to charge what they
wished for the additional channels offered such as
sports, films and data-transmission.[69]

The technology, economics and politics of
broadcasting are changing so rapidly that it is
still too soon to predict whether over-the-air
broadcasting in its present form will remain in competition with cable transmission and direct reception of satellite signals. For example, the networks themselves have moved quickly into using
satellites to transmit to their affiliated stations,
and could conceivably, if they saw it as more profitable, someday abandon the affiliates for direct-
broadcasting to residential receivers. The per-

formance of the national cable channels continues to
be unprofitable; just two of the twenty or so
channels that depend on advertising revenue remain
profitable.[70] The built-in market of over 180
million telephone homes for AT&T and local telephone
companies to offer data services give them a formidable advantage against which other companies might
find it impossible to compete.

Thus, with the advent of the newer technologies,
the political game is deepening and broadening, and
it is possible that as the industry changes and new
coalitions emerge, the players in the political process will also shift into new alignments, resulting
in other regulatory balances. It is now apparent
that any attempt to curtail regulation at the
Federal level could lead to efforts at the sub-
Federal, at the levels of State and municipal juris-
ductions. Some cities have already justified their
right to regulate cable television programmes because the cable lines are strung along common roads
or use the facilities of regulated utilities. Moreover, in a recent ruling, a Federal US District
Judge ruled as unconstitutional a local ordinance to
enable city officials to censor cable television.[71]
If S.66 (or similar legislation to deregulate cable
TV at the local level) does not become law and if
initiative to regulate broadcasting and cable activities is otherwise loosened at the Federal level,
it is possible that the legal basis for such decisions might have to be reconsidered.

In conclusion, a serious study of broadcasting
regulation in the United States should alert people
to the obvious: What Congress (and its creature, the
FCC) gives, it can take away. Rather than predic-
ting an end to regulation, the struggle over regulations will continue to engage the various groups
with vested interests in providing entertainment and
information. Thus, in the 1980s, it is possible
that broadcasting in the US will face less regulation at the Federal level but increased regulation
at the sub-Federal and supra-Federal levels. If
UNESCO or ITU were to implement agencies that would
actually regulate how information flows over borders,
US-based media conglomerates might not, for the first
time, be free to choose higher profits over public
interest. Who will define the public interest and
how it will be defined in those circumstances await
future ideological battles. How the US ethos of free
enterprise, embodied in the conglomerates, will fare
in a world in which communication activities would
be subject to regulation by other nations or inter-

national agencies should be a fascinating subject
of study.

United States: A System of Minimal Regulation

References

1. The literature on the broadcasting of politics is so vast that it is impossible to cite it all. For a recent overview with an excellent bibliography see David Paletz and Robert Entman, *Media, Politics, Power*, New York, The Free Press, 1982.

2. The Federal Trade Commission (FTC) is the agency authorised to regulate commercial advertisements on television in the name of consumer protection. The FCC is the major regulatory agency for broadcasting and as such its duties and structure will be briefly reviewed in the body of this chapter. Both agencies have been frequently criticised. For more details see Sidney W Head, Broadcasting in America: *A Survey of Television and Radio*, 3rd Edition, Boston, Houghton Mifflin Company, 1976, especially pp.411-412 and 429-431. For a review of recent political issues relating to advertising which concern broadcasters see NAB, *Broadcasting and Government*, Washington, DC, National Association of Broadcasters, 1982, pp.40-48.

3. The whole amendment reads: 'Congress shall make no law respecting an establishment of a religion, or prohibiting the free exercise thereof; or abridging the freedom of speech or of the press; or the right of the people to assemble, and to petition the government for a redress of greviances.'

4. Two laws, the Sherman Anti-trust Act and the Clayton Anti-trust Act, give the Department of Justice the right to sue media corporations which they define as monopolistic. What constitutes a trust or monopoly varies according to the industry; for example, cable and over-the-air broadcasting are subject to different rules. See NAB, *Broadcasting and Government*, pp.48-52 and Head, *Broadcasting in America*, pp.390-395 and 421.

5. Other corporate funds include revenue from cable fees, especially pay-TV film channels. The national government and individual State governments support public television in the US, but stations in this system also get funds from the business world through grants. Public stations also raise money through subscriptions and fundraisers such as auctions. The Carnegie Commission Report, *A Public Trust*, New York, Bantam Books, 1979, p.341, reports that about 25% of the funding comes from these sources.

6. In particular, see Herbert Schiller's work, especially *Mass Communications and American Empire*, New York, Augustus M Kelley, 1969.

191

7. Willard D Rowland Jr, 'The Illusion of Fulfillment: The Broadcast Reform Movement',*Journalism
Monographs*, no 79, December 1982.
8. Muriel G Cantor, 'The Organization and Production of Prime Time Television', in D Pearl et al
(eds.), *Television and Behavior: Ten Years of Scientific Progress and Implication for the Eighties*,
Washington, DC, Government Printing Office, 1982,
pp.349-361.
9. *Ibid*, p.353.
10. Public television was established by the
Public Broadcasting Act of 1967 with Congress appro-
priating money for the system. Before 1967 there
was little support from the national government for
what was known as educational television. See The
Carnegie Commission Report, *A Public Trust*, pp.33-65.
11. Stations, of course, produce some programming locally. In particular, most network-affiliated
television stations produce two or more news shows
daily and often produce 'talk' shows which are
broadcast usually during the morning hours.
12. ABC is the only network producing daily
soap operas. For more details see Muriel G Cantor
and Suzanne Pingree, *The Soap Opera*, Beverly Hills,
Sage Publications, 1983. All the networks produce
daily news shows.
13. Sally Bedell Smith, 'Is It Time for a
Fourth TV Network?', *New York Times*, August 28 1983,
Section 2.
14. Fred Friendly, *The Good Guys, the Bad Guys
and the First Amendment: Free Speech vs Fairness in
Broadcast*, New York, Random House, 1975.
15. Jeremy Tunstall, *The Media are American*,
New York, Columbia University Press, 1977; Muriel G
Cantor, *Prime-Time Television: Content and Control*,
Beverly Hills, Sage Publications, 1980, p.13.
16. Except where otherwise noted the material
for this section was derived from FCC, Network
Inquiry Special Staff, 'Historical Evolution of the
Commercial Network Broadcast System', mimeo draft,
October 1979; Erik Barnouw, *A Tower in Babel: A
History of Broadcasting in the United States, Volume
I - to 1933*, New York, Oxford University Press,
1966; Gleason L Archer, *History of Radio: to 1926*,
New York, American Historical Society, 1938; Gleason
L Archer, *Big Business and Radio*, New York, American
Historical Society, 1939; J Fred MacDonald, *Radio
Programming in American Life from 1920 to 1960*,
Chicago, Nelson-Hall, 1979.
17. Head, *Broadcasting in America*, p.120.
18. MacDonald, *Radio Programming in American*

Life, p.76.

19. Erik Barnouw, *Tube of Plenty*, London, Oxford University Press, 1975, p.466.

20. Head, *Broadcasting in America*, pp.109-110.

21. Barnouw, *A Tower in Babel*, pp.154-156.

22. *Ibid*, p.121.

23. Most of the material in this paragraph came from Erik Barnouw, *The Sponsor: Notes on a Modern Potentate*, London, Oxford University Press, 1978. See page 15 for both of the quotations found here.

24. The source of this information is FCC, 'The FCC in Brief', FCC, Information Bulletin, June 1982. In addition the document was verified through a telephone conversation with a FCC public relations person.

25. Erwin G Krasnow, Lawrence D Longley and Herbert A Terry, *The Politics of Broadcast Regulation*, 3rd Edition, New York, St Martin's Press, 1982, p.15.

26. Newton Minnow, a former FCC Commissioner, for example, makes that point explicitly in Krasnow et al, *The Politics of Broadcast Regulation*, 'Preface'.

27. See Friendly, *The Good Guys* ... throughout and Head, *Broadcasting in America*, pp.323-324.

28. FCC, *The Communications Act of 1934 with Amendments and Index Thereto*, Washington, DC, Government Printing Office, 1971, p.58.

29. *Ibid*, pp.51-52.

30. *Ibid*, p.52. The exact words in the Law are: 'Nothing in the foregoing sentence shall be construed as relieving broadcasters ... from the obligation imposed upon them under this Act to operate in the public interest and to afford reasonable opportunity for the discussion of conflicting views on issues of public importance.'

31. Rowland, 'The Illusion of Fulfillment', p.26.

32. *Red Lion Broadcasting, Inc v Federal Communications Commission*, Supreme Court of the United States, 395 US 367, 1969.

33. *Ibid*.

34. Willard D Rowland, Jr, *The Politics of TV Violence*, Beverly Hills, Sage Publications, 1983, pp.253-289; NAB, *Broadcasting and Government*, pp. vii and 1-11.

35. Krasnow et al, *The Politics of Broadcast Regulation*, p.17.

36. Rowland, *The Politics of TV Violence*, pp. 242-243.

37. NAB, *Broadcasting and Government*, pp.1-11.

38. Cantor, *Prime-Time Television*, pp.45 and 54.

39. Head, *Broadcasting in America*, pp.305-306.

40. The Prime-Time Access Rule was adopted by the FCC in 1970. This rule, along with the Financial Interest and Syndication Rules, was part of a package intended to decrease network dominance in prime-time programming. It prohibits network affiliates in the top 50 markets from broadcasting network programming for more than three of the four hours of prime-time (7.00 to 11.00 pm). This rule is being reviewed and may be repealed as part of the move to deregulate television. See NAB, *Broadcasting and Government*, pp.36-37, and Cantor, *Prime-Time Television*, p.49.

41. The material for this section comes from Cantor, *Prime-Time Television*, p.49-50; Rowland, *The Politics of TV Violence*, pp.239-246; and Geoffrey Cowan, *See No Evil: The Backstage Battle Over Sex and Violence on Television*, New York, Simon and Schuster, 1979.

42. 'Networks Win Financial Interest/Syndication Battle', *Broadcasting*, August 8 1983, pp.27-30.

43. FCC, *Report and Order of the Commission on Network Television Broadcasting*, Second Series, Washington, DC, Vol 23, May-July 1970.

44. *Washington Post*, 'FCC Hands Network Victory, Votes to Life Syndication Rule', August 5 1983.

45. Karen V Eustis, 'Syndication Wars: The Networks vs the Independent Producers', Unpublished paper, Los Angeles, March 10 1983.

46. Conversation with an official spokesman of the A C Nielsen Co in January 1983.

47. *Broadcasting*, August 8 1983, pp.28 and 29.

48. *Washington Post*, 'Film Makers Win Round in Fight with Networks', October 20 1983.

49. *Ibid.*

50. *Washington Post*, 'FCC Hands Network Victory', October 20 1983.

51. *Washington Post*, 'Reagan Briefed on TV Issue', October 21 1983.

52. See Carnegie Commission Report, *A Public Trust*, and Harry J Skornia, *Television and Society: An Inquest and Agenda for Improvement*, New York, McGraw-Hill Book Company, 1965.

53. Head, *Broadcasting in America*, pp.195-197.

54. NAB, *Broadcasting and Government*, p.x states, 'While passage of legislation to eliminate "equal time" requirements, the fairness doctrine, or the "reasonable access" provisions will remain a remote possibility, broadcasters' arguments will

receive serious consideration (in 1982).' Any bill
introduced in either House of Congress to eliminate
the Fairness Doctrine is unlikely to be considered
seriously before the 1984 Presidential Election.

55. This account is drawn primarily from 'US
team back from Geneva, pleased with itself and ITU',
Broadcasting, July 25 1983, pp.26-27. *Broadcasting*
is the 'trade' journal of the broadcasting industry
in the US. However, *DBS News*, a newsletter published in Washington, DC (Special Issue, Phillips
Publishing, Inc, Mid-July 1983), claims that the
reason the US was blocked in its proposal to set a
60% higher ceiling on signal strength was the fear
by some nations that it could then be picked up by
the smaller home-dishes. Lower-strength signals
would need the larger earth stations which would
then require cable distribution, easier for governments to control and regulate.

56. International Commission for the Study of
Communications Problems, *Interim Report on Communications Problems in Modern Society*, Paris, UNESCO,
1978.

57. The full title is: 'The Declaration of
Fundamental Principles Concerning the Contribution
of the Mass Media to Strengthen Peace and International Understanding, the Promotion of Human Rights
and to Countering Radicalism, Apartheit and Incite-
ment to War.'

58. Sean MacBride, President, *Many Voices, One
World*, Final Report of the International Commission
for the Study of Communications Problems, London,
Kogan Page/New York, Unipub/Paris, UNESCO, 1980,
p.141.

59. MacBride, *Many Voices, One World*, p.XVIII.

60. MacBride, *Many Voices, One World*, p.111.

61. From an article in *The New York Times*,
August 28 1983, on the promotion of Barry Diller
from Chairman of Paramount Pictures to head of the
leisure-time group of Gulf and Western. Before
Paramount, Diller worked for a large talent agency
and then ABC, where he became the vice-president in
charge of prime-time entertainment, a career sug-
gestive of the inter-mix of media interests and controls that has evolved.

62. MacBride, *Many Voices, One World*, pp.111
and 261.

63. John H. Clippinger, 'The Hidden Agenda',
Journal of Communication, 29:1, Winter 1979, p.198.

64. NAB, *Broadcasting and Government*, p.32.

65. US Congress, Senate Print 98-22, 'Long-
Range Goals in International Telecommunications and

Information - An Outline for United States Policy', March 11 1983. (Government Printing Office: 052-070-05841-2).

66. 'Fowler exhorts countries to embrace technical change', *Broadcasting*, October 10 1983, p.87.

67. 'UN: new satellite principles', *Intermedia*, 11:1, January 1983, p.9.

68. 'Cable TV wants fewer regulations', *USA Today*, June 15 1983; 'Senate Approved Cable TV Deregulation', *The Washington Post*, June 15 1983.

69. 'Cities, Cable Operators Reach Agreement', *Congressional Quarterly*, March 26 1983, p.637.

70. Ben Brown, 'Speciality cable sinks in red tape', *USA Today*, July 22 1983.

71. 'Judge rules cities can't censor cable TV', *USA Today*, August 3 1983.

Chapter Six

CANADA: NATION-BUILDING THREATENED BY THE U.S.-
DOMINATED MEDIA?

Richard Collins

Canada offers students of broadcasting a site for
investigating a number of general problems of broadcasting policy as well as a distinctive broadcasting
formation of some complexity but great fascination.
For Canada has the problems of both a large and a
small country, of an advanced and a developing
society, but above all of a nation whose identity is
always in question. What holds Canada together?
     The country has two official languages and sub-
stantial linguistic minorities speaking Italian,
German, Ukranian, native Indian and Inuit languages,
Greek and Chinese. It is the second largest nation
state in the world stretching nearly three thousand
miles north-south and four thousand miles east-west,
spanning seven time zones, with a population of
almost 23 million largely dwelling in a strip two
hundred miles deep north of the US/Canada border embracing three metropolises but with a substantial
scattered rural population. The geography of Canada
is such that although east-west water communications
stretching from the Atlantic to the Rocky Mountains
facilitated early exploration and exploitation of a
large land area, in much of the country north-south
connections are as convenient as east-west. Physical
communications with the United States are, in western and Atlantic Canada, as easy or easier than they
are with central Canada.
     Perhaps most importantly the economic interests
of the Canadian regions diverge and one of the enduring tasks of the Federal government has been to
mediate between these interests, though that mediation has often, though not invariably, been in the
interests of central Canada, i.e. the two most populous provinces of Ontario and Quebec. The National
policy of the nineteenth century (1878) privileged
the interests of manufacturing and finance - princi-

197

pally in southern Ontario and Laurentian Quebec -
over those of primary producers. The oil and gas
regime of recent Canadian Federal governments has
necessitated Canadian producers - notably in Alberta
- selling to Canadian consumers - principally in
Ontario and Quebec - at below world prices. On the
other hand the Crow Rate (the price at which the
railways haul grain to the ports) has been set at a
level favouring the farmers of the prairies and has
not enabled the railways to invest sufficiently in
the maintenance and improvement of their infrastructure. Economic interests are then a potent
force for the focussing of regional perceptions of a
common identity opposed to actions taken by the
Federal government in the name of Canada, but which
have characteristically favoured the populous and
powerful central Canadian regions.

To say that the unity of Canada is in crisis is
a truism: in Quebec and Alberta separatist politicians have entered office, the provinces take each
other and the Federal government to court and the
passage to bilingualism in Ontario and Manitoba is
exceeded in conflict only by Quebec's passage to
monolingualism. The dominant Liberal party holds no
seats in the Federal House of Commons from ridings
(constituencies) west of Winnipeg and its virtual
monopoly in Quebec Federal politics (one non-Liberal
member of the House of Commons) contrasts with its
comprehensive subordination to the separatist Parti
Quebecois (PQ) in the Quebec National Assembly (the
provincial legislature). Yet Canada survives. The
1976 victory of the PQ with its sails set for
separatism has been followed by the rejection of
this policy by the population of Quebec in the 1980
referendum. Recent polls in Quebec indicate substantial Francophone dissatisfaction with the provincial government's hard-line policy towards the
use of the English language in Quebec and Anglophone
institutions. Provinces fight out their disagree-
ments with each other and with the Federal government in Canadian courts - within a Canadian institutional framework. There is substantial popular
assent to nation-building investments and policies;
whilst westerners may be alienated and resent central hegemony, they still fly Maple Leaf flags outside their homes.

Canadian identity may be problematic, but it is
less problematic than would be Albertan, United
States, British colonial or even Quebec national
identity, even though Canadian identity is characteristically defined by what it is not: not American,

not British, not French. As Wilden puts it, Canada is 'Notland': a country whose limits of action, identity and geography are defined by others - nowhere more so than in communications.[1]

Given the centrifugal forces at work in Canada, a consistent theme in Canadian history and public policy has been that of nation-building: the construction of an infrastructure, an economic and political regime and ideology that will establish and maintain the imaginary unity of the Canadian nation. In this constant activity of national construction and self-definition, communications and the activity of the state - principally at Federal but also at provincial level - in facilitating inter-Canadian communications have long been central.

For example, the construction of the Inter Colonial Railway (opened 1876) between the Atlantic provinces and central Canada was part of the Confederation agreement and the accession of British Columbia to the Canadian confederation was conditional on the construction of an east-west transcontinental railway to link British Columbia to central Canada. The alignment of these railways was determined by military and economic judgements regarding the threat to Canadian interests from the United States as well as by geography. In the judgement of Sir John A MacDonald, the first Prime Minister of the Dominion of Canada, a condition of Canada's existence was the assertion of east-west transcontinental links and the construction of a communication infrastructure to realise them.

Since confederation, efficient communications and the state's role in communication have been consistently regarded by Canadian policy makers and scholars as a condition of Canada's continued existence. Whether the concern is with physical communication (the Canadian Pacific and National railways, the Trans Canada Highway or the development of Trans Canada Airlines, later Air Canada, as a Crown Corporation) or with the communication of information (the regulation of the telephone and telegraph systems, the establishment of the National Film Board of Canada and the Canadian Broadcasting Corporation or the dollar-for-dollar matching grants from Federal government to newspapers establishing news bureaux outside their home provinces or abroad), Canada has always had communication as a matter of great importance on the public policy agenda. Canada is exceptional in having a Ministry of Communications and federal (and provincial) resources are devoted to the production of, in general very good

199

quality, research and communication policy formation.

The historical importance of communications infrastructure in the formation of the Canadian state, the primacy ceded to communication in Canadian political and academic discourse following Harold Innis and Marshall McLuhan, combined with the technological fix exposure to Daniel Bell's prophecies of a post-industrial information society, have created in Canada a kind of national obsession with communication policy and Canadian communication sovereignty. Whether one considers this obsession to be rooted in a correct apprehension of a real threat or in an imaginary fear that irrationally strikes residents of 'Notland' depends on one's judgement as to the importance of communications in the maintenance of the Canadian state and Canadian sovereignty. In any event there can be no doubt that historically broadcasting in Canada has been used for nation-building purposes. In particular, this concern with the establishment and maintenance of a Canadian identity has manifested itself in a fear of cultural domination via the broadcasting media by Canada's powerful southern neighbour, the USA.

The provisions of the 1968 Broadcasting Act are particularly revealing in this respect. For example, under the terms of section 3, 'Broadcasting Policy for Canada', it is stated that

> The Canadian broadcasting system should be effectively owned and controlled by Canadians so as to safeguard, enrich and strengthen the cultural, political, social and economic fabric of Canada; ... the programming provided by each broadcaster should be of high standard, using predominantly Canadian creative and other resources; there should be provided, through a corporation established by Parliament for the purpose, a national broadcasting service that is predominantly Canadian in content and character; and the national broadcasting service should ... contribute to the development of national unity and provide for continuing expression of Canadian identity. [2]

Despite these provisions, however, broadcasting in Canada is, and has been since its inception in Montreal in 1919, surbordinated to foreign interests. The global trends identified by Schiller[3], Tunstall[4] and Smith[5] of US dominance in world information

flows are nowhere more potently exemplified than in
Canadian broadcasting. The history of Canadian
broadcasting (we shall use this somewhat misleading
term in the absence of a comprehensible alternative
that embraces the phenomena of cable, satellite,
terrestrial microwave and broadcast distribution of
audiovisual information signals) from 1919 to 1983
is one of subordination to the United States. Moreover, the lack of communication sovereignty ex-
perienced by Canada in its relations with the United
States is reproduced within Canada where the problem is always with the bigger neighbour next door:
Anglophone Canadian culture dominates Francophone,
Ontario dominates Atlantic and western Anglophones,
the native Indian and Inuit people are subordinated
to the dominant Francophone or Anglophone culture
and broadcasting systems, and so on. To help understand the Canadian fear of US domination and the
concomitant normative emphasis on nation-building in
Canada through broadcasting, indeed to comprehend
fully the contemporary nature of Canadian broadcasting, we must first look at the history of radio and
television in this North American society.

THE HISTORICAL DEVELOPMENT OF BROADCASTING IN CANADA

Radio broadcasting began in Canada in 1920 when the
Canadian Marconi Company began service from its
Montreal station XWA (later CFCF). By 1923 probably
34 radio stations were transmitting in Canada and
556 in the United States. As the Director of the
Radio Services of the Canadian Government observed,
'the aether disregards all boundaries'.[6] From the
inception of broadcasting in Canada to the present
day the Canadian experience has been decisively
shaped by developments south of the border. By
1932, the year of the establishment of the Canadian
Radio Broadcasting Commission (CRBC) under the
Canadian Radio Broadcasting Act of the same year
(the first step taken by the government of Canada
to direct the development of broadcasting), the
combined radiated power of US broadcasters was
680,000 watts, while that of Canadian broadcasters
was less than 50,000 watts.[7] Peers instances the
popularity of US stations with Canadian listeners:

> Nine tenths of the radio fans in this Dominion
> hear three or four times as many United States
> stations as Canadian. Few fans, no matter in
> what part of Canada they live, can regularly

pick up more than three or four different
Canadian stations; any fan with a good set can
"log" a score of American stations.[8]

In 1928 the first Royal Commission on broadcasting in Canada, the Aird Commission, was appointed
and it reported in 1929, a decade after the licensing
of Canada's first radio station. Many of the concerns
of the Aird Commission have become perennials in
Canadian broadcasting policy, but of particular
interest is the commission's concern with the two
major paradigms of broadcasting organisation: the US
model of, supposedly, free competition among stations for audiences and revenue on the one hand and
the European public service model of state licensed
and funded monopoly on the other. In their analysis
of the Canadian situation the members of the Aird
Commission found themselves drawn to the European
solution (particularly to the instances of Germany
which offered a model of Reich/Land relations that
had potential for Federal/Provincial relations and
the UK's monopoly incorporated in the BBC). However,
the Commission was reporting on a system that had
developed on essentially American lines, of competition among stations in profitable markets for
audiences and advertising revenue, and which was in
danger of becoming wholly American in nature. In
their visit to NBC (National Broadcasting Company)
in New York members of the commission were disturbed
by NBC management's reassurance that the company intended to extend its service, and the same quality
of service as that enjoyed in the United States, to
Canada. In 1929 the two principal Toronto stations
joined US networks: station CFRB joined CBS
(Columbia Broadcasting System) and station CKGW responded by joining the NBC Red network. In Montreal
station CKAC similarly joined CBS in 1929 and the
pioneer Canadian station CFCF (owned by Canadian
Marconi in which RCA - Radio Corporation of America
- had an interest) affiliated to NBC in 1930. Radio
stations serving the two great Canadian metropolises,
Toronto and Montreal, accounted for half the total
radiated power of transmitters in Canada.
    The Aird Report led - in the teeth of opposi-
tion from the vested interests of Canadian commercial broadcasters represented by their trade
association the CAB (Canadian Association of Broadcasters) - to the establishment of a national system
of broadcasting in Canada. Statements made by one
of the members of the commission (C. Bowman) argued
that only a national publicly financed system could

be genuinely Canadian:

> The drift under private enterprise is tending
> towards dependence upon United States sources.
> Contracts are being made between Canadian
> broadcasting agencies and the more powerful
> broadcasting interests of the United States.
> Increasing dependence upon such contracts would
> lead broadcasting on this continent into the
> same position as the motion picture industry
> has reached, after years of fruitless endeavour
> to establish Canadian independence in the pro-
> duction of films.

For

> privately owned Canadian broadcasting stations,
> with nothing like the revenue available to the
> larger stations in the United States, cannot
> hope to compete beyond a very limited audience
> which in itself would be insufficient to sup-
> port broadcasting worthy of Canada ... The cost
> of equipping Canada with radio stations to com-
> pare with the most popular stations in the
> United States would be more than Canadian radio
> advertising would support.[9]

Bowman's arguments that Canadian interests and
experience were not being represented in a broadcasting system that was substantially American and that
the revenues raised in a distribution system (here
radio broadcasting) governed by competition among a
plurality of stations for limited resources would
not permit the production of programming capable of
attracting and serving audiences competed for by US
signals were correct and prescient. He identified
the structural situation that has obtained in
Canadian broadcasting to date and which has prevailed because at the crucial points of decision in
Canadian broadcasting history the issue of the fundamental irreconcilability of commercial imperatives
of profit maximisation with the achievement of
Canadian nationalistic, cultural and political goals
was always fudged. Neither commercial nor national
goals were ever decisevely chosen. Nor, perhaps,
given the problematic nature of Canadian national
identity and the general assent to the capitalist
order in Canada, could such a choice ever be made.
The 'conflict within his soul'[10] attributed by
Graham Spry to the Conservative Prime Minister R.B.
Bennett's commitment both to private ownership *and*

Canadian statist, nationalistic action is a conflict
that is pervasive within Canada - characteristic
perhaps of a prosperous capitalist economy occupying
a relatively subordinate position in the world
economic order.

The report of the Aird Commission was followed
by a period of intense debate, lobbying and political action which resulted in the promulgation of the
Broadcasting Act of 1932, the establishment of the
first public body concerned with broadcasting in
Canada, the Canadian Radio Broadcasting Commission,
and a much quoted statement by the Prime Minister
that exemplifies the enduring contradiction in
Canadian communications policy between the noble
articulation of intelligent policy and a refusal of
the necessary changes in the status quo required to
realise the stated policy goals.

> This country must be assured of complete con-
> trol of broadcasting from Canadian sources,
> free from foreign interference or influence.
> Without such control radio broadcasting can
> never become a great agency for communication
> of matters of national concern and for the dif-
> fusion of national thought and ideals, and
> without such control it can never be the agency
> by which national consciousness may be fostered
> and sustained and national unity still further
> strengthened. Secondly, no other scheme than
> that of public ownership can ensure to the
> people of this country, without regard to class
> or place, equal enjoyment of the benefits and
> pleasures of radio broadcasting. Then there is
> a third factor, ... the use of the air ... that
> lies over the soil or land of Canada is a
> natural resource over which we have complete
> jurisdiction under the recent decision of the
> privy council (referring to the confirmation of
> federal prerogatives in broadcasting challenged
> by provincial governments - *author*). I cannot
> think that any government would be warranted in
> leaving the air to private exploitation and not
> reserving it for development for the use of the
> people.[11]

Bennet's lofty sentiments notwithstanding, the
CRBC was established for the fulfilment of compel-
ling national goals with a budget insufficient to con-
struct an adequate network of transmitters for the
proposed national service or to induce private
broadcasters to sell airtime for the broadcast of

CRBC programmes. Dissatisfaction with the regime
established for the CRBC was orchestrated and arti-
culated by the Canadian Radio League, which had been
established by a number of patriotic and influential
young Canadian activists to press for a broadcasting
order through which the goals of Canadian nationalism could be realised. The Radio League, now
called the Broadcasting League, was established 'to
create a radio broadcasting system which can draw
the different parts of Canada together, which can
use the air not only for indirect advertising but
more essentially for educational and public purposes.'[12] The opposition of the Radio League, arti-
culated in political attacks on the Liberal party by
the Conservatives, resulted in the newly elected
Liberal government for 1936 legislating to establish
the Canadian Broadcasting Corporation, the CBC.

The Canadian Broadcasting Act of 1936 established a corporation modelled on the BBC and appointed as general manager the director of public relations of the BBC, Gladstone Murray, in preference to
the two alternatives: Reginald Brophy, an employee
of NBC New York, and Harry Sedgwick, the president
of the Canadian Association of Broadcasters. Support
for the public service ethos was further evidenced
by the appointment of Alan Plaunt, the President of
the Canadian Radio League, to the first board of the
CBC.

The first priority for the new corporation was
the establishment of an effective national distribution system for Canadian reception of Canadian radio
programming. The daunting and costly task of achieving coverage of 84% of the population of the nation
was completed in 1939. Comprehensive coverage (if
coverage excluding 16% of the population can be
called comprehensive) was achieved in partnership
with some commercial broadcasters, whereby the
private stations became affiliates of the CBC network and sold advertising and served audiences with
CBC programmes. In addition, the programming for
the extended network included programmes sponsored
by advertisers and much American production which
could be purchased at a price far below that required to produce Canadian material of comparable appeal
and production values. Thus CBC was in competition
with Canadian commercial broadcasters both as a
purchaser of programmes from third parties (principally the United States) and of Canadian talent, as
well as for advertising revenues and audiences.
Programming and purchasing policy, though in parts
distinctive, was forced into a convergence with that

of the private broadcasters, with the commercial broadcasters seeking to maximise audiences for the least expenditure on programming (and therefore affiliating to the US radio networks and securing programmes from the USA) and thus maximise profits, while CBC was compelled to programme its schedules at the lowest cost (tending similarly to seek products from the USA) because of the constraints imposed by a shortage of funds resulting from heavy expenditure in constructing and operating its national transmission and distribution system.

The CBC thus developed as a public sector and public service broadcaster heavily influenced by the model of Reith's BBC though in a distinctively different fashion. In many ways CBC's initial development was one following the model of the US radio networks: a central organisation owning and operating transmitters in major metropolitan areas making available programming produced at the centre to remote, affiliated, privately-owned stations that themselves produced some of their own programming. Unlike the US networks though, CBC (although drawing some of its revenues from the sale of audiences to advertisers) was publicly financed and charged with the achievement of national political and cultural goals both through its own programming and through the powers to regulate the commercial broadcasters of Canada.

The recurrent criticism of the CBC from the commercial broadcasters in Canada was that it was both 'cop and competitor', for the new corporation retained a feature inherited from its predecessor, the CRBC, of regulating the whole of the Canadian broadcasting system as well as participating as a major state funded element within that system. The anomaly of cop and competitor was not rectified until 1958 with the establishment of the Board of Broadcast Governors separate from the CBC. Essentially what now appears as anomalous was an expression of the ideology of broadcasting in Canada as a *single* system, a viewpoint reiterated by the 1968 Broadcasting Act. 'Broadcasting undertakings in Canada ... constitute a single system, herein referred to as the Canadian broadcasting system, comprising public and private elements.'[13] No government, however, was prepared to fund the national service and curb the power of the commercial broadcasters in order to realise such a single system. Moreover, while the notion of a single system has persisted, acting as a rallying flag for nationalists who have sought to orchestrate the whole of

Canadian broadcasting, public and private, for the achievement of nationalist goals, in fact Canadian broadcasting has never been a single system and this is even more true of the post-television era.

The second world war, particularly in its early stages when the United States was not a combatant, orientated Canadian listeners to Canadian radio and particularly to the national CBC service. US programming priorities as a non-belligerent (and even as a belligerent) were different from the interests of Canadians and the resources available to the CBC as by far the largest single element in the Canadian broadcasting system meant that its war news and foreign coverage were superior to that any private broadcaster could offer. Like the BBC, CBC had a good war, though its balancing act as 'cop or competitor' became increasingly precarious.

In 1949 a commission of enquiry into the arts and culture in Canada including broadcasting, the Massey commission, was established. Its report, published in 1951, largely supported the CBC for its achievement of three pre-eminent goals: 'An adequate coverage of the entire population, opportunities for Canadian talent and for Canadian self-expression generally, and successful resistance to the absorption of Canada into the general cultural pattern of the United States.'

The inadequacies of the CBC were those of insufficiently rigorous regulation of commercial broadcasting and of 'reticence' as to publicising itself. Massey therefore substantially endorsed the notion of the single national system, approved CBC's practice as a broadcaster and only condemned CBC as a regulator. For Massey it seems CBC's faults were those of being too soft a cop and too quiet a competitor. However, Massey's endorsement of the CBC (qualified by the minority report of one member, Dr. Surveyor) and his argument for the extension of the CBC's hegemony over radio in Canada were based on assumptions that a new broadcasting technology, television, was to expose as erroneous. The Massey Commission argued that; 'the principal grievance of the private broadcasters is based ... on a false assumption that broadcasting in Canada is an industry. Broadcasting in Canada in our view is a public service directed and controlled in the public interest by a body responsible to Parliament.'14 Television was to demonstrate that the private broadcasters were correct. Even if their truth was not the whole truth, it was part of the truth. Broadcasting is an industry, an industry of a particular kind, a cultural industry with many differences to the steel or shoe industry, but an industry nonetheless.

The commercial broadcasters and other Canadian interests were anxious to establish television in Canada as early as possible. CBC, however, helped by the support given it by the Massey commission, was able to block private television broadcasting, but was until 1952 unable to command the revenues to initiate its own television service. Its pious priorities were set out in the late 40s:

> The Board believes that in line with fundamental radio policies laid down by Parliament for radio broadcasting, television should be developed so as to be of benefit to the greatest possible number of people, so that public channels should be used in the public interest and with the overall aim of stimulating Canadian national life and not merely of broadcasting non-Canadian visual material in this country. The Board will strive for the maximum provision of Canadian television for Canadians.[15]

CBC's inability to command public funds adequate to the achievement of the national goals it espoused, combined with its political influence and licensing power enabling it to block the development of commercial television, created a vacuum into which, of course, the cross border signals of the US TV networks flowed. Thus, television in Canada characteristically began before Canadian television. At the inception of CBC's services in September 1952 - in Toronto and Montreal only - there were 146,000 television receivers in Canada tuned to American stations and the first cable network was established in London Ontario to distribute US signals to subscribers.

The history of radio in Canada was replicated by television. American signals were imported over the air from powerful transmitters in US border settlements like Buffalo, Burlington and Bellingham built to deliver Canadian audiences to US advertisers and by cable to Canadians in towns unable to receive a satisfactory signal with a home aerial. Again the resources made available by government to the CBC to institute a national system of Canadian television were inadequate for the task and substantially less than those committed by private capital to the commercial section of the supposedly single

Canadian broadcasting system. By 1958 44 private television stations were on the air in Canada as opposed to 8 CBC. Ellis remarks:

> When CBFT Montreal and CBLT Toronto finally began broadcasting in September 1952, it emerged that their production facilities and even more significant, their coverage, has been seriously compromised by the need to keep within the government's unrealistic allocation of funds. The CBC's ability to "compete" with the private sector was impaired even before private TV station licences were being granted.[16]

In spite of funding inadequate for the establishment of a national television distribution system and the production of substantially Canadian programming, CBC television achieved much in the 1950s. Its English language drama production section sold 35 television dramas to the BBC to spearhead the BBC's fight back against commercial television in the U.K. Meanwhile Francophone services of CBC - Radio Canada developed the *Tele-roman* format with such success in the legendary series *La Famille Plouffe* that:

> Hockey schedules in St. Jerome, Joliette and Quebec City have been shifted to avoid games on Wednesdays. In Valleyfield the start of games is delayed until after 9pm. Throughout Quebec theatre owners complain that attendance drops when the Plouffes are on the air ... In Montreal 81% of all television sets owned by French language viewers are tuned to the Wednesday night show, according to the Elliott Haynes survey.[17]

CBC's achievements, however, satisfied few Canadians. Sections of the population lacked a television service, others had access to only one channel, and in the border areas and those served by the growing cable system Canadian channels and programming were outweighed by productions from the USA. The commercial broadcasters were to be excluded from establishing a television service, the Massey Commission had recommended, until after CBC had developed national programming in the two official languages available. But in order to make available a national television service as rapidly as possible, the government instituted a policy of licensing private broadcasters in areas unserved by CBC and declining to license second stations in markets already served

by a Canadian television broadcaster until national
single channel coverage had been achieved. The
effect of this attempt to shotgun a national network
based on co-operation between CBC and commercial
broadcasters was disastrous. CBC were excluded from
extending their services to a number of provincial
capitals (because private broadcasters had the initial licence) and private interests were excluded
from the major metropolitan markets. Absence of
service in major Canadian centres of population, the
existence of competition for audiences from the US
networks in border areas, the conflict of interests
between CBC, the commercial broadcasters and advertisers and the continuing anomaly of CBC acting as
'cop and competitor' provided fecund provocations
for discontent.

The Fowler Royal Commission on Broadcasting,
appointed in 1955, reported in 1957. The report recommended the establishment of a regulatory board
independent of the CBC - the Board of Broadcast
Governors (BBG) appointed by the government. It
also favoured funding mechanisms for CBC that would
separate its funding from direct influence by
government and which would, hopefully, provide CBC
with the resources necessary to establish a national
television distribution infrastructure and to fill
its schedules with substantial amounts of quality
Canadian programming. Fowler also reiterated the
pious, orthodox litany of a single national broadcasting system of mixed ownership with CBC assuming
the role of 'central factor' in the system.

Implementing or not the Fowler report was to
become the prerogative of a new Conservative government returned in 1958 with close links to a number
of commercial broadcasting interests. Essentially
the elements of Fowler that were appropriated by
the Conservatives were those that enlarged the
rights of commercial broadcasting and reduced those
of CBC. The 1958 Broadcasting Act established a
Board of Broadcast Governors, maintained CBC's
direct financial dependence on government and removed from the provisions of the Broadcasting Act
referring to CBC's aims and objectives any responsibility for the fulfilment of national purposes and
responsibilities.

The BBG licensed second television stations in
a number of Canadian cities on application from
commercial interests (notably in Toronto where CFTO
was established by the Baton group financed by J D
Eaton, 'reportedly the most generous of all Tory
campaign bankrollers'[18] and in Edmonton where the

CBC secured the licence for the second station).
The BBG were soon considering requests from commercial interests for the licensing of a network of
commercial television stations throughout Canada and
the establishment of a Canadian national commercial
system to compete with the CBC.

The commercial network, CTV, developed as a
system owned by its affiliates. It was licensed and
began operations in 1961 with eight affiliated members, though of these only those not subjected to
competition from the United States enjoyed satisfactory revenues. But in the three major Canadian
markets, Montreal, Toronto and Vancouver, there was
trouble. In Vancouver the BBG was forced to authorise the sale of 24% of the equity in CHAN-TV to
foreign capital (the US Famous Players and British
ATV), while in Toronto the dominant interest,
Bassett and Eaton, attempted to replace a leading
minority shareholder, Aldred, by the ABC network, a
United States company owned by ABC-Paramount giving
ABC 25% of the equity (though only 18.8% of the
voting stock). These initiatives provided an opportunity for Graham Spry, the standard bearer for
Canadian nationalism in broadcasting, to publicise
elements of foreign ownership in the Canadian broadcasting system. Spry documented US and UK stakes in
the ownership of the Quebec and Montreal stations
and in Kitchener, Windsor, Vancouver, Ottawa,
Pembroke, Cornwall, Halifax and the proposed stake
in CFTO Toronto, the leading member of the CTV network. The BBG refused to allow ABC to take a stake
in CFTO, though subsequently CFTO borrowed a reported $2.5m from ABC in return for which ABC took
three seats on the CFTO board and a share in the
station's profits.

The effect of the expansion of Canadian television distribution was, as Spry predicted, 'to
cream off the easiest advertising revenues in competition with the CBC in the major Canadian markets
with some 65% of the population.'[19] This resulted
in the squeezing of CBC's production budgets, with
the CBC having to compete with commercial broadcasters either by producing programming in Canada
and enduring revenues and profits squeezes or purchasing programming from US producers and filling
the schedules with cheap, attractive foreign product. The brief period in the 1950s in which - in
spite of expenditure on constructing a distribution
infrastructure - the CBC had been able to channel
substantial revenues into programme production in
Canada came to an end with the establishment of the

second network and the expansion of distribution
capacity, the fragmentation of audiences and the
disaggregation of revenues that had financed *Les
Plouffes* and the television dramas sold to the BBC.
In order to protect the Canadian production industry,
and even more importantly, national, cultural, political and ideological ends, the BBG promulgated the
first 'Canadian content' regulations, attempting to
inhibit by regulation the tendency, which it had
fostered by the licensing of an expanded television
distribution system, to secure television programming from the US rather than Canadian sources. The
first Canadian content requirements of the BBG were
for a minimum of 45% rising by April 1962 to a minimum of 55% home-produced content. The long story of
negotiation between a regulator charged with maintaining a Canadian element in Canadian broadcasting
and a commercial television industry with strong
financial incentives to minimise the exposure of its
audiences to Canadian programming had begun. The
structural processes that the BBG had initiated with
the licensing of second stations and the CTV network
were, in the coming decades, to be amplified by the
growth of cable distribution of broadcast television
in Canada and the consequential penetration of the
US networks into markets that the technology of
terrestrial broadcasting had not permitted them to
enter.

The customary retrospect of broadcasting historians on the BBG is to regard it as a classic
instance of a regulatory agency 'captured' by the
interests it was supposed to police. This view
though is one that proceeds from the axiom that
Canadian national interest and identity are dependent
on an effective policy of Canadian content and control in communications. Through that optic the era
of the BBG is one of a regulator complicit with a
group of traitors within the gates - the commercial
broadcasters - in constituting the Canadian broadcasting industry as a channel for the distribution
of US programming. This analysis of the commercial
broadcasting interest and its regulatory lapdog as
comprador capitalists profiting from the delivery of
their compatriots' attention and identity to foreign
interests is open to a number of challenges. For
instance, it could be argued that Canadian national
interest and identity are not vitally dependent on
communication policy - Canada and Canadian nationalism have survived in robust health in spite of the
substantial non-Canadian presence and interest in
the Canadian broadcasting system since 1919. Indeed

Canadian communication policy may be seen from a standpoint different to that of the customary cultural nationalist one as having consistently commanded the assent of Canadians for a broadcasting system based on the profit motive and the importation of programming for consumption by Canadians at substantially less than the economic cost of production. In other words, the policy has been one of consumers and distributor enjoying an abundant supply of information goods free of the task of paying an economic price for them.

Hull rather argues that the BBG mediated relatively successfully between the interests of commercial broadcasters and those of the national interest and that deficiencies in its stewardship stemmed from inadequacies in the Broadcasting Act of 1958 and the lack of ministerial concern with communications issues, rather than from the BBG itself.[20] Moreover, the promulgation of Canadian content regulations, even though softened by the BBG under pressure from commercial broadcasters, was definitely not in the interests of the commercial television and radio industry. The controversial nature of the regime of the Board of Broadcast Governors is due to the board presiding over, and in part promoting, a crucial divide in Canadian broadcasting. The shift was from a national system dominated by the CBC to a system where commercial interests - at first the commercial broadcasters, but latterly and increasingly the cable industry - achieved dominance in Canadian broadcasting as, essentially, distribution conduits for American programming checked only by the modest inhibitions enjoined by the regulator. That such a fundamental shift had taken place was recognised by the appointment of Robert Fowler (who had chaired the Royal Commission of 1955-7) to head an advisory committee on broadcasting in 1964. The second Fowler report urged - in a somewhat Utopian fashion - that government define clearly its intentions for broadcasting and create effective instruments for the promulgation of its policies: 'In the past Parliament has not stated the goals and purposes for the Canadian broadcasting system with sufficient clarity and precision, and this has been more responsible than anything else for the confusion in the system and the continuing dissatisfaction which has led to an endless series of investigations of it.'[21] The twin thrusts of Fowler's recommendations identified by Ellis - clear policy objectives and regulatory restructuring - were taken into the government's 1966 Broadcasting White Paper and the 1968 Act.

The 1968 Act is clearly based on the assumption that Canadian identity and nationhood are dependent on the Canadianness of its communication systems. The Minister's statement introducing the Bill in Parliament included the following passage:

> The most important of these principles is surely that which established that the air waves, which must be shared between public and private broadcasters, are public property and that they constitute a single broadcasting system. It is impossible to exaggerate the importance of broadcasting as a means of preserving and strengthening the cultural, social, political and economic fabric of Canada.[22]

A new regulatory agency was created to enforce the goals enjoined on broadcasters by the 1968 Act - the CRTC, Canadian Radio Television Commission (later the Canadian Radio-Television and Telecommunications Commission), which replaced the BBG. In setting out a broadcasting policy for Canada and by creating the CRTC, the 1968 Act fulfilled the recommendations of Fowler, but broadcasting in Canada and in particular the relations of the new regulator with its clients have been no less troubled post-68 than they were previously. For the Act, reflecting the minister's analysis and intention, was based on the fallacious theology of a single broadcasting system - the view that Canadian national integrity necessitates a Canadian communication system and that regulation and legislation can prescribe and control the forms of Canadian communication development. Fortunately or unfortunately, communications in Canada have been extremely hard for government to control because of Canada's proximity to the United States and its ability readily to import communication goods, coupled with the rapid development of communication technologies unforeseen by legislators. The 1968 Act for instance does not consider a technology that had been in place in Canada for sixteen years - cable television - let alone those developments, like broadcasting satellites, which are now exercising the minds of Canadian policy makers.

CABLE TELEVISION

Cable television in Canada developed as a system for the distribution of broadcast television signals from the United States to subscribers unable to

214

receive these signals over the air with a domestic
receiving aerial. There are markets in which local
topography precludes reception of any television
signals (including Canadian) with a domestic receiving aerial, but the most important reason for
the general penetration of cable distribution in
Canada is its delivery of foreign signals. The
countries that vie with Canada for the status of
being the most extensively cabled in the world (the
small countries of Europe: Belgium, the Netherlands,
Swizerland) share a common experience: a small population relative to neighbouring countries with a
common language, which means that domestic broadcasters have low revenues for programme production
compared to those enjoyed by the neighbouring broadcaster. Thus CBC, supported from the state budget
and a share in the revenues from the sale of television advertising in Canada with a tenth of the
population of the neighbouring United States, has
much in common with the Dutch broadcasting authority
NOS neighbouring West Germany. Dutch and Canadian
viewers can, by subscribing to cable, enjoy television funded by revenues approximately ten times
larger than the domestic service. Thus, audiences
in the Netherlands for the German ARD and ZDF services are as high as those in Canada for the
American CBS and NBC.

The consumption of American television distributed by cable in Canada is a phenomenon in which
the three agents directly involved all benefit. The
subscriber for an average annual subscription of $64
receives signals that are usually unavailable over
the air (and may include Canadian signals in addition to the principal benefit of the American PBS,
CBS, NBC and ABC channels) and reception at least
equal and usually much superior to that available
over the air; the cable operator receives an annual
average rate of return of 24%, though Babe gives the
example of an operator enjoying returns in excess of
700% on equity[23]; and the originator of the signals
- the US network - though receiving nothing from the
cable operator (who therefore gets the major product
sold gratis) enjoys larger audiences which may be
sold to advertisers. In the case of PBS (Public
Broadcasting Service) the American broadcaster benefits from Canadian donations (United States PBS
stations received via cable in Nova Scotia and
Alberta draw over 40% of their financial support
from Canadian donors). This is not surprising,
given that PBS reception extends viewer choice more
than proportionally: 'In Toronto, one PBS station

215

adds more to viewer choice than four US commercial stations. Not surprisingly, the effect of cable on the average number of options is greatest where cable introduces a PBS station to a market, such as Halifax or Calgary, that has a limited number of stations available over the air.'[24]

Given then that cable offers such benefits, why is it frequently identified in Europe and Canada as a major problem? Many regard trans-border flows of television programming as a kind of pollution of the airwaves - an involuntary and unwelcome import like acid rain. For any provision of new services, and hence any extension of choice, fragments the audience and diminishes the revenue base for existing services. Thus revenues available for production and programming tend to decline unless either more television is consumed (and viewing hours tend to be fairly inelastic - even in a Canadian winter only so much time can be devoted to television viewing, with Canadians already watching an average of 23 hours per week)[25] or premium rates are paid as in the renting of cassettes or videodiscs or for pay television. This rationale lies behind the licensing of pay television in Canada in 1982. Given this general tendency for revenues accruing to each station to decline with additional services, broadcasters are compelled to procure their programming from sources that provide the highest appeal to viewers at the lowest costs - in most cases from United States producers.

The major US broadcasters enjoy the largest domestic market in the world (ten times that of the Canadian market) and one that is remarkably chauvinistic in its interests and resistant to penetration by foreign production. Thus US producers are able to amortise high production costs fully in their domestic market and treat export markets as a source of jam for the bread, selling high quality and high production values programming at dumping prices into non-US markets. Canada has long been the most important export market for US film. American producers of television programmes continue to be able to sell at dumping prices undercutting Canadian producers (though because of competition amongst Canadian purchasers, the prices paid by Canadian broadcasters - while much lower than the cost of comparable home-produced programming - is high in comparison to the prices paid by British or West German broadcasters).

The typical programme imported from the US by

the Canadian networks during the 1974/75 season
(and the situation has not changed since[26])
could be purchased for about $2000 per half
hour, although the cost to the US producer
would be about $125,000. With a much smaller
market the Canadian producer spends about
$30,000 on a similar type of programme. It is
scarcely surprising that Canadian viewers regard a programme costing $30,000 to produce as
inferior to one costing $125,000. When two
specific programmes of the same type are compared, we find examples such as *Excuse my
French*, a Canadian situation comedy, with an
estimated revenue of $16,000 and production
costs of $30,000 per episode and *M*A*S*H* which
brought in an estimated revenue of $24,000 for
a purchase cost per episode of about $2,000.[27]

McFadyen, Hoskins and Gillen also point out that:
'An extra hour a day of prime time Canadian programming adds $4.4 million to $6.8 million to a television station's expenditure. As their expenses on
average are $5.6 million a year, this represents
about a doubling of their financial outlay. It is
scarcely surprising that Canadian television broadcasters are reluctant to invest in Canadian programming.'[28]
     Cable television then has expanded the distri-
bution capacity of the Canadian television industry,
fragmented audiences and the revenue base of
Canadian broadcasters and amplified the long term
structural imbalance between US and Canadian broadcasting. In 1977, 62.35% of Anglophone Canada had
access to four *US* television channels, while only
45.61% of Anglophone Canada had access to 4 *Canadian*
television channels.[29] Broadcasting interests -
whether CBC or commercial broadcasters - have custo-
marily deplored this state of affairs. The Canadian
Association of Broadcasters (CAB), the trade association of commercial broadcasters, stated: 'The
critical source of funding for commercial broadcast
programmes depends on advertising revenue and the
generation of this revenue is seriously affected by
growing numbers of alternative viewing opportunities,
notably those represented by US stations and other
programming services carried by cable.'[30]
     The CAB's protests and its playing the nationa-
list cause are more than slightly disingenuous, for
the commercial broadcasters are themselves major
carriers of US programming. A variety of regulations - the deletion of commercials on US signals

carried by cable, the passing of bill C58 removing
tax deductible benefits for Canadian corporations
advertising on US stations and the simultaneous substitution policy whereby when a programme is scheduled by both Canadian and US stations a cable
operator is required to substitute the Canadian for
the US signal - have been promulgated to protect the
revenues from the sale of advertising accruing to
Canadian broadcasters.

Canada has, as the Minister of Communications
Francis Fox said in *Towards a New National Broadcasting Policy:*

> The finest technical infrastructure for broad-
> casting in the world. Canada also has the
> world's most advanced system of domestic com-
> munications satellites which is employed to
> distribute radio and television programming.
> Satellite, microwave and cable technologies
> have made possible major achievements in exten-
> ding broadcasting services in both official
> languages to all but a small minority of
> Canadians.

More debatably he argued,

> And this elaborate technical infrastructure,
> which on a per capita basis is more extensive
> than that of any country in the world, is
> effectively owned and controlled by Canadians.[31]

This distribution system has been created by the
two interests operating in the supposedly single,
national system. The public sector - notably CBC,
but in recent years a number of the provinces as
well (principally Ontario and Quebec but also
Alberta, Saskatchewan and British Columbia) - has
created a transmission and distribution system for
the pursuit of public service and Canadian (or
Quebec) goals. The private sector, whether the commercial broadcasters or the cable industry, have
created subject to the market and regulation by the
CBC, BBG or CRTC their transmission and distribution
system for profit generated largely by the delivery
of American production - the US networks by the
cable operators and US programming by the commercial
broadcasters. American and other foreign, principally British, programming is by no means absent
from public sector stations, whether CBC owned and
operated, CBC affiliates or run by the provinces
(the latter are nominally educational but increas-

ingly, particularly TV Ontario and Radio Quebec,
provide a genuine alternative service). The public
sector, however, exists for the achievement of goals
unattainable by scheduling exclusively foreign programming, whereas the goals of the private sector
could best be met by scheduling entirely programming
produced outside Canada.

The Federal Cultural Policy Review Committee
(the Applebaum Hebert or Applebert report) argues
that broadcasting policy is the most developed expression of a pervasive Canadian condition:

> Cultural policy has not been entirely success-
> ful in encouraging the best use of the human
> creative resources Canada has in abundance. As
> a democratic and cosmopolitan country we have
> thrown open our borders to foreign cultural
> products and not given ourselves sufficient
> opportunity to enjoy the fruits of our own cul-
> tural labour. It is a telling state of affairs
> that our broadcasting system boasts the most
> sophisticated transmission hardware in the
> world - satellites, interactive cable, teletext
> - while Canadian viewers spend 80% of their
> viewing time watching foreign programmes on
> television. Broadcasting may provide the most
> striking illustration of this point, but it is
> by no means the only one. Our response to this
> dilemma is not, however, to come down on the
> side of protectionism, but rather to press home
> the point as forcefully as we can that federal
> cultural policy has largely favoured physical
> plant and organisational development over
> artistic creativity and achievement.[32]

The CRTC (see Table 6.1) established the extent
to which Canadian broadcasters offered Canadian viewers Canadian programming in the 8-10.00 pm prime
time period during 1978-79.[33] The Francophone and
Anglophone services of the CBC/Radio Canada led the
field, followed by a rather unrepresentative Toronto
independent station CITY (in Calgary, Edmonton, Winnipeg and Vancouver independent TV stations' Canadian
prime varied between 22.8% and 28.5%), then came the
Francophone commercial network, the two main non-CTV
commercial broadcasters in Southern Ontario (the
premium Anglophone market) and finally the major
Anglophone commercial broadcaster, the CTV network.

In 1981 the then President of the CBC, Al
Johnson, assessed the availability and consumption
of foreign and Canadian television programmes in

different categories (see Tables 6.2 and 6.3). [34]

Table 6.1: Percentage of Canadian Produced Content in Peak Time Programming for 1978-79.

Radio Canada	71.4
CBC	68.5
CITY	40.0
TVA	28.5
Global	22.8
CHCH Hamilton	22.8
CTV	5.7

Table 6.2: *Anglophone television:* Percentage of Broadcast Time and Viewing Time for Various Types of Canadian/foreign programming 1979-80.

Broadcasting Time			Viewing Time	
Canadian	Foreign		Canadian	Foreign
33	67	All programmes	26	74
62	38	News	89	11
67	33	Public Affairs	71	29
60	40	Sports	79	21
4	96	Drama	3	97
31	69	Variety/Music/Quiz	20	80

Overall there is a tendency for Anglophone Canadians to prefer foreign programming, but in certain areas - news, public affairs and sport - there is a tendency to prefer Canadian production. For drama, music and variety, which tend to have high production budgets and are the most watched programmes in the schedules, foreign programmes are preferred. For Francophones the situation is different. Here we find a much more marked tendency for Francophones to prefer Canadian productions, though Table 6.3 is misleading in that it does not consider Francophone viewers' consumption of Anglophone programmes. The degree of cultural self-consciousness and perception of unity among Canadian Francophones

Table 6.3: *Francophone television:* Percentage of Broadcast Time and Viewing Time for Various Types of Canadian/Foreign Programming 1979-80.

| Broadcasting Time | | | Viewing Time | |
Canadian	Foreign		Canadian	Foreign
64	36	All programmes	62	38
100	0	News	100	0
97	3	Public Affairs	98	2
89	11	Sports	96	4
12	88	Drama	20	80
78	22	Variety/Music/ Quiz	82	18

is clearly a decisive difference. In 1974 the then head of the French services division of CBC/Radio Canada said:

> Before television we had no medium of expres-
> sion that was truly our own; we had almost no
> movies, no theatre, no balladeers, we were
> always trailing others. Then practically over-
> night, television gave us all that. Here, one
> could apply to television what journalist Andre
> Laurendau said of the situational comedy *Ti-Coq:*
> "A nation used to the fact that the stories
> told are always happening 'elsewhere' and al-
> ways involving 'foreigners' has now recognised
> itself in television with immense pleasure,"
> and "in that sense there is no doubt that tele-
> vision has been an essential factor in helping
> French Canada to identify and define
> itself." [35]

The principal strategy for the achievement of the ends of the 1968 Broadcasting Act - 'to safe-guard, enrich and strengthen the cultural, political, social and economic fabric of Canada' through the notionally 'single system' - is the Canadian content regulations of the CRTC. Other potential powers, such as the granting and withdrawal of licences, have not been much used, though the CRTC, in an in-novatory decision of potentially enormous importance in 1979, renewed the network licence for the CTV commercial, national, Anglophone network on the con-dition that it scheduled 26 hours of original

Canadian drama in 1981-82. This decision of the
CRTC, the subject of appeal by the CTV through the
courts, was vindicated as an implementation of
Section 3 of the 1968 Broadcasting Act by the Supreme Court in 1982.
    Canadian content regulations were introduced by
the BBG in 1959 and changes are currently being proposed by the CRTC. The regulations now provide that
60% of all programming broadcast on television be
Canadian and that betwen 6 p.m. and midnight, the
main viewing hours, 60% of CBC and 50% of private
broadcasters' programming be Canadian. Canadian
content is broadly defined: co-productions with
Commonwealth or Francophone countries qualify as
Canadian if 30% of the budget is spent in Canada or
on Canadian participation, while other co-productions qualify if 50% is spent on qualifying expenditure (these percentages have varied at different
periods of Canadian content regulations). Programmes of 'general interest to Canadians' qualify
as Canadian content, including the world series and
the United States President's State of the Union
message. An off-the-record unattributable and possibly apocryphal story told to the author by a
Canadian broadcaster in 1981 concerned another broadcaster who fulfilled Canadian content requirements
by training a camera on an aquarium of swimming fish
- Canadian fish and so Canadian content!
    There is also some evidence to suggest that the
regulations are not observed (intuitively this seems
likely in a system so large and difficult to police
with such high incentives for evasion of the regulations). For example, in 1981-82 the CRTC charged
four of the 1,229 television broadcasters in Canada
with violation of the content regulations. One was
found not guilty by a provincial judge, another had
the charge dismissed on a technicality and the CRTC
dropped the other two charges. However, the problem the regulations were designed to meet and that
'Applebert' identifies as persistent is clearly in
evidence.
    In January 1983 the CRTC published a policy
statement of its intentions for Canadian content in
television. The CRTC notes that CBC exceeds its
Canadian content requirements and intends to raise
its Canadian content to 80%. But there has been:

    An unacceptable decline in the amount of
    Canadian programming scheduled by a number of
    private television broadcasters serving major
    markets during the hours of heavy viewing be-

between 7.30 - 10.30 pm. In addition there is
an under-representation of some forms of programming particularly in the areas of entertainment and children's programming. Canadian
dramatic productions are virtually non-existent
on private English language television, which
is dominated by foreign entertainment programs
and this is particularly the case during the
mid-evening hours. Drama currently accounts
for 49% of all viewing time on English language
television and 66% of the viewing time between
7.30 pm and 10.30 pm. However only 5% of drama
scheduled is Canadian produced, and Canadian
drama represents only 2% of the total time
spent by Canadians viewing dramatic productions.[36]

To meet these problems (which are much less
marked for Francophone television than for Anglophone) the CRTC proposed to introduce a points system which would give 'weighted points for the contribution of actors, singers and other performers' and
'take into account the various contributions of the
production team, from the producer and editor to the
set designer and camera operator.'[37] It is also considering introducing a 35% quota for the mid-evening
hours, changing the annual period over which Canadian content is assessed to two semi-annual periods
(to avoid the practice of filling the low viewing
summer months with Canadian programmes and filling
the high viewing winter months with foreign production) and to give a 50% Canadian Content credit to
programmes made outside Canada and not in French,
English, Inuktitut or Canadian Indian languages
which are then dubbed or lip synchronised in Canada.

A minor, but in the current circumstances of
vigorous promotion of cable television in Britain,
much hyped stimulus to production in Canada is the
CRTC requirement that one channel of a cable system
and 8% of its expenditure be devoted to community
programming. The CRTC established that two thirds
of all programming fell into the 'locally originated
automated programming category' (e.g. airport arri-
vals and departures, weather reports, etc.) and one
quarter 'community video/audio programming'[38] and
that a declining portion of productions were 'hands
on' community made productions.[39] No figures were
offered for audiences for community programmes
(popular lore has it that they are so small as to be
unmeasurable), but the CRTC estimates that 20,000
individuals (i.e. less than 0.1% of the population

of Canada) were involved in 'accessing the community channel' as producers.[40]

SATELLITE BROADCASTING

In the early 1970s the government of Canada created Telesat Canada. Owned by the government and the principal telecommunications carriers of Canada, Telesat operates the domestic communication satellite system of Canada which is used *inter alia*, for the distribution of television signals across Canada by CBC for re-broadcasting by terrestrial transmitters. In 1981 the CRTC licensed Canadian Satellite Communications (CANCOM) to provide a satellite to home television and radio distribution systems. The licensing of CANCOM was influenced by three principal factors: the desire to stimulate the communications satellite industry in Canada for reasons of industrial policy; the existence of an estimated 800,000 homes that can only be adequately provided with television services by DBS (Direct Broadcasting Satellites) because they are in small communities, isolated farms or in remote areas[41]; and the perceived need for a Canadian service to compete with the unauthorised reception of US satellite 'superstation' programmes. This reception of US satellite signals has become extremely common in Canada even when strictly illegal. Bars, hotels and motels in urban areas attract clients on the basis of offering viewing of US satellite signals, principally from the Satcom 1 satellite.

CANCOM was licensed to deliver four Canadian television signals (3 Anglophone and 1 Francophone) and eight radio signals (2 native language, 2 French and 4 English); but in 1983 the CRTC licensed CANCOM to add the 3 + 1 package to its services (3 + 1 is the United States CBS, NBC, ABC networks and PBS). The CRTC's rationale for this decision was that licensing CANCOM to deliver US television signals (the principal market being cable operators hitherto unable to offer them due to the high cost of terrestrial microwave transport of the signals) would enable CANCOM to keep the cost of its Canadian services low. Essentially CANCOM has been licensed as a 'cable in the sky' system with a potential franchise of 800,000 subscribers delivering both Canadian and US signals to subscribers. The major difference is that some markets served by CANCOM may have already been consuming US production but were unable to receive Canadian television. Yet the net effect of the 1981 and 1983 CANCOM decisions seems

to have been to deliver US television to Canadians
who have hitherto been unable to receive it and to
expose Canadian broadcasters and programme makers to
sharpened foreign competition. As Lyman points out:

> The outcome of major technological evolution
> can be a negative one for Canada's cultural in-
> dustries. Too much emphasis on technology and
> the implementation of new delivery infrastruc-
> tures may direct investment away from program-
> ming, i.e. investment in Canadian production.
> A specific example is the licensing of the
> Atlantic regional pay-TV network whose poten-
> tial subscriber base is so small that the CRTC
> imposed as a condition of licence a very low
> proportional commitment to Canadian programming
> (15% of gross revenues as opposed to 50% for
> the Ontario regional license holder).[42]

Just as radio, television and cable offered distribution technologies that enabled new markets to be
served with cultural goods and created market relationships that favoured non-Canadian producers of
those goods, so too are broadcasting satellites. The
Canadian state has invested heavily in satellite
production and development and has a technology that
may potentially lower broadcasting distribution
costs dramatically, but it seems likely that the
cultural goods that will circulate through the new
low cost distribution systems will not be principally Canadian. In his presentation to the CRTC
seeking approval (in the event denied) for a second
CBC national television channel, CBC 2 - Télé 2, Al
Johnson talked of the large economies available from
the new distribution technologies: 'We propose ...
to use the new mode of distribution - by satellite
to cable. Not, by the way, simply because this is
the new technological mode, but because the construction of parallel conventional distribution
systems would cost over $80 million while satellite
to cable distribution costs only $3.5 million per
year.'[43]
The economies of the new distribution technology are evident enough. However, they are not
being applied to existing services, but rather to
make possible additional services. The CRTC's '3 +
1' decision recognises that by now a necessary condition of delivering Canadian signals to Canadians
(in the absence of public funding further to the
$477 million of the Federal budget for CBC, the $20
million for TV Ontario, $36 million for Radio Quebec

and the more modest funding for provincial broadcasting in Alberta, British Columbia and Saskatchewan) is the supply of American signals. Audiences
will pay for US services, but are less ready to pay
for their Canadian equivalent.

PAY TELEVISION

The Pay TV licensing decision of the CRTC in 1982,
referred to by Lyman above, is one that institutes a
system for delivering cultural goods to consumers by
completely eschewing the broadcasting distribution
system which has been dominant in radio and television in Canada since 1919. Similarly it institu-
tionalises a wholly new kind of financial relationship between consumers and distributors of cultural
goods. Pay TV is available only to cable subscribers (though actually and potentially there is a
very high penetration of cable in Canadian markets).
In 1981 4,593,015 households were cable subscribers
out of a total of 6,190,560 households wired in
franchised areas covering 6,600,375 households.[44]
Unlike broadcast radio and television, reception of
which incurs no direct costs after purchase of the
receiving apparatus, the Pay TV system delivers
programmes only to those who pay a separate subscription. Pay TV was licensed: (a) to contribute
to the realisation of the objectives set out in the
Broadcasting Act and to strengthen the Canadian
broadcasting system; (b) to increase the diversity
of programming available to Canadians; and (c) to
make available high quality Canadian programming
from new programming sources by providing new opportunities and revenue sources for Canadian producers
currently unable to gain access to the broadcasting
system.[45]
    To achieve these goals the CRTC licensed a
'national general interest service' *First Choice
Canadian Communications Corporation* in French and
English; 'regional general interest services' in
Alberta *(Alberta Independent Pay Television)*,
Ontario *(Ontario Independent Pay Television)* and the
Atlantic Region *(Star Channel Services)*; a 'speciality' (performing arts) service, the *Lively Arts
Market Building* (LAMB), for national distribution
from Toronto; and a regional multilingual service,
World View Television, for British Columbia.
    The CRTC's decision has attracted hostile
comment - both at the time of its delivery and subsequently in the light of the activities of the
successful licensees. Much of the initial adverse

comment was directed at the Commission's reversal of
its conclusion in its Report on Pay Television that
a single national pay television network be established.[46] The judgement of the report and of commentators (see *inter alios* Audley[47], Woodrow and
Woodside[48] and the minority opinion of CRTC Commissioners Gagnon and Grace[49]) is that too many birds
have been launched and that a plurality of pay services will fragment audiences and revenues, bid up
the costs of programming (again largely emanating
from the United States), siphon programming from
broadcast television to Pay TV and prefer audiences
in some regions of Canada at the expense of others.
Lyman succinctly expresses the central proposition
of the critics:

> The fundamental flaw in the CRTC's licensing
> scenario lies in the incomplete economic equa-
> tion that seems to lie behind it. While the
> objectives are laudable in terms of support of
> Canadian programming ... it will prove almost
> impossible for Pay TV operators both to live up
> to the conditions of licence and to stimulate
> competitive Canadian programming - unless
> either the national or regional licence-holder
> drives the other out of the market in a parti-
> cular geographic area. It appears that pay-TV
> in Canada will continue the tradition of broad-
> casting as a conduit for American entertainment
> programming.[50]

Experience supports the critic's judgement and
not that of the CRTC. For example, the arts channel
went into receivership in June 1983. The Alberta
and Ontario regional pay systems now operate under a
common title, *Superchannel*, offering competition to
the supposedly national system in two crucial Anglophone markets. In the other major Anglophone market,
British Columbia, *First Choice's* competition is not
so fierce, but *World View* is permitted to offer 40%
of its total scheduling time and of prime time in
English. There seems no reason to suppose that
World View will be less successful than the commercial broadcasters in fulfilling the CRTC's requirements while still maximising audiences and revenues
on US programming. *First Choice* is required to
offer national distribution of Anglophone and Francophone programming. West of Winnipeg it is reported
to have subscribers to its Francophone services
measured in double figures, the revenues from whom
are trifling when set against the costs of satellite

transponders for ensuring national availability of
Francophone programming. In licensing Pay TV operations the CRTC recognised the differences in the
licencees' abilities to programme Canadian content
whilst maintaining economic viability. Accordingly
the Atlantic region licensee, *Star Channel*, was required to commit only 15% of gross revenues to
Canadian content, while the Ontario licensee, *Ontario
Independent Pay Television*, was required to commit
50%. *First Choice* was required to commit not less
than 45% of total revenues to Canadian programmes
and is partially fulfilling that requirement by co-
producing in Canada with Playboy Enterprises' Canadian 'adult' (i.e. pornographic) programmes – *First
Choice* promotes itself as the 'Playboy Channel.' The
development is logical enough, since only porno-
graphy can command sufficient revenues from the
fragmented Canadian audience to make Canadian programming economically viable for *First Choice*. Pay
TV, no less than the development of a plurality of
Canadian broadcast television channels or the importation and distribution of US television signals by
cable or satellite, fragments the potential audience
and lowers the revenue base for programming. It exemplifies the persistence of the condition of 'Tech-
nopia Canadensis' diagnosed by the ex-Minister of
Communications, David MacDonald: 'A condition of intense focus on hardware and new technologies causing
an inability to see long range effects.'[51]

CONCLUSION

The most recent developments in the Canadian broadcasting system, CANCOM and Pay TV, will exemplify
MacDonald's diagnosis. It is clear that there is a
continuing contradiction between the aspirations defined by the Canadian state in legislation for
Canada and its broadcasting system on the one hand
and those of the Canadians who (outside the public
sector) own and operate the broadcasting system on
the other. The CRTC, charged by the Federal government with the responsibility of creating a broadcasting system that serves the national objectives
prescribed in the Broadcasting Act, sets out in the
Pay TV Decision an explicit set of objectives for
Pay TV. However, the system that the CRTC sanc-
tions by its licenses cannot realise those objectives nor, given that its role is reactive and regulatory, can the CRTC set in place a Pay TV or broadcasting order which could realise the objectives of
the 1968 Broadcasting Act and Decision 82 – 240. The

broadcasting system has overexpanded its distribution capacity, reducing the revenues per hour available for programming finance and necessitating the purchase of production from sources offering the highest audience gratification for the lowest cost.

Each new technological initiative accelerates the spiral of decline by sucking in more and more foreign production and thereby making the conditions of existence of Canadian production harder and harder to achieve. However, it has to be recognised that this process has been remarkably consistent; perhaps it is what Canadians want. Certainly there is no evidence that suggests a regime necessary to achieve the aims of the Broadcasting Act would enjoy popular support. Such a regime would involve reducing the number of signals available to Canadians, ceasing the importation of US signals and the purchase of US programming, directing the revenues generated in the broadcasting system into production not shareholders' pockets and increasing the allocations from the public purse for broadcasting. Of the measures in the latest Canadian Federal policy statement in *Towards a New National Broadcasting Policy*, only increased allocations from the state budget is proposed. The other measures are directed towards stimulating the hardware industries and removing restrictions on programme reception. Probably no more could be done - the structural inhibitions to establishing a *Canadian* broadcasting system in Canada are by now too strong. All that can be done is to recognise that the notion of a single national system is an antique fiction and to continue support for the public sector and those parts of the private sector that can be recruited or coerced into serving the laudable ends of the 1968 Broadcasting Act.

At the same time, although one may recognise that hegemony in its own national culture and communications system is a legitimate political goal for any state, there is no evidence offered by the case of Canada that loss of national cohesion and identity attends the absence of that hegemony. From outside the dominant, Innis-inspired Canadian approach, the history of broadcasting in Canada can be seen very plausibly as evidence that national sovereignty, indeed nationhood itself, is not dependent on a distinctive national orientation in the communication system. Canadian broadcasting may effectively be American, but Canada is not thereby a part of the United States. 'Notland' is still somewhere.

References

1. A. Wilden, *The Imaginary Canadian*, Vancouver, 1980.
2. 1968 Broadcasting Act, Section 3.
3. H. Schiller, *Mass Communications and American Empire*, New York, 1969.
4. J. Tunstall, *The Media are American*, London, 1977.
5. A. Smith, *The Geopolitics of Information: How Western Culture Dominates the World*, London, 1980.
6. F. Peers, *The Politics of Canadian Broadcasting 1920-51*, Toronto, 1969, p.6.
7. D. Ellis, *Evolution of the Canadian Broadcasting System*, Hull, 1979, p.2.
8. Elton Johnson, October 15 1924, quoted in Peers, *The Politics of Canadian Broadcasting 1920-51*, p.20.
9. C. Bowman, articles in the *Ottawa Citizen*, December 27-31 1929, quoted in Peers, *The Politics of Canadian Broadcasting 1920-51*, pp.53-54.
10. Ellis, *Evolution of the Canadian Broadcasting System*, p.10.
11. House of Commons debate, May 18 1932, quoted in Ellis, *Evolution of the Canadian Broadcasting System*, p.8.
12. Peers, *The Politics of Canadian Broadcasting 1920-51*, p.65.
13. 1968 Broadcasting Act, Section 3.
14. Massey Report, p.283, quoted in Ellis, *Evolution of the Canadian Broadcasting System*, p.31.
15. F. Peers, *The Public eye: television and the politics of Canadian broadcasting 1952-68*, Toronto, 1979, p.10.
16. Ellis, *Evolution of the Canadian Broadcasting System*, p.35.
17. Peers, *The public eye*, p.54.
18. *Time*, April 11 1960, quoted in Peers, *The public eye*, p.230.
19. Peers, *The public eye*, p.239.
20. W. Hull, 'Captive or victim? The Board of Broadcast Governors and Bernstein's Law 1958-68', paper presented to the annual meeting of the Canadian Political Science Association, June 1983.
21. Ellis, *Evolution of the Canadian Broadcasting System*, p.60.
22. House of Commons debate, October 17 1967, quoted in Ellis, *Evolution of the Canadian Broadcasting System*, p.69.
23. S. McFadyen, C. Hoskins and D. Gillen,

Canadian Broadcasting: Market Structure and Economic Performance, Montreal, 1980, p.242; R. Babe, *Canadian Television Broadcasting: Structure, Performance and Regulation*, Hull, 1979, p.128.
    24. McFadyen, Hoskins and Gillen, *Canadian Broadcasting*, p.214.
    25. Canadian Broadcasting Corporation, CB2/Télé 2, 'A proposal for national non-commercial satellite delivered CBC television services', 1980, p.7.
    26. Department of Communications, 'Towards a New National Broadcasting Policy', Ottawa, 1983.
    27. CRTC background paper, 'The economics of Canadian television production', Ottawa, 1976, quoted in McFadyen, Hoskins and Gillen, *Canadian Broadcasting*, p.197.
    28. McFadyen, Hoskins and Gillen, *Canadian Broadcasting*, p.159.
    29. CRTC, 'Canadian Broadcasting and Telecommunications: past experience and future options', 1980, p.23.
    30. Canadian Association of Broadcasters, 'Brief to the Federal Cultural Policy Review Committee', 1981, p.49.
    31. Department of Communications, 'Towards a New National Broadcasting Policy', Ottawa, 1983.
    32. L. Applebaum and J. Hebert, *Report of the Federal Cultural Policy Review Committee*, Ottawa, 1982, p.6.
    33. CRTC, 'Canadian Broadcasting and Telecommunications: past experience and future options', 1980, p.23.
    34. A. Johnson, 'Canadian programming on television. Do Canadians want it?', Talk to the Broadcast Executives Society, February 1981, CBC mimeo.
    35. R. David, 'The role of the French network', CBC mimeo, undated.
    36. CRTC, 'Policy statement on Canadian content in television', 1983, pp.6-7.
    37. CRTC, 'Policy statement on Canadian content in television', p.14.
    38. CRTC, 'Survey of the community channel', 1979, p.4.
    39. CRTC, 'Survey of the community channel', p.38.
    40. CRTC, 'Survey of the community channel', p.29.
    41. A. Curran, 'Canada goes for the middle range in television satellites', *Intermedia*, vol.9 no.4, July, 1981.
    42. P. Lyman, *Canada's Video Revolution*, Toronto, 1983, p.95.

43. A. Johnson, 'CBC 2 and Télé 2', CBC documents, Ottawa, 1981, p.5.
44. CRTC, 'Annual Report', Ottawa, 1982, p.61.
45. CRTC, 'Decision 82-240 Pay Television', March 1982, p.1.
46. CRTC, 'Report on Pay Television', March 1978.
47. P. Audley, *Canada's Cultural Industries*, Toronto, 1983.
48. R. Woodrow and K. Woodside, *The Introduction of Pay TV in Canada*, Montreal, 1982.
49. CRTC, 'Decision 82-240 Pay Television', March 1982.
50. P. Lyman, *Canada's Video Revolution*, p.79.
51. R. Woodrow and K. Woodside, *The Introduction of Pay TV in Canada*, p.161.

The author wishes to acknowledge his particular debt to the work of Ellis and Peers in the writing of this chapter.

Chapter Seven

AUSTRALIA: BROADCASTING IN THE POLITICAL BATTLE

Richard Harding

The Australian Constitution confers a wide range of
enumerated powers upon the central (Commonwealth)
government. One such power (section 51v) is to
'make laws ... with respect to ... postal, telegra-
phic, telephonic and other like services'. This
power is supplemented by the incidental power (section 51 xxxix) - to legislate with respect to
'matters incidental to the execution of any power
vested by the Constitution in the Parliament...' In
drafting this clause, the Founding Fathers could
hardly have had television, cable, satellite broadcasting, teletext, videotex and so on in mind. Even
'steam radio' was barely imaginable in 1900. Thus a
primary issue in seeking to understand the development of Australian broadcasting and telecommunications is this: where does the law-making power, and
thus political responsibility and control, reside?
     The first case to confront this problem was
R. v. Brislan, ex parte Williams (54 Commonwealth
Law Reports 262). It reached the High Court in 1935,
twelve years after regular radio broadcasting had
begun in Australia. Mrs. Williams, a resident of a
depressed area of Sydney, had been discovered by
inspectors from the Postmaster-General (PMG) listening to a five-valve, all-electric, wireless receiving set connected to an indoor aerial. She was
tuned to a 'B Class' (commercial) broadcaster. Under
the Wireless Telegraphy Act (a Commonwealth Statute)
such transmissions could only lawfully be received
by persons holding a current wireless listener's
licence. Mrs. Williams had no such licence. Her
prosecution became a test case in which the crucial
question was the extent of Commonwealth legislative
power over broadcasting.
     The High Court held that the Act was a valid
exercise of the power conferred by section 51v of

the Constitution. In doing so, it rejected two
propositions of immense potential significance to
the future development of Australian broadcasting
law. The first proposition was that, as the common
characteristic of posts, telegraphs and telephones
was *intercommunication at the behest of either party*,
wireless broadcasting being a one-way process (*at*
the listener) was not a 'like service'. Logically,
and in the context of the known technology of the
time, it was a strong argument. Had the High Court
been able to gaze into a technological crystal-ball,
they would of course have seen inter-communication
(talk-back radio, videotex) as a future component of
broadcasting. However, their reasons for rejecting
this argument were somewhat more mundane. One was
that, quite simply, radio broadcasting was a form of
telephony inasmuch as a special *receiver* was needed
for it to be effective: this factor, rather than the
potential for *inter*-communication, served to identify the class of activities covered by section 51v.
The other was the kind of reason beloved of lawyers
- that there was an available precedent of high
authority to follow. This was the Privy Council
case of *In Re Regulation and Control of Radio Communication in Canada*(1932) in which it had been
held that the word 'telegraphs' in section 92(10) of
the Canadian Constitution encompassed radio broadcasting and was thus within federal power. It is
interesting that at about the same time judicial decisions were allocating power over broadcasting to
the central governments in the two British Commonwealth nations with the greatest land-masses and the
most complex ethnic mix. Subconsciously, perhaps,
but unequivocally the way was being paved for broadcasting to become an instrument of national unification and identity.
   The second argument which was rejected was as
follows: that, in referring to 'services' the Constitution contemplated *publicly-provided* services.
This argument, if successful, would have fundamentally affected the balance that has subsequently
come into existence between broadcasting financed
directly from the public purse, namely the Australian Broadcasting Commission (ABC), and that financed through the private sector. However, this argument was unanimously rejected. Latham said (at 276-
7):

   It seems to me to be impossible to attach any
   definite meaning to section 51v short of that
   which gives full and complete power to Parlia-

ment to provide or to abstain from providing
the services mentioned, to provide them upon
such conditions of licences and payment as it
thinks proper or to permit other people to provide them, subject or not subject to conditions
or to prohibit the provision of such facilities
altogether.

This decision, then, cleared the Constitutional
decks. Broadcasting laws and regulations were exclusively a matter for Commonwealth (i.e. central)
legislation and administration. If this point needed
any underlining, this was done in 1965 (when the High
Court held that the Commonwealth had power to establish a corporation, viz. the ABC, and also the power
to regulate its programme-making facilities) and in
1966 (when it was held that the ownership and control provisions of the Broadcasting and Television
Act with regard to commercial broadcasting were
validly enacted). Each of these decisions drew upon
the incidental power as well as the principal Constitutional head.
    The political history of the development of
Australian broadcasting and telecommunications is
thus an aspect of Commonwealth political history.
This is not to deny, in a federation where Common-
wealth-State relations have historically been immensely important, State influence on Commonwealth
policies. But any such influence has necessarily
been indirect, peripheral and fortuitous.[1] In terms
of policy formulation and implementation, broadcasting in Australia has been a matter for central
government. It is at this level that the political
battle has been fought.

A HISTORY OF THE DEVELOPMENT OF AUSTRALIAN BROAD-
CASTING

Early experiments in broadcasting, between 1900 and
1905, culminated in the passage of the Wireless
Telegraphy Act. This vested control of wireless
broadcasting in the PMG; the main operational importance was navigational and the principal technology morse code. The First World War held back the
development of general broadcasting, though it en-
hanced security-related communications systems.
Indeed, administration of the Act temporarily passed
to the Naval Department. However, in 1920 in response to the first public demonstration of radio,
broadcasting control was reposed once more in the
PMG. In 1923 the first 'sealed set' system (one

where listeners paid a subscription to have their
sets sealed to a particular station) was introduced.
During that year, four sealed set stations were
established 2SB, 2FC, 3AR and 6WF. (The numeral pre-
fix indicates the State of operation in Australia.
New South Wales is 2; Victoria 3; Queensland 4;
South Australia 5; Western Australia 6; Tasmania 7;
and the Northern Territory 8).

However, the sealed set system was hardly designed to popularise broadcasting. After a year's
operation, the four stations had a total of only
1,400 licence-holders between them. Accordingly, in
1924 the government tried another approach, that of
the open set. Two classes of station were created
by regulations made under the Act: 'A Class', to be
financed predominantly from revenue collected by the
PMG for listeners' licences; and 'B Class' to be
financed from advertising, to which at this stage
there were no limitations.

This new scheme did the trick, with broadcasting and listeners alike responding enthusiastically.
Within two years, eight 'A Class' and twelve 'B
class' stations were on the air. Between 1924 and
1928 wireless was establishing itself as part of
everyday Australian life so that by 1928 approximately 270,000 householders held licences.[2] The
quality of the product seemed to be improving also;
indeed, in these early halcyon days there briefly
seemed to be a direct correlation between quality
and profitability, a factor which encouraged further
investment. However, enormous technical problems
had yet to be overcome. If broadcasting were seen
as a way of linking city to country and vice-versa,
it was not working out in practice.

Substantially for this reason and in recognition of the need to invest public money to serve the
public interest in those areas of broadcasting which
could not be relied upon to be profitable, the
Commonwealth government acquired during 1929-30 all
'A Class' licences. These were designated 'national'
and were to be operated by the PMG with programmes
supplied by the Australian Broadcasting Company.
The aim was to create new national stations in
country areas to receive this service. The Australian Broadcasting Company had been one of the most
successful of the commercial operators. Yet, paradoxically, this arrangement was to be the foundation
stone of the non-commercial Australian Broadcasting
Commission. Meanwhile, 'B Class' stations - now
designated 'commercial' - continued to be regulated
under the Wireless Telegraphy Act, with their

commercial position protected.

In 1932 the Australian Broadcasting Commission Act was passed, establishing a national publicly-funded, non-profit-making broadcasting organisation. Its stations were initially to be the former 'A Class' stations. Inglis describes the ABC, in its 1932 manifestation, as a 'thoroughly imperial artifact'. He continues:

> The government had decided, as the Postmaster-General told the House, "to follow the British system as closely as Australian conditions will permit". The British Broadcasting Corporation consisted of a Chairman, a Vice-Chairman and three others called "Governors" who appointed a Director-General, as the Australian Commissioners did a General Manager, and other staff. The Corporation got all its revenue from licence fees. It too could be instructed by the Postmaster-General to broadcast or not to broadcast items. There were differences. BBC Governors were paid much more than ABC Commissioners ... In Britain the Corporation, not the PMG, was responsible for its technical services, from studio to transmitter, as the Commission might have been had someone other than the head of the PMG drafted the Bill. One large undebated difference was that the BBC was founded by a charter, deriving its authority not from parliament but from the King-in-Council. The archaic instrument was chosen in order to put the broadcasters at a distance from parliament. There was no Act for Members of Parliament to invoke or amend, only the charter to be renewed, with or without alteration, whenever it ran out (initially, after ten years); and when members tried to ask parliamentary questions about the BBC, the Speaker nearly always stopped them. This device was inimitable: a Dominion government could no more create a corporation in the name of the Governor-General than it could have his jewellery protected by Beefeaters. There was one difference still greater. The BBC had the air of the kingdom to itself. The ABC had to induce listeners not only to get a receiver and switch it on, but to turn in to a "national" station rather than to any of its increasingly numerous and vigorous competitors.[3]

To Inglis' list should be added one further point - that from the outset the employment structure within the ABC was to mirror that of the public sector bureaucracy. Over the succeeding half-century, it would develop to a point where seniority outweighed merit in promotion, where the concept of tenure cemented into the organisation the idle and the incompetent, and where management could be circumscribed by the Public Service Arbitrator and overruled by various appellate procedures.[4] Curiously, even in 1983 when the ABC underwent its first ever major re-structuring, many of these features remained undisturbed, apparently sacrosanct.

Meanwhile, commercial broadcasting developed apace. Between 1929 and 1936 the number of stations grew from 12 to 73. In 1930 the first industry organisation - the Australian Federation of Commercial Broadcasting - was set up, forerunner of the very powerful lobby groups which came to have the ear of Liberal governments during the post-war period and in particular during the 1970s. In 1935 limitations were placed on the number and distribution of commercial stations which could be owned by a single company or individual. This seemed to be a strong manifestation of the value that Australian broadcasting should not only be a dual system, but also that the commercial part of that system should be diverse and pluralist. However, a more cynical view was that a private enterprise government wished to ensure that a greater number of its supporters could obtain a slice of what was becoming an increasingly profitable pie. In 1942, a new statute - the Australian Broadcasting Act - was passed to modernise the system of broadcasting control. This framework was completed in 1948 by the creation of the Australian Broadcasting Control Board, a regulatory body for commercial broadcasting. In its most important functions - granting, renewal or transfer of licences - its role was, however, merely an advisory one to the government of the day.

The ABC was also moving ahead. Not only had war-time emphasised the role of communications for bringing about national unity, but also censorship and propaganda (Radio Australia, the ABC's external service, had been set up in 1939) had highlighted the crucial value and need for an independent and comprehensive national information service. Accordingly, in 1946 the Australian Broadcasting Act (which also now provided the legislative framework for ABC affairs) was amended by the Chifley Labour government so as to *require* the Commission to employ its own news-gathering staff. This move, the culmination of a bitter struggle both with the newspaper proprietors (who feared that their own power and profits could be undermined) and within the ABC itself[5], has undoubtedly been vindicated by the passage of time.[6] In 1983, when the ABC was being restructured, it was surprising to find another Labour government prepared to water down this obligation somewhat.

The other major move which occurred in 1946 was the decision that Parliament should be broadcast. The ABC itself was the prime mover in this[7], an arrangement which has subsequently become a programmer's nightmare.[8] Nevertheless, it was an important symbol of the growing awareness that Australia as a nation should be presented to the population via the national broadcaster: broadcasting was seen as a useful tool for nation-building purposes.

In 1948 it was decided that the ABC should be funded by annual appropriation rather than directly from licence fees. The mechanics of funding have always been debated as if they are absolutely crucial to independence. The Annan Committee in Britain, for example, was uncompromising:

> ... the best way of financing the BBC is by continuing the licence fee. The only possible alternative is a direct grant from the Exchequer from taxation, and we reject this because we think it will undermine the BBC's independence.[9]

However, in Australia because of the vast areas to be serviced, the consequential need for immense capital investment and the operational inevitability of setting up 'mini-ABCs' in each State, licence-fee funding was already inadequate in 1948 and was certain to remain so. There was really no alternative, so the problem of undermined independence simply had to be coped with. Licence fees continued to be charged and collected until 1974, but they went into general revenue and were not specifically earmarked for the ABC.

The next major development was the introduction of television. In the early 1950s there was surprisingly little enthusiasm for this. Sir Robert Menzies - Churchillian in his vanities if in no other way - regarded television as an offensive gimmick, telling one interviewer that he hoped 'this thing will not come to Australia within my term of office.'[10] The newspaper proprietors, his natural allies, at this stage could only see it in terms of its threat to newspaper sales; though later they

were to reap unimagined profits from the new technology. Only the equipment manufacturers seemed
anxious to hasten its development.

However, as television spread through the developed nations and with the Melbourne Olympics drawing near, a favourable decision was inevitable. The
only real question - one mirrored a quarter of a
century later with regard to the domestic satellite
system and the development of radiated over-the-air
subscription television (RSTV) and cable television
(CTV) - was the balance to be struck between the
national and the commercial sectors. With the
Liberals in power, the commercial sector emerged
well on top - a fact vividly symbolised by the fact
that the very first public television transmission
in Australia was from a commercial station, owned
almost inevitably by a press baron.

In more detail, the pattern to be adopted was
that the ABC should have no more than one station in
each capital city and should have the primary
initial responsibility for covering the unprofitable
country areas, whereas there would be no less than
two commercial licences for each capital city. By
the 1970s this had become three in all mainland
capitals except Perth. This arrangement 'doomed the
ABC as a tastemaker'.[11] The contrast with the BBC's
position in the UK is, of course, obvious and sharp.

If we pause at this point in the narrative, the
two key themes which were henceforth to dominate
Australian broadcasting can now be identified: broadcasting as a means of influencing opinion and broadcasting as a highly lucrative business. Subsequently
they will intermingle so as to be, at times, virtually indistinguishable. Debates carried on in the
name of profits are not infrequently really about
power, and vice-versa. This will be particularly so
in the 1970s - a turbulent period of optimism
followed by disillusionment and deep political anger
in Australia.

Before coming to this, however, let us complete
the outward history of events. The important High
Court decisions of 1965 and 1966 have already been
referred to; they served to entrench the dual
(national/commercial) system of broadcasting which
had been developing for the previous forty years.
In 1970 the east-west microwave link was opened,
bringing Western Australia into modern telecommunications contact with the eastern and most populated
part of the continent. In 1974 the Whitlam Labour
government gave the go-ahead to FM broadcasting on
the VHF band; in 1975 ethnic broadcasting began; and

in the same year colour television transmission
started. These last three matters require fuller
exposition.

In opening up FM broadcasting, the Whitlam
government made not just a technological advance but
a conceptual breakthrough in the system of Australian broadcasting. This decision created a third
sector, public broadcasting, financed not directly
from the public purse nor from advertising revenue
but from the resources of community groups banding
together for this purpose. Of the first 14 such
stations, 9 were on the FM band and only 5 on the
already-overcrowded AM band.

In the following year ethnic broadcasting became the fourth sector in the broadcasting system.
Australia is a nation of immigrants and from 1945
onwards the influx has increasingly been from non-
English-speaking countries. Broadcasting was slow
to respond to the changing profile of potential
listeners or viewers. Indeed, as these migrants
were almost inevitably clustered at the lower end of
the socio-economic scale, commercial broadcasters -
being captives of advertisers - made no attempt at
all to cater for their needs as there would be no
profit in doing so.

The ABC for its part, had been founded as an
antipodean BBC - its programmes imperial in their
focus and its accents British in their timbre.
Inglis notes, with regard to 1932, that 'the announ-
cers ... were rolling stones with English or near-
English voices', though by 1939 'the ABC did tolerate a broader local accent in sporting commentators
and on regional stations.'[12] The Commission was
simply not attuned to the differing cultural needs
of migrants. It preferred, from 1949 onwards, to
approach the problem from the other end, with a
long-running programme called *English for New
Australians*. For all this, it was the ABC - admit-
tedly goaded by a Labour government which had depended for its election upon the ethnic vote in greater
Melbourne - which first responded to the changing
needs. Early in 1975 it established in Melbourne a
radio station, 3ZZ, which was 'access' in its structure and which was in fact utilised predominantly by
ethnic community groups. At its zenith the station
was broadcasting in no less than 32 languages, including English. At almost the same time, two ethnic stations - 2EA and 3EA - were set up under the
umbrella of public broadcasting. By 1977 from these
small beginnings there had grown a fully-fledged,
publicly-funded radio and television service. It

was confined still to the major cities, Sydney and
Melbourne, but in principle could extend throughout
the continent.

As regards the introduction of colour television, Australian viewers took to it like ducks to
water - spurred on as with the first establishment
of monochrome television by an imminent Olympic
Games, this time in Montreal. Saturation coverage
was achieved in two years. In the early 1980s the
market-penetration of video-recorders has been no
less dramatic.

In summary, then, the Australian broadcasting
system now contains four elements: national, commercial, public and ethnic. With regard to radio, the
breakdown is as follows: first, the ABC has four
national networks, a major overseas network (Radio
Australia) and a Sydney-based rock station (2JJJ);
secondly, commercial broadcasters operate 134 stations - 36 in capital cities and 98 in other towns
and country areas; thirdly, there are now 49 public
broadcasting stations, distributed through capital
cities, suburbs, country towns and remote areas such
as mining sites. The licences are held by educational institutions, churches, aboriginal groups and
other community interests; and finally, ethnic
broadcasting - under the aegis of the Special Broadcasting Service - which is still confined to Melbourne, Sydney and the Sydney satellite cities of
Newcastle and Wollongong. Plans to extend the network to the other mainland cities are well-advanced.
These should be stimulated by the fact that ethnic
groups, frustrated by delay, are now seeking public
broadcasting licences - moves which, if successful,
would undermine government policy.

With regard to television, the pattern is as
follows: first, the ABC has one network reaching
across the whole nation. Ten of the 217 stations
necessary to complete this network have local studio
facilities and thus a capacity to vary and localise
the national network output; secondly, there are 50
commercial stations - 15 in metropolitan areas and
35 in smaller towns and country areas. Three networks - Seven (Fairfax and the Herald group), Nine
(Packer) and Ten (Murdoch) - have come to dominate
the metropolitan areas, though some commercial
stations remain 'independent'; thirdly, there are no
public broadcasting television stations, though the
law makes provision for their future development.
Applications for licences have been lodged in Sydney,
Melbourne, Adelaide and Perth. However, the government has not allocated any wavelengths at this stage

and so the licensing authority - the Australian
Broadcasting Tribunal - cannot yet proceed with
these applications; finally, ethnic television stations exist in Sydney and Melbourne. Their output
is substantially the same. There is pressure for
the network to be extended in due course to the
other mainland capitals, and the law makes provision
for this eventuality.

Clearly, then, the national and the commercial
sectors are still predominant, with the public and
ethnic sectors as yet relatively underdeveloped. The
politics of Australian broadcasting is principally
the politics of the relationship of the national and
commercial sectors with each other, with successive
governments and with the agencies responsible for
other aspects of telecommunications. But the two
minor strands cannot be ignored; they are now woven
into the fabric. A decade ago neither of these sectors existed. A decade ago, also, Australia was
still marking time technologically, whilst today it
is poised for fundamental change. The natural point
at which to take up political analysis in more
detail is 1972 - the year in which a Labour government was elected to office after twenty-three years
of unbroken Liberal party rule.

BROADCASTING AND THE WHITLAM GOVERNMENT: 1972-1975

Whitlam's election in December 1972 was facilitated
by a breach in the predominantly rightist ranks of
the major commercial media with the temporary defec-
tion of Rupert Murdoch. Consequently, for some
months preceding the 1972 election, Labour policies
were being presented fairly, even sympathetically,
to a considerable proportion of the newspaper-read-
ing public, particularly in the crucially important
electoral area of greater Sydney. During the campaign itself, Labour continued to receive generous
coverage from Murdoch; by contrast, the Liberal
leadership and policies sometimes found themselves
the subject of ridicule and hostility.[13]

In the event, with so many factors in its
favour - a demoralised government, a credible leader,
the Vietnam war, a recession and the support of some
of the press (not just Murdoch) - Labour only just
managed to win, gaining a swing of a mere 2.5 per
cent on its 1969 vote. Whilst it is impossible to
isolate the precise significance of any one factor,
common sense suggests that the absence of universal
media hostility, indeed the positive support of some
parts of the media, must have assisted Labour. Quite

possibly, without that support the Australian electorate, with its native conservatism, might still have returned the right-wing Coalition to power.

Of course, Whitlam realised that he could not rely upon Murdoch to defect again - a perception graphically borne out in 1975 when the Murdoch press did all it could to destabilise the government and, once it had been dismissed, conducted so vitriolic a campaign against Labour that its own journalists struck in protest. Labour's media strategy, therefore, was broadly to diversify media outlets, to create effective alternatives to the normally monolithic and anti-Labour commercial media and to impose some quality control upon the operations of the latter. Necessarily, in the context of the electronic media, these objectives involved strengthening the ABC as the only non-commercial broadcasting organisation with experience and know-how, so as to make it a more effective counterweight to commercial radio and television. Key issues in control of the commercial stations were an increase in Australian content and the creation of effective disciplinary powers for the Australian Broadcasting Control Board. In a word, Labour's policies would come to threaten both the power and the profits of the commercial broadcasters.

It is important, as a background, to appreciate that in Australia there was then, and still is, massive cross-ownership between the print and the electronic media.[14] The Annan Report noted that 'in Australia, newspaper interests have gained control of television stations with very sharp repercussions upon political expression and news.'[15] Whilst warning against exaggerating the risk of cross-ownership, Annan nevertheless firmly recommended the adoption in Britain of ownership rules far more restrictive than those prevailing in Australia. At any rate, Whitlam's dilemma was that in trying to curb the activities of the electronic media, he was certain to arouse the antagonism of the press and its owners.

The first problem tackled by the Labour government was that of the ABC's finances. To be publicly funded is inevitably, at least in the perception of the recipient, to be under-funded. This perception depends, of course, upon one's criterion for measurement: the quantity and quality of tasks which one should be performing. Certainly, the ABC possessed cbligations far beyond those prevailing on the commercial stations - news gathering, educational broadcasting, running six orchestras and a

national training orchestra, broadcasting through
Radio Australia, maintaining overseas offices and
generally developing Australian talent at all levels.
The funds - $70 million in the Liberal's last year -
were spread very thinly.

Whitlam's response to the ABC's under-funding
was to pour money into the organisation: $92 million
for 1973-74, $122 million for 1974-75 and, puta-
tively, $140 million for 1975-76. The Commission
was enabled to increase its staff, from 6,000 in
December 1972 to 7,500 by November 1975. With all
this went, as one would expect, an expansion of
activities, into areas which threatened the power
and the profits of the commercial broadcasting sector.

For example, the government allocated the ABC
a frequency on the AM band to open a rock station,
2JJ (now known as 2JJJ, three letters in the call-
sign indicating that it broadcasts on FM). From its
very first moment on the air, playing a record censored by the commercial stations, it became a thorn
in the side of commercial broadcasters and politicians of the Right. Although able to reach only
half of the Sydney area because of transmitter deficiencies, its ratings soon reached 8%. This undermined the standard commercial justification for
banal and unadventurous programming - 'We must be
giving listeners what they want or else they wouldn't
listen to us any more.' Anti-ads (Come to cancer
country', etc.), notice of demonstrations and dissemination of community service information contras-
ted starkly with the neat, conformist and materia-
list messages constantly peddled by the commercial
stations. 2JJ rapidly became a living, on-the-air
reproof to the musical crassness and social flip-
pancy of commercial radio as well as a critic of
establishment values.

Labour also, as mentioned above, facilitated
the establishment of access radio - communication by
the people for the people. Australians had grown
accustomed to broadcasting *at* the people, and this
new access approach made some people feel very un-
comfortable. Their reaction was, in retrospect,
predictable enough, to attack 3ZZ and its elected
Planning Committee for its supposed leftist bias.
The ABC as the umbrella organisation had acquired
not simply another radio station but a 24 hour-a-
day presence which symbolised the demand for diversity and change in society. The Right and their
media allies, which for the previous quarter of a
century had thrived on the celebration of the status

245

quo, were angry and resentful.

FM radio likewise became a focus for resentment on the part of the Right and its sympathisers. In 1972 not a single FM station had been operating in Australia. This was for technical reasons: television had been allocated to VHF rather than UHF. Labour quickly moved to clear the VHF band, and announced that FM radio stations would be established. As already stated, the establishment of the public broadcasting sector was in this way made possible. But there were, of course, far more wavelengths available than public broadcasters would take up. Within the Labour party, there was a strong grass roots feeling that 'the interests which have controlled traditional AM radio for so long should get no slice of the enlarged radio cake.'[16] It was thus no real surprise that the 1975 Labour party conference formally resolved that no FM licences should be allocated to the commercial sector. To commercial broadcasting interests this decision 'revealed the Australian Labour party's deep and violent antagonism to the independent media'.[17] By contrast the ABC was to be the first recipient of stations on the FM band, a national network for fine music to be known as ABC-FM. The government's decision to enhance the role of the ABC thus made the Commission the most prominent symbol for the resentment of the commercial broadcasting sector.

There were other matters which promoted opposition from the commercial sector. One was Labour's decision to provide for a staff-elected Commissioner - incipient democracy, no less, raising its head in the workplace. Another was the growth of a new programme, *Lateline*, a current affairs format whose slant was avowedly Leftist. Its guru, Allen Ashbolt, publicly defended its ideological position on the basis that 'balance' *within* a single programme was 'merely a device for protecting the status quo and preserving inequality and injustice, while trying to project an image of democratic fairness'.[18] Its programmes enraged the Right and their rage was expressed in the press outlets owned by commercial broadcasters. One commentator claimed: 'At taxpayers' expense, the most rabid left-wing propaganda is permitted.' Another joined in: 'Even if the ABC does not take its order from Canberra, its bright young trendies ... take their cue from a trendy Labour government.' Australian society seemed to be changing; the ABC was in the forefront of that change; and the apologists of the Right showed that this was more than could readily be stomached.

All these changes were occurring against a backdrop of a deliberate, government-inspired policy of increasing Australian content, particularly in the expensive medium of television. Product is cheap to buy, expensive to make: a rough working ratio is one to ten. In 1972-73 the ABC's Australian content had been 54%; in 1973-74, as Labour's policies began to take effect, there was a slight increase in terms of hours of transmission though the percentage remained the same; but by 1974-75 it had increased by 400 hours a year and was up to 61%. In that same year, the ABC spent approximately $3 million on ready-made overseas programmes, whilst the commercial stations were spending about $29 million to enable them to sustain a *non-Australian* content of just over 50%.

Of course, the issue was not simply a financial one. It was really about commercial broadcasters being willing participants in a cultural cringe which seemed to mirror and epitomise Australia's political postures of the previous twenty-five years - for example, obsequious involvement in a US adventure in Vietnam. The commercial sector was thus a willing actor in the Americanisation of Australian broadcasting output. The issue was also about taking resources from a society without putting sufficient back in.

The Australian content debate manifested itself, for the commercial sector, in the creation of a 'points system' by which to measure performance. As a condition of their licence, commercial television stations had to acquire a certain number of points, computed according to a formula which took account of the time, the type and the duration of the broadcast. It was widely ridiculed - half an hour of an Australian reading Australian poetry at peak time would, it was said, see a station right for the remainder of the week - and widely resented. At about the same time, the Australian music performance quota for commercial radio was increased to 15%.

Labour also sought to clarify some ambiguities as to the precise powers of the Australian Broadcasting Control Board: for example, whether it could require an adequate and comprehensive programming mix from licensees. On those few past occasions when the Board had bared its teeth, the commercial broadcasting industry had managed to treat it with contempt. Labour thus moved to make licence renewal - hitherto a rubber-stamp formality - a genuine review process, a matter for public hearing, evidence and argument. Public accountability was being sought for the utilisation of a scarce public resource, the airwaves.

Reaction was strong. The Fairfax group denounced Labour's proposals as 'Big Brother for TV', while the industry lobby organisation claimed that they would lead to 'total control by a government board of television programming'. At the same time, Labour's administrative reorganisation, which moved broadcasting policy from the PMG to a new Department of the Media, was denounced as a first stage in news manipulation. Accordingly, in December 1974 and again in April 1975, commercial media interests were able to prevail upon their political allies to block Labour's legislation in the Senate, where they held a majority.[19]

Later in 1975, the Opposition used its Senate majority to defer dealing with the question of Supply. As government money began to run out, the political crisis increased. On November 11 1975, with three weeks' Supply still remaining, the Governor-General dismissed the Whitlam Ministry from office and installed the Leader of the Opposition, Mr. Malcolm Fraser, as Prime Minister. Many volumes have since been written about the Governor-General's action. Suffice to say for present purposes that Whitlam had a secure working majority in the House of Representatives, that to dismiss a government in such circumstances was unprecedented, that the country came to the brink of major political violence as a consequence and that in the hours and days following the move the role of the media was of crucial importance. The ABC, as national broadcaster, was inevitably in the forefront of the political battle to come.[20]

In fact, the ABC had been under sustained pressure from the Opposition for the previous year, pressure which had become intense and continuous in the week preceding November 11.[21] The Commission Chairman, Professor R.I. Downing, was deeply worried by the hounding the ABC was receiving; it is not fanciful to suppose that this pressure could have been a factor triggering the heart attack which killed him on November 10.[22] As for their dealings with the commercial sector, in a move which makes one speculate that they must have suspected what was about to happen, the Opposition had booked all available political advertising time for the period November 11 to December 13 (the date set by the Governor-General for a General Election which Fraser

would go into as Prime Minister).[23]
    During the campaign itself, the right-wing
coalition pressure upon the Chairman-less ABC was
unrelenting. The caretaker Minister for the Media
was Mr. Peter Nixon, skilful architect of the year-
long campaign against the ABC. On November 12 he
fulminated:

> Never in its history will the ABC come under
> such close scrutiny as during the election
> campaign. ABC News and Current Affairs must
> expect unprecedented watchfulness by the
> National Country Party and the Liberal Party.

Senior management - always at heart pragmatic and
never entirely comfortable with the new forces
which Labour had set free within the organisation -
reacted conservatively. The order went down the
line - every political programme must be balanced
internally. Thus, during the most dramatic political crisis and election campaign since Federation,
the ABC, the national broadcaster and the only independent information service in Australia, was
neutered - which is a far different thing from being
neutral.[24] The commercial stations and their
siamese twins, the press, felt no such inhibitions.
The political media traffic was one-way. On December 13, Labour was annihilated.

FRASER FAVOURS THE COMMERCIAL SECTOR: 1975-1983

The ABC had come to be the most important and visible manifestation of Labour's policy in relation to
the media. Accordingly, Fraser's objective - and it
was very much his own rather than that of the
various ministers successively responsible[25] - was
to tame and punish it. This policy suited the commercial sector well and so was doubly attractive.
    The story of Fraser's relationship with the ABC
has been told in great detail in various places.[26]
What will emerge from the skeleton account which
follows is the extent to which Fraser's policies
were the exact obverse of Labour's. There were, it
seemed, no shared values which would underpin the
sort of evolutionary and carefully constructed development which a national broadcasting organisation
needs. In this respect Australia's political history of broadcasting has been more volatile than
that of the UK, Canada or New Zealand.
    Let us begin with money. It was stated earlier
that the appropriation for 1975-76 had been $140

million. In fact, the procedure invariably followed
was to make an initial appropriation - in this case
$132 million - on the basis that there would be sup-
plementation later to take account of increased
fixed costs. It was calculated that this would be
of the order of $8 million. Financial planning
quite properly proceeded, therefore, on the basis of
a total annual appropriation of $140 million. But
in January 1976, half-way through the financial year
(which in Australia runs from July 1 to June 30) the
government announced that not only would there be no
supplementation, but also that $1 million of the
appropriation already made was to be confiscated.
For the balance of the year, therefore, the ABC was
to make savings at the rate of about 12%. In a context where employees were for the most part unsack-
able, where ongoing obligations had been entered
into on the basis of decisions made months or even
years previously and where no overdraft or borrowing
capacity was legally possible, this requirement was
devastating. For the remainder of the year, the
whole energy of the national broadcasting organisation was expended simply upon achieving financial
survival.

What savings could be made? There were behind-
the-scenes hints that ABC-FM or 2JJ should go, moves
which would have delighted Fraser's commercial
friends. But the Commission - still with one exception Whitlam appointees - was not prepared to curry
political favour in this way. Moreover, it still
hoped that the cut-back would be a one-off move
made for authentic financial reasons rather than the
first move in a continuing politically-motivated
vendetta. Accordingly, the Commission simply thin-
ned out all of the ABC's activities. But the
following year there were further swingeing cuts.
Although the pressure lifted from about 1980, during
the Fraser years the ABC was to endure 30% cuts in
funding in real terms and a 20% reduction in staff
numbers. This reduction was, by government decree,
to be achieved by way of 'natural wastage' - a process which distorts the employment profile of any
organisation and consequently brings about even
greater inefficiency. Thus Fraser's claim, echoed
by the commercial broadcasting sector, that the ABC
was wasteful and inefficient was very much a self-
fulfilling prophecy.

Meanwhile, an inquiry into the broadcasting industry was set up, to be conducted by a public ser-
vant, Mr. Fred Green. The procedure was to be semi-
private, in that no submissions were to be subjected

to public scrutiny or argument. Within the ABC, the perception was strong that a quick and painful hatchet-job was about to be perpetrated.

In the event, the Report turned out to be less threatening than had been feared.[27] However, there were two recommendations which struck at the very heart of the ABC's independence. The first was that its performance should periodically be reviewed by a new body, the Australian Broadcasting Tribunal, which was to be set up to regulate commercial broadcasting and whose members would be closely associated with that sector of the industry. The second was to reduce the number of Commissioners, a proposal which would necessarily involve sacking at least two of the existing Whitlam-appointed members.

Whilst all this was going on, Fraser appointed as Chairman of the Commission a man whose whole background and value structure seemed to be antagonistic to the sort of organisation the ABC was trying to be. This was Sir Henry Bland. Bland had formerly been Secretary of the Department of Defence, was closely associated with Australia's involvement in the Vietnam War and had until a few months previously been Chairman of the Administrative Review Committee. In this role he was thought to have had a major input into the decision to cut back ABC finances and staff.[28] The choice was certainly an unusual one.

If the ABC still saw itself as a source of public debate about matters of public concern, Bland quickly indicated his own hostility to such a role:

> As one who has had to listen to so many people for so often, I couldn't care less if there were no current affairs programmes ... *State of the Nation* has been a bit of a disaster ... *TDT* has been scraping the barrel ... indeed, I know that in some cases *TDT* has gone out and created news and then rushed along next night and filmed the result of their stimulation of the previous day.[29]

If such programmes could not be avoided altogether, then at least they must be internally balanced. He stated:

> The argument was that (the ABC), in the totality of its programmes, did present all points of view. I do not believe this. It is not satisfactory to me to have the contrary view expressed at some other time.[30]

As for external broadcasting, Bland as a former
architect of defence and foreign policy could see it
only in terms of state propaganda:

> How on earth does anybody imagine that Radio
> Australia could go its own way? How can any-
> body imagine that Radio Australia can put out
> programmes in direct contradiction to govern-
> ment policy, foreign policy ...? Radio Austra-
> lia, you wouldn't imagine, would report on what
> some ratbag said on the Yarra Bank ... (Yarra
> Bank is the Melbourne equivalent of Speakers'
> Corner in Hyde Park - author's note). I'm not
> troubled by Radio Australia sitting down with
> somebody from Overseas Trade who says, "we're
> sending a delegation to Kashmir ... will you
> give it a mention?" and Radio Australia in its
> normal way putting together something about
> it.[31]

Such robust attitudes could only ultimately lead
to climactic confrontation. This duly occurred with
regard to the 1976 Boyer Lectures, the ABC equivalent
of the Reith Lectures. At its November 1975 meeting
the Commission had decided to invite Australia's
most distinguished historian, Professor C. Manning
Clark, to be the 1976 Lecturer. In accordance with
normal practice the exact topic was left to be settled in consultation with the head of the responsible department. This was Radio Special Projects,
whose head was Allen Ashbolt - the guru, it will be
recalled, of *Lateline*.

On September 20 1976, before Clark's lectures
had been recorded, a public meeting was held at the
Sydney Town Hall to discuss the theme 'Kerr and the
Consequences'. Clark was one of the principal spea-
kers; his theme was that the events of November 11
1975 would be seen by historians as having constituted a major stimulus towards the growth of Australian Republicanism. *Lateline* took a live cut, including Clark's speech, from the meeting and broadcast it nationally. Ashbolt's justification for
doing so, if one were needed, was that,

> the meeting was so unusual as to be historic.
> It probably marked the beginning of a movement
> in this country towards republicanism and over-
> all reform of the Constitution. The national
> service had ... a national duty to record it,
> broadcast it, report on it and discuss it ...
> The *Lateline* programme has immense archival

value, and ... future historians will be grate-
ful for the ABC's sense of historical judgment.

It is doubtful whether Bland would have heard the
broadcast live; but evidently Senator Carrick, the
government's Senate spokesman on media matters, was
informed of its general thrust. In a statement a
few days later, he attacked Clark, the Republican
movement and the ABC.

Bland was now brought into the matter. The
Assistant General Manager (Radio) was told to require Ashbolt to clear Clark's scripts with management before the Boyer Lectures were recorded or put
on the air. There could be no purpose for doing so
other than censorship. The order provoked a furore.
At its October meeting the Commission (still dominated by Whitlam appointees) overruled Bland.[32]

This incident undoubtedly marked a turning-
point in Bland's relationship with Fraser. It was
the final event in a series that united the staff,
senior management, the Commission, the general
public and even the normally anti-ABC press against
him - and thus by extension against Fraser. Never
a sentimentalist, Fraser decided that Bland must go.
And if he were to go, he must be provoked into
resigning. Accordingly, in early December he attacked Bland in Parliament. Bland, characterising
this as an attack on the independence of the ABC
itself, resigned in high dudgeon.[33]

Henceforth, a different approach was to be
taken. Fraser appointed as Chairman Mr. John
Norgard, a bluff and mild-mannered technocrat whose
avowed aim was 'to get the ABC out of the headlines'.
Norgard was furnished, following amendment of the
Act, with sufficient new Commissioners to put the
Whitlam rump into a minority and just enough funds
to get the organisation moving again, albeit almost
imperceptibly. Quietly and effectively, he began
to tame the ABC. *Lateline* was taken off the air;
another left-leaning programme, the *Terry Lane Show*,
was canned; and most significantly 3ZZ was closed
down altogether. When transmission ceased on July 16
1977, ABC management called in Commonwealth police
to remove the staff - a graphic illustration of the
stage that democratic broadcasting had now reached
in Australia.[34] A year later, with the support of
the Norgard Commission, the government announced
that the broadcasting staff would no longer be permitted to elect their own Commissioner.

Norgard took the ABC through till the end of
1981. Nothing much changed. A few important

battles were quietly lost: for example, the question of ownership of the domestic satellite system and the argument that rights to major sporting events should by law be non-exclusive. (Whilst they could be exclusive, the ABC could never match the commercials in the bidding). Australian television production gently declined; indeed, as early as 1976, many writers, cameramen and lighting operators had headed off to the Australian cinema industry. The ABC for its part had lost any capacity to excite or surprise.

In 1980 the government set up a Committee of Inquiry into the ABC under the Chairmanship of a businessman, Mr. Alick Dix. Assiduously it gathered an immense range of information about the workings of the complex organisation.[35] Its May 1981 Report came forward with some useful recommendations: for example, that money earned from merchandising should be retained rather than set off against the annual appropriation, as hitherto had been the case; that various procedures be adopted to improve industrial relations within the ABC; and that there would be seven-yearly independent reviews of the total Australian broadcasting system. But some other recommendations were calculated to reduce even further the independence of the ABC, most notably that news should be taken from the agencies, thus inevitably reducing the ABC's own news-gathering potential, and that corporate sponsorship should be encouraged thus tending to make the ABC a prisoner of private enterprise.

More importantly, the general thrust of the document was politically naive. Having identified and highlighted failures of management, Dix's report seemed to legitimise Fraser's interference in ABC affairs as having been predominantly occasioned by the value-neutral factor of incompetent management. Wittingly or unwittingly, the Dix Report was a whitewash for politically-motivated interference sustained since 1975.

In 1982 Fraser prepared to implement the Report. The Australian Broadcasting Corporation Bill omitted one threatening Dix recommendation - corporate sponsorship. But it introduced two other aspects no less detrimental in their potential effect. These were, first, the specific exclusion of the ABC from direct participation in CTV and, secondly, the creation of an immensely bureaucratic Complaints Commission. This Commission was to be not for the industry generally but specifically for the ABC. If implemented, the proposal would have created two classes of broadcaster: one, the ABC, looking constantly over its shoulder and the other, the commercial stations, free to get on with the job of broadcasting as they saw fit.

The 1982 Bill was left to lie on the Table. Providentially for the ABC, the Fraser government was defeated at the polls before the matter could proceed. But by then Fraser had turned the vibrant organisation which he had inherited into a hesitant and dis-spirited shadow of its former self. At the same time, his government had favoured the role of the ABC's main rival - the commercial broadcasting sector.

Overall, the commercial stations enjoyed a charmed run between 1975 and 1983. First, the weakening of the ABC shielded them from unflattering contrasts of the sort which had been manifest until 1975. Even Fraser's act of saving the ABC from sponsorship was more an act of saving the commercial stations from competition for funds. This was because the ABC, despite its low television ratings (c.12%), draws its audiences mainly from the higher socio-economic levels. It provides in fact a ready-made target audience for up-market promotions, rather like the colour supplements of the quality Sunday papers in Britain. The Australian television industry has, somewhat oddly, never taken account of the factor of the spending power of the audience being delivered to advertisers; McNair-Anderson ratings are simply head-counts. This seems to be a fundamental flaw in the economics of the industry and one which could hardly have survived the entry of the ABC into competition for funds.

Secondly, FM broadcasting was opened up to the commercial sector. Although initially unprofitable, it is already apparent that it will, in the large city markets, displace AM as the main radio technology.

Thirdly, self-regulation was substantially adopted as the means of programme control. The Tribunal, set up by Fraser following the Green Report, possessed a wide range of powers which it could have exercised. However, the 1977 inquiry conducted by the Tribunal[36] produced a report the industry could readily live with. There would be broad guidelines, legally enforceable, as to such matters as the frequency and duration of advertising, programme standards and Australian content; but except at the leading edges these would be interpreted and applied by the industry itself.[37] The only substantial inroad into this approach related to children's pro-

gramming - a classic case of tipping one's hat to
middle-class liberals.

Fourthly, the government was never reluctant to
amend the law for the convenience of its allies if,
for example, an embarrassing argument took the Tribunal by surprise or it made an unexpected decision.
Thus when Rupert Murdoch was seeking Tribunal approval to take over control of TEN-10, Sydney, he ran
into the argument that, for the purposes of the Act,
he was a foreign resident and thus disqualified from
holding a licence. As it turned out, the Tribunal
rejected this argument on the evidence. Nevertheless, it was an embarrassment, for demonstrably Mr.
Murdoch was not an Australian resident in quite the
same way as are most Australians. Without hesita-
tion, the Government proceeded to change the law so
as to provide that an Australian *national* was con-
clusively presumed to be an Australian *resident* for
the purposes of the ownership and control provisions.

The other example also concerned Murdoch,
though the other network operators (Packer and Fair-
fax/Herald) also benefited from the outcome. At the
time Murdoch was seeking to take over ATV-10, Melbourne, the Act provided that the Tribunal, in considering whether to permit licence transfers, should
'maintain such ownership and control as ... in its
opinion best accord with the public interest'. The
Tribunal took the view, urged upon it by public
interest groups who were at that time accorded standing, that ownership by the same interests of
stations in the two major markets was contrary to
the public interest because of its implications for
uniformity of programming.[38] This decision, if sustained, would have eroded the legal base of networking. In fact the decision was reversed on appeal.
But Fraser was taking no chances. The Act was amended so as to exclude from the notion of 'public
interest' the issue of the supposed programming
effect of ownership patterns.

The question of networking brings us, fifthly,
to government support by inaction. The philosophy
of the Broadcasting and Television Act purportedly
is that, even if cross-ownership between the print
and the electronic media is unavoidable in the
Australian situation, at least there should be
strict limits upon multiple ownership. This philosophy goes right back to the 1935 regulations, mentioned earlier. Diversity and localisation were
presented from the outset as key values, so that
when television started it was provided that no person or company should own or control or have a

'prescribed interest' in more than two stations. Yet what is the reality? It is that there have developed three metropolitan networks - arrangements whereby stations in capital cities other than Sydney and Melbourne become associated with the Seven, Nine or Ten networks operating from bases in those cities.

The precise details of these sorts of arrangement vary. Sometimes they will go so far as to permit the dominant station to impose national advertising for networked programmes; sometimes they oblige the 'slave station' to purchase and put on the air programmes (usually soap operas) which have already failed dismally elsewhere; sometimes the arrangement takes in the 'slave stations's' own 'slave station' in a country area. But the general objective is a common one - that the 'slave station' shall both supplement and become dependent upon the greater purchasing power of the network operator. For the latter the benefit is to spread costs and increase profitability; for the 'slave station' ready access to the best part of the network's programming is offset by the inevitable erosion of its sense of responsibility and responsiveness to the local market which it has been licensed to serve.

Far from tackling, or encouraging the Tribunal to tackle, the public interest questions underlying networking, Fraser positively encouraged it by limiting legal challenge. Moreover, it was decided that the networks would have access to the domestic satellite system so as to create the economic pressure which would tend to bring country stations within direct network dominance. Thus, if Australian broadcasting output is generally being Americanised, within Australia that output is becoming more uniform.

Finally, it was mentioned that at the time of the ATV-10 hearings, public interest groups, such as Justice in Broadcasting, had standing to be heard, lead evidence and oppose the application. The owners successfully challenged the exercise of this right in two separate legal proceedings. The standing of persons other than those asserting property interests was left in legal limbo; and that is where Fraser let it remain.[39] This was consistent with his policy in relation to the Broadcasting Information Office. The Green Report had recommended that such an office be established to monitor and record the performance of commercial broadcasters - to provide, in fact, information as to compliance with or breach of licence conditions. Obviously, the industry itself did not need the office; on the

contrary its users would have been those very public
interest groups and researchers which normally lack
the resources to document their causes of concern.
Fraser set up the office in a statutory sense; but
he never allocated funds for its operation and so it
was stillborn.

In summary, commercial broadcasting flourished
under Fraser. Between 1975 and 1983 other industries - mining, motor vehicle manufacturing, transport, retailing, etc. - underwent a major shakeout.
Yet commercial broadcasting remained consistently
profitable, with its profits almost keeping pace
with inflation. A sure indicator of the financial
attraction of the industry was the number of corporate raids and licence transfers occurring during
the period. Between 1975 and 1983 there was a shift
in the pattern of these raids. At the beginning of
the period broadcasting had still been a business
predominantly for broadcasters and the media; by
the end the market raiders included conglomerate enterprises for whom broadcasting was simply another
business activity, to be taken up or dropped according to general business criteria: another example
of Australian broadcasting mirroring the American
system. Of course, the picture was complicated by
the increasing tendency for the traditional media
owners themselves to diversify activities.[40] This
raised a new crop of potential problems, which Fraser
was content to ignore.

The bait that attracted the conglomerates into
competition with the more traditional media owners
was the expectation of a profits bonanza from the
new media technologies. Control or ownership of a
radio or television station would be the natural
launching-pad for participation in CTV, RSTV, the
domestic satellite system (AUSSAT) and videotex. A
series of governmental and administrative decisions
put these at the mercy of private enterprise.

First, with regard to cable television and RSTV,
in 1980 the Tribunal was instructed by the government to conduct an inquiry into their development.
Its August 1982 Report was a commercial broadcaster's dream.[41] The main recommendations were as
follows. It was proposed, unequivocally, that both
systems should be developed as quickly as was feasible. This should be done in a manner which took
account of existing commercial television patterns.
The ABC, for its part, should be excluded entirely
from RSTV and gain limited access at most to CTV.
Telecom - the national common carrier - should not
be the carrier for CTV reticulation systems; these

should be made over to private enterprise. With regard to CTV there would be one cable only for any
given area and the licence should relate to the
whole cable. There would be no *enforceable legal
obligation* for the licensee to make channels on that
cable available to the ABC., public interest or community groups, etc., though it was stated that there
was an expectation that he would endeavour to do so.
The licence should be for fifteen years, an unprecedented period of business monopoly, and would be
renewable for further ten-year periods. Comparable
provisions were recommended for RSTV.

These recommendations were made against a backdrop where it had already been announced that AUSSAT
would be privately owned. Obviously, ready access
to the satellite was a precondition of the national
networking of CTV (cable) and RSTV (subscription
television) and also of traditional television. A
Board of Directors for AUSSAT had already been
appointed, its membership reflecting the predominant
commercial broadcasting interests. The ABC was not
represented; its position was to be that of a sup-
plicant as to both access and cost.

At about the same time, an Inquiry into Telecom was recommending that the profitable parts of
that public utility should be sold off to private
enterprise.[42] Cross-subsidisation would cease. One
of the more profitable parts was the national broad-
band system (only completed, as mentioned above, in
1970). This was used extensively by commercial
broadcasters (who from 1985 would control the satellite system) and also by the ABC. The ABC's commercial vulnerability, once the broad-band system
was in the hands of private enterprise, would be
exacerbated. Videotex - still at the planning
stage but certain to be based on the British system
- was expected to be profitable; Telecom accordingly
would have no part of it.

This model of business regulation of the telecommunications industries was peddled as being *deregulation*. In reality, of course, it was no such
thing. Rather, it would have been regulation of the
whole system for the benefit of sectional interests
- those whose raison d'etre is to make profits and
whose habit of mind is to exercise power.

THE RETURN OF LABOUR: 1983

With his media package ready to put in place, Fraser
called an early General Election - like a turkey
calling an early Christmas, as one commentator

presciently noted. In March 1983 Labour under a new
leader, Mr. Bob Hawke, was voted into office.

And so the pendulum began to swing again. With
regard to the new technologies, it was soon announced that AUSSAT would be 100% publicly-owned; that
the profitable parts of Telecom would not be hived
off; that Videotex would be developed through Telecom; that CTV would be put on ice for some years inasmuch as the capital investment required would dis-
tort the national need for developmental finance;
and that further thought would be given to the development of RSTV. The ABC was to have primary use of
the transponders on the first satellite to be put in
place; the expectation was that it would develop two
further national radio networks and push its television network into the remotest corners of the
continent.

New legislation - the Australian Broadcasting
Corporation Act - created a fresh charter for the
ABC, one which would encourage efficient business
practices and modern management approaches. The
Complaints Commissioner idea was dropped; instead
the ABC would employ community liaison officers. The
Commission was replaced by a Board of Directors, one
of whom would be staff-elected. This notion seemed
to have become almost a symbol of the value struggle
underlying Australian media policy. But one concession was made in all this; although the legislation did not positively require it, all the other
Directors were vetted by an all-party Committee of
Parliament. The discontinuity introduced by Whitlam
(who did not re-appoint a single Liberal appointee)
and Fraser (who reciprocated) was seen as something
to be avoided.

Disappointingly, the new Act picked up the Dix
recommendation that the ABC should be allowed to use
the domestic news agencies. Also, it did little to
disturb the entrenched public service positions and
standards of existing employees. But it was a start,
and after the government had announced a major in-
fusion of funds, no observer could be in doubt that
the aim was to restore the Corporation to a position
of major influence in the total broadcasting system.

No major changes were made at once to the
structure of commercial broadcasting. However, new
appointments to the Tribunal led inexorably to
changes in policy - most notably at this stage a
reduction in the quantity and frequency of television advertising. Self-regulation would no longer
suffice.

CONCLUSION

The politics of broadcasting is a crucial aspect of the politics of modern democratic societies. In some states the prevailing political style to a degree obfuscates this; media policies are treated as if they were merely technocratic and comparatively value-free. In Australia, particularly since the extraordinary events of November 11 1975, this charade is no longer sustainable, and both sides know it. To be sure there are some peripheral, though not insignificant, areas - public and ethnic broadcasting - where some common ground exists so that development can be evolutionary. But at the centre, broadcasting policy has become one of the most visible areas in the struggle to gain and retain political power. Broadcasting in Australia is very much a part of a tough, crude and committed political battle, a battle to be continued over the "new" media of cable, satellite and pay television.

References

1. M. Armstrong, *Broadcasting Law and Policy in Australia*, Sydney, Butterworths, 1982, chapter 1.
2. K. Inglis, *This is the ABC*, Melbourne, Melbourne University Press, 1983, p.9.
3. Inglis, *This is the ABC*, pp.19-20.
4. R. Harding, *Outside Interference: The Politics of Australian Broadcasting*, Melbourne, Macmillan, 1979, chapter 10. A. Dix, *The ABC in Review: National Broadcasting in the Eighties*, Canberra, Australian Government Publishing Service, 1981, paras. 57-68, chapters 6, 20 and 22.
5. Inglis, *This is the ABC*, pp.129-131.
6. Dix, *The ABC in Review*, chapter 10.
7. Inglis, *This is the ABC*, pp.128-129.
8. Harding, *Outside Interference*, p.42.
9. *Report of the Committee on the Future of Broadcasting*, (Chairman: Lord Annan), HMSO Cmnd, 6753, 1977, p.132. Hereafter referred to as *The Annan Report*.
10. Inglis, *This is the ABC*, p.193.
11. S. Hall, *Superstory: 20 years of Australian Television*, Melbourne, Macmillan, 1976, p.18.
12. Inglis, *This is the ABC*, pp.22 and 73.
13. L. Oakes and D. Solomon, *The Making of an Australian Prime Minister*, Melbourne, Cheshire, 1973, p.275.
14. *Annual Report of the Australian Broadcasting Tribunal 1977, incorporating the 29th Annual Report of the Australian Broadcasting Control Board 1976*, Canberra, Australian Government Publishing Service, 1978, Appendix K. W. Bonney and H. Wilson, *Australia's Commercial Media*, Melbourne, Macmillan, 1983, chapter 3.
15. *The Annan Report*, p.198.
16. Harding, *Outside Interference*, p.10.
17. *Ibid*, p.11.
18. A. Ashbolt, *Meanjin Quarterly*, Melbourne, 1977, pp.255-257. Inglis, *This is the ABC*, pp.361-363.
19. Harding, *Outside Interference*, pp.18-28.
20. E. Luttwak, *Coup d'Etat: A Practical Handbook*, London, Allen Lane, 1968, pp.112-113.
21. Harding, *Outside Interference*, pp.17-19 and 29-31. Inglis, *This is the ABC*, pp.383-385.
22. Inglis, *This is the ABC*, pp.383-385.
23. Harding, *Outside Interference*, p.34.
24. Inglis, *This is the ABC*, pp.385-388. Harding, *Outside Interference*, pp.31-34.
25. Harding, *Outside Interference*, chapter 9.

26. *Ibid.*, chapters 3-9. Inglis, *This is the ABC*, Chapter 8. J. Dugdale, *Radio Power: A History of 3ZZ*, Melbourne, Hyland House, 1979, passim.
27. Harding, *Outside Interference*, chapter 7. Inglis, *This is the ABC*, pp.400-401. F. Green, *Australian Broadcasting: A Report on the Structure of the Australian Broadcasting System and Associated Matters*, Canberra, Australian Government Publishing Service, 1976, passim.
28. Inglis, *This is the ABC*, p.394.
29. Harding, *Outside Interference*, p.69.
30. *Ibid*, pp.69-70.
31. *Ibid*, p.70.
32. Inglis, *This is the ABC*, pp.397-398. Harding, *Outside Interference*, pp. 72-75.
33. Inglis, *This is the ABC*, pp.403-405. Harding, *Outside Interference*, pp.82-85.
34. Dugdale, *Radio Power*, passim.
35. Dix, *The ABC in Review*, passim.
36. *Self Regulation for Broadcasters: A Report of the Australian Broadcasting Tribunal*, Canberra, Australian Government Publishing Service, 1977, passim.
37. Bonney and Wilson, *Australia's Commercial Media*, pp.146-151.
38. *Ibid.*, pp.76-80.
39. Armstrong, *Broadcasting Law and Policy in Australia*, pp.179-184.
40. Bonney and Wilson, *Australia's Commercial Media*, pp.66-69.
41. *Cable and Subscription Television Services for Australia: A Report*, Canberra, Australian Government Publishing Service, 1982. passim.
42. J. Davidson, *Report of the Committee of Inquiry into Telecommunications Services in Australia*, Canberra, Australian Government Publishing Service, 1982, passim.

Chapter Eight

JAPAN: BROADCASTING IN A NEW DEMOCRACY

Michael Tracey

In the latest volume of his history of the BBC Asa
Briggs writes 'There is still need to compare in
depth British experience with that of other countries: British broadcasting is part of a bigger,
still largely unwritten, story.'[1] It is also to a
considerable extent the history of public service
broadcasting, existing in a state of creative tension with a commercial broadcasting system. My own
research has examined this fascinating but puzzling
idea in three cultures: Japan, Germany and Britain.
In this chapter I will be discussing the particular
case of Japan, but in these opening remarks I wish
to consider it for a moment in the context of something of the other two cultures as well.
      For the vast majority of people in these
liberal democratic societies the experience of
political life lies in their experience of broadcasting, and particularly of television. Their
citizenship, the extent to which they are informed,
the things about which they are informed, the
people about whom they are informed, all this becomes contingent upon their 'viewership'. In a
liberal democracy then, which depends for its vita-
lity and strength on its citizens being adequately
informed and involved, enormous responsibility is
placed on those broadcasting organisations which
provide the vital link in that political process.
Even more than that though, they have become the
articulators and disseminators of the national experience: they hold a mirror up to the nation's
face, often to its pain. Yet even amid the ill-
defined way in which they go about their business
they embody a purpose and a role which were quite
self-consciously created, which provide the only
purpose for their being in existence and which become eroded a little more as each day passes.

Writing about public service broadcasting is no
longer words in an essay: it is an obituary, a re-
quiem for an idea.
     Decent definitions of public service broad-
casting are thin on the ground, but as good as any
is that by Sir Ian Jacob shortly before he retired
as Director General of the BBC in 1959. It was, he
said:

> ... a compound of a system of control, an atti-
> tude of mind, and an aim, which if successfully
> achieved results in a service which cannot be
> given by any other means. The system of con-
> trol is full independence, or the maximum de-
> gree of independence that Parliament will
> accord. The attitude of mind is an intelligent
> one capable of attracting to the service the
> highest quality of character and intellect. The
> aim is to give the best and the most comprehen-
> sive service of broadcasting to the public that
> is possible. The motive that underlies the
> whole operation is a vital factor; it must not
> be vitiated by political or commercial conside-
> rations.[2]

In Britain the idea of public broadcasting emerged
relatively gently out of parliamentary scrutiny and
Reithian practice. In Japan and Germany it was
self-consciously created by conquerors. An idea was
implanted in these broadcasting systems partly because of the general desire of the Allies to divorce
broadcasting from the state as part of their effort
to prevent an emergence of a powerful, centralised
state, and partly because the implanting was being
done by men whose model was, very loosely, the BBC.
The impulse towards the public service model was
such that the Americans were even willing to reject
the premises upon which their own domestic broadcasting was based. Thus the public corporation
emerged, the *Anstalt des Offentlichen Rechts* in
Germany and NHK in Japan. In fact, it would be true
to say that it seems as if public service broadcasting was founded on an ideal, and its history has
been one of efforts to prevent a political and commercial reality catching up with that ideal. Before
looking at Japan's broadcasting system, however, I
shall first give some background material on the
political reconstruction of Japan after world war
two.

THE RECONSTRUCTION OF POSTWAR JAPAN: THE MAKING OF
A CLONE CULTURE

In Japan while there are pre-war antecedents, the
contemporary story begins with the American Occupation and in particular their mission to create a
clone culture. In the first instance NHK and later
the commercial television system were the result of
prescriptions laid down after 1945.
 The United States had taken the dominant role
in determining and executing policy in the occupation of Japan. This simply reflected the principal
part American military forces had played in the
latter's defeat. Not surprisingly, as a document
from an American official historian notes, the natural outcome of the preponderant influence of the
United States in formulating policy for the occupation 'was that the ultimate goal towards which
Japan was to be guided was democracy in the traditional Western sense.'[3] The determination that this
was the ultimate goal reflected a prevailing concept
of the purpose of an occupation of a conquered
country: 'This concept derives from the realisations
that mere military disarmament will not suffice to
prevent future aggression, and that therefore the
attitudes which sanction aggression and the new institutions which foster such attitudes must be
eliminated and new attitudes and institutions favouring the peaceful conduct of relations with the international community established.' The initial
purpose of occupying then was 'to bring about the
minimum political and legal changes that were indis-
pensable for the elimination of militarism, imperialism and other features that had promoted
aggression.'
 It must also be said that the purpose of creating what were in effect clone cultures was not just
to prevent the renewal of aggression. The Japanese
and German people were crushed in 1945 and to
imagine them as a future threat was fanciful. As
important in the 'occupying' mind was that if they
were not rebuilt in the liberal democratic mould
they could readily be subverted to Communism. This
threat was more real in Germany, but in both Europe
and the Far East one can readily see within the
policies of occupation the division of the world
into rival camps. It was within this geopolitical
struggle that Japanese communications policy was
developed.
 The Instrument of Surrender based on the
Potsdam Declaration provided the legal basis for the

occupation of Japan. Japan's surrender under the terms of the Declaration was unconditional and the Allies did not recognise any contractual relationships with Japan: the terms of the Declaration were considered as principles which the Allies felt morally but not legally bound to observe. The terms stated that once Japan fulfilled the conditions required by Allied policy objectives, the occupying forces would be withdrawn and Japan would once again enjoy full sovereignty.

Occupation policy for the achievement of what was described as a 'peaceful and responsible government that conformed to the democratic principles' rested upon the assumption that a tendency toward democratic development was latent in Japanese society. This view was reflected in the Potsdam Declaration which specified that 'the Japanese Government shall remove all obstacles to the revival and strengthening of democratic tendencies among the Japanese people.' In similar fashion United States policy required that the Japanese people should be encouraged to develop 'a desire for individual liberties and respect for fundamental human rights and to form democratic and representative organisations.'

A second major assumption which guided the occupation was that the reforms and institutions selected and used in the effort to democratise political, economic and social life must coincide with and satisfy Japanese aspirations. Only insofar as the Japanese leaders and people recognised the goals of the occupation as desirable was it felt that there could be hope that the alterations accomplished by the occupation would endure.

Finally, it was recognised that new patterns of behaviour could not be imposed as rigid and static forms upon Japanese society, but must be capable of growth and adaptation in the hands of the Japanese themselves both during the occupation and after its end. General Douglas MacArthur, Supreme Commander of the Occupying Forces, argued that the political and economic freedom advocated by the occupation was based upon concepts of the rights and dignity of the individual. He adhered therefore to the policy that the Japanese as individuals and as groups should be given every opportunity to work out their own solutions to political, governmental, social and educational problems. Furthermore, he insisted that even though 'imperfections' might be found to exist, there should be no demand for alteration of actions which had been taken by the Japanese within

the framework of democratic procedures and which
conformed to democratic principles.

The establishment of basic conditions for the
growth of democratic government as well as the
occupation's philosophy of fundamental human rights
required the abrogation of laws and practices and
the elimination of agencies which had suppressed
those civil liberties and human rights. The first
months of the occupation were characterised by overt
and corrective SCAP action in the form of sweeping
directives which ordered the government to abrogate
and immediately suspend all laws, decrees, orders,
ordinances and regulations restricting political,
civil and religious liberties. Unrestricted discussion of the Emperor, the imperial institution and
the Japanese government was to be allowed; restrictions on the collection and dissemination of information were to be removed; and all legal discrimina-
tions on the basis of race, nationality, creed or
political opinions were abolished. The press was
freed from government control and restrictions on
the freedom of communication and expression removed.
Political prisoners were released. Police abuses
were eliminated and oppressive police agencies
abolished. State support of religion was prohibited,
thereby bringing about a separation of religion from
the state since it was felt it had been misused for
political ends, and also conforming to the cherished
American notion of the separation of Church and
state.

The 'reformation' of Japan obviously meant that
the political leadership of the war years, which was
held to have been oppressive abroad and totalitarian
at home, had to be removed and excluded from public
life, to prevent, as one document described it, 'the
resistance and sabotage which could normally be expected from these persons and to permit the development of new leadership capable of infusing a new
spirit and vigor into government and politics more
attuned to Japan's changed circumstances.'

In two formal directives issued on January 4
1946 SCAP directed the government to identify and
abolish all secret ultranationalistic and terrorist
organisations, to prevent their future re-creation
and to take necessary steps to remove and exclude
from public office all persons who had been influential in promoting militarism and militant nationalism. The Japanese government under its own ordinances prepared and administrered the entire programme subject to SCAP review. Designated as the
'purge', the programme was inaugurated on the

national level immediately following the issue of
the directives. Incumbents of, or candidates for,
important government positions were removed or
barred. Of major importance was the screening and
barring of unacceptable candidates for Diet membership in the election held in April 1946, especially
significant as the new Diet was to be responsible
for constitutional revision. A second phase of the
purge initiated in 1947 removed and excluded ultra-
nationalists from positions of leadership in pre-
fectoral, city and village governments. In a third
phase, begun late in 1947, the purge was applied to
persons holding important positions in financial,
commercial and industrial enterprises and in public
information media. It was a cleansing operation
exactly parallelling the process of de-Nazification
in Germany.

Concurrently with measures to remove obstacles
to the development of a democratic government and
society, SCAP initiated positive steps to incorpo-
rate democratic concepts and institutions in Japanese life. MacArthur believed that the democratisa-
tion of the legal basis of the government required,
as a first step, the liberalisation of the Meiji
Constitution and so informed the Prime Minister,
Prince Haruhiko Higashi-kuni, in September 1945. In
October the Supreme Commander reiterated his view
regarding the Constitution in an interview with
Prime Minister Kijuro Shidehara who had succeeded
Higashi-kuni. MacArthur declared that in the
achievement of the Potsdam Declaration, 'the traditional social order under which the Japanese people
have been subjugated for centuries will be corrected.
This will unquestionably involve a liberalisation of
the Constitution.'

The Meiji Constitution was held to be unsatisfactory as a framework and guide for democratic
development since it appeared irreconcilable with
the political realities of the change of the Emper-
or's position under the impact of occupation, the
postulate of a truly representative government and
the emphasis of the Potsdam Declaration and Allied
policy upon fundamental human rights which were
constitutionally granted the people only 'within the
limits of the law'.

To ensure that the current views of the Japanese people were brought to bear upon the revision of
the Constitution, an election for members of the
lower house of the Diet was held in April 1946. For
this election the electorate was broadened by the
enfranchisement of women and the lowering of the

voting age to 20 years. To maintain legal continuity, the new Constitution was enacted as a revision
of the Meiji Constitution and revision procedures
observed the forms required by that document. In
substance, however, the amended Constitution was a
completely new charter.

The new Constitution established representative
parliamentary government with sovereignty in the
hands of the people. The Emperor was stripped of
his former sovereignty and became the symbol of the
state. Powers related to government were denied him
and his 'acts in matters of state' became merely
formal and ceremonial. The National Diet, a bicame-
ral elected body, was made the highest organ of
government with the lower house superior to the
upper. The Diet was vested with final authority
over national finances; and the constitutional provision specified that 'power to exercise national
finance shall be exercised as the Diet shall determine'.

Executive power was vested in the Cabinet
headed by a Prime Minister formally appointed by the
Emperor upon designation by the Diet from among its
members. The Prime Minister appointed the members
of his Cabinet, a majority of whom must be members
of the Diet. The Cabinet was, and is, responsible
to the Diet and if it loses the confidence of the
Diet must resign or dissolve the House of Representatives and call a new general election of members
of the House of Representatives.

The judiciary was made an independent third
branch of the government, eliminating the former
subordination of the courts to the executive branch
of the government. The Supreme Court was vested
with the rule-making power to determine procedures
and practices and with the power of judicial review
regarding the constitutionality of legislative as
well as administrative acts.

The Constitution guaranteed unconditionally all
civil liberties, as well as the right to work, to
engage in collective bargaining, to receive protection against economic exploitation, and to enjoy
complete social equality including equality of the
sexes. As mentioned previously, Church and state
were separated. Finally, war was renounced as a
sovereign right of the nation; armed forces and war
potential were not to be maintained and it was
specified that the 'right of belligerency of the
state will not be recognised'. This provision,
arising from the experience of military defeat and
surrender, marked a radical and unique departure in

constitutional development.

The basic legal codes, civil and criminal, were
revised to conform to the provisions of the new
Constitution. Lèse-majesté was eliminated from the
criminal code, as were all restrictions on the legal
status of women as wives and mothers abolished from
the civil code. The 'house' system was replaced in
civil law by the modern small family. Provision was
made for the equal sharing of succession to property
among descendants regardless of sex, with an en-
titlement of the surviving spouse, whether husband
or wife, to legal shares.

Inevitably a great deal of thought had been
given to the position of the Emperor within Japanese
society and therefore his possible role in a post-
surrender Japan. The archives are full of accounts
of views which ranged from on the one hand that he
be strung up, to the other that he became an integral part of the rebuilding of the society.

The central feature of the Japanese 'Emperor'
system as viewed through American eyes, was the sen-
timental attachment of the masses to the person of
the Emperor, whom they regarded as deeply and personally concerned for their welfare and whose task
they sought to ease by complying to the best of
their ability with the orders issued in his name.
His lofty and secluded position, combined with his
distant past, surrounded him with an aura of pseudo-
divinity, invoking reverence and awe. Nevertheless,
respect for his authority and obedience to his will
resulted from what one report in February 1946 described as 'a very human affection which the people
felt for him, and which they believed he felt for
them, and relatively little from fear or supersti-
tion.'

The basic attachment remained intact, even in
defeat:

> The Emperor's reported opposition to the war,
> his decision to conclude peace over the oppo-
> sition of the military, his reported distress
> at the people's suffering, his difficult posi-
> tion under the occupation and willingness to
> humble himself even further in the popular
> interest by calling hat in hand on the nation's
> conqueror and his known desire, stronger than
> that of his ministers, for the growth of demo-
> cratic institutions in Japan have confirmed in
> the people's eyes his concern and affection for
> them. His New Year's Day Rescript denying any
> claim to divinity detracted not in the least

from their devotion to him, but merely carried
further a process beginning months earlier with
his surrender broadcast when, as one Japanese
put it, "the Emperor came down from a position
high in the skies and became the real father
of our nation".

The Japanese then were believed by the United States
ófficials to maintain an instinctive dependence and
confidence in the Emperor, in a way in which they
did not for any government or any other individual
or groups:

> With him they feel essential unity and harmony
> can be maintained and Japan may eventually re-
> gain a measure of prosperity and self-respect,
> while without him they foresee disunity and
> disaster.

The figure put on this by US officials was that
something like 95% of the Japanese population wanted
the 'Emperor' institution retained in some form.
The view of the liberal wing of Japanese
society went so far as to suggest that without the
Emperor the introduction of democratic structures
and processes would be impossible. The occupation
forces in Japan were then in the rather fortunate
position of possessing, in the person of the
Emperor, the core of what we would recognise as a
constitutional monarchy. Whereas in Germany all
semblance of a political structure had disappeared
with the allied powers therefore having to start
from scratch, in Japan a vital, skeletal structure
remained.
It was within this context that the Occupying
Forces developed their policy towards the development of Japanese broadcasting. Glimpses of the
documents produced at the time illustrate the point.
In August 1946 one official report observed:

> From its inception in 1926 until VJ Day 1945
> the Broadcasting Corporation of Japan served as
> a propaganda medium for the Japanese warlords.
> At the cessation of hostilities the broadcas-
> ting facilities of Japan, consisting of three
> networks totalling 58 stations, were utilised
> by SCAP for the purpose of expediting the
> mission of the occupation. SCAP is now using
> two of the networks to insure public under-
> standing of all directives, policies and plans
> for the political, economic and social

272

rehabilitation of Japan. This is being accomplished a) by broadcasting complete news coverage and explanations of all directives of SCAP, b) by giving voice to sound Japanese political and reconstruction thought, and c) by taking steps to minimise Japanese government control of radio, thereby establishing it as a reliable and trustworthy source of news, information, education and entertainment for the Japanese people.[4]

Other documents spoke of the primary functions of broadcasting in Japan as advancement of Japan as a democratic nation: 'information, education and entertainment' (that Reithian trilogy intoned apparently unselfconsciously) were the goals set. 'In order to achieve this, broadcasting must attain high standards. This required freedom of the medium and assumption of full responsibilities' and so on. In short, broadcasting in Japan was being placed at the heart of this society as one of the instruments of social engineering. The whole character of contemporary Japanese broadcasting - its organisation, range of programmes, relationship to its audience and corporate ethos - stems from the seeds sown by SCAP. The total ecology of broadcasting, however, also has specifically to include commercial broadcasting. Moreover, in the future it will have to include the evolution of broadcasting into a 'hightech' world of new systems communications.

BROADCASTING IN JAPAN: HISTORY AND ORGANISATION

Both the pre- and post-war character of Japanese broadcasting were, to a certain extent, born out of national disaster. After the 1923 Tokyo earthquake there was a strong feeling that a more efficient information system provided by broadcasting would have averted some of the confusion which followed in the wake. Steps were therefore taken by the Ministry of Communications to organise a system of radio broadcasting and in the same year an ordinance was established by the government authorising and creating the supervisory structure for radio broadcasting.

The first Japanese broadcasting signals were transmitted by the Tokyo Broadcasting Station on March 22 1925. In 1926 three temporary stations which had been established in Tokyo, Osaka and Nagoya were merged to form NHK. This was established as a public utility, privately managed, but

under the close supervision of the government. Up
until that point the only law governing the use of
radio waves was the 1915 Wireless Telegraphy Law.
The source of finance of the new NHK was local,
through fees collected from listeners. This structure prevailed from 1925 to 1945, though it was also
one geared primarily to the exposition of official
voices and views.

From 1945 to 1950 the NHK continued to function,
but under the close supervision of SCAP. Censorship
and tight editorial control were maintained and the
organisation was purged of elements held by the
occupying power to be unacceptable on grounds of
attitude or past behaviour. On November 11 1946 a
new Japanese government was promulgated, with a
commitment to pacifism, a doctrine of popular sovereignty and a respect for fundamental human rights.
Article 21 of the promulgation guaranteed freedom of
'speech, press and all other forms of expression'.
At the same moment censorship by SCAP was abolished.

On May 3 1947 the new Constitution of Japan
came into effect. In the months before that date
SCAP GHQ instructed the Communications ministry to
revise existing laws and regulations regarding
broadcasting and communications so as to reflect
'the spirit' of the new Constitution. In the eyes
of its makers NHK was to be many things, but it was
not to be a governmental poodle.

On December 22 1949 three related Bills were
published, coming into law on June 1 1950 as:

    (i)   the Radio Law
   (ii)   the Broadcasting Law
  (iii)   the Radio Regulatory Commission Establish-
          ment Law

As of that day the old Nippon Hoso Kyokai juridical
body was dissolved and the new NHK established. The
substance of the new legislation was as follows:

(i) The Radio Law: This replaced the old Wireless
Telegraphy Law, becoming thereby the principal
legislative enactment regulating radio communications. Its central purpose was the efficient ordering of the utilisation of radio waves. It had,
therefore, a mainly technical function.

(ii) The Broadcast Law: This states that 'broadcasting enterprises are subject to regulation by the
Broadcast Law in respect of programming and other
business matters. This is because it is necessary

to regulate broadcasting so as to meet the public welfare and to strive for sound development thereof in view of its powerful influence on our daily life'.

The Law established a dual system of broadcasting with on the one hand the NHK as the public organisation opposed by commercial private broadcasting organisations on the other. NHK was to be established as a corporate body in charge of public broadcasting services, responsible for its operations to the National Diet.

The Broadcast Law also laid down a number of important prescriptions. It established, for example, that broadcasters:

> (a) shall not disturb the public security and good morals and manners; (b) shall be politically impartial; (c) shall broadcast news without distorting facts; and (d) as regards controversial issues shall clarify the issues from all angles possible.

The Law also laid down the basic guidelines for broadcasters' programming policies, insisting that they 'shall provide cultural and educational programmes, as well as news and entertainment programmes, maintaining harmony in their scheduling policies'.

The most immediately obvious feature of the law to those familiar with British broadcasting is the way in which it defined NHK as being autonomous, neither state-owned nor commercially based, funded by a listening fee. The various articles refer to the need to care for the public welfare (Article 1, item 1); to ensure freedom of expression by guaranteeing the impartiality, integrity and autonomy of broadcasting (Article 1, item 2); and to safeguard that broadcasting contributes to the development of a healthy democracy (Article 1, item 3). Even the delicate relationship between institutional autonomy, formal law and informal commitments shows some clear, even remarkable, parallels between NHK and the BBC. This is even more surprising given that there is little evidence from within archival sources to indicate any self-conscious pursuit of the BBC model - as there had so obviously been in Germany.

(iii) Radio Regulatory Commission Establishment Law: This was modelled on the independent regulatory commission system in the United States. The Commission was empowered to regulate the emission of radio waves and generally supervise broadcasting through its quasi-legal function.

The key features to note about the significance of these laws were that, firstly, NHK was no longer a monopoly, secondly, broadcasting was distanced from government control and, finally, that NHK was to be funded by direct financial support from subscribers.[5]

In April 1951 provisional licences were granted to 10 commercial radio companies. The first television service was inaugurated by the Nippon Television Network (NTN) in August 1952, followed by NHK's first television service in February 1953. By the early 1950s, then, the basic structure, organisation and purpose of the whole of Japanese broadcasting was complete.

JAPANESE BROADCASTING TODAY

The relationship between broadcasting and the Japanese telecommunications structure can be represented schematically. (See Table 8.1). The relationship between NHK and the government can also be represented schematically to show the various interfaces between the institution and the state's statutory powers. (See Table 8.2).

The key to understanding any broadcasting system within the world's liberal democracies lies in seeing the ways in which the system of political relationships within which the broadcasting institution is placed interlocks with pressures which flow from its financial basis. Wherever one looks in those societies, broadcasting lies at the focal point for those competing pressures from the economic and political spheres.

The obvious immediate effect of the creation of the commercial broadcasting stations was to create an environment of competition for NHK. That of course was the whole intention, but what was not clear was the way in which this would ultimately affect the programming policy of the public service system.

There is an obvious analogy here with the situation which emerged in Great Britain in 1954. The difference, however, is that commercial television there was cocooned within a public service framework. The effect of that was to blunt the more rapacious impulses that beat within the hearts of commercial television entrepreneurs. No such condition did or does exist in Japan.

Table 8.1: Telecommunications Regulatory Structure6

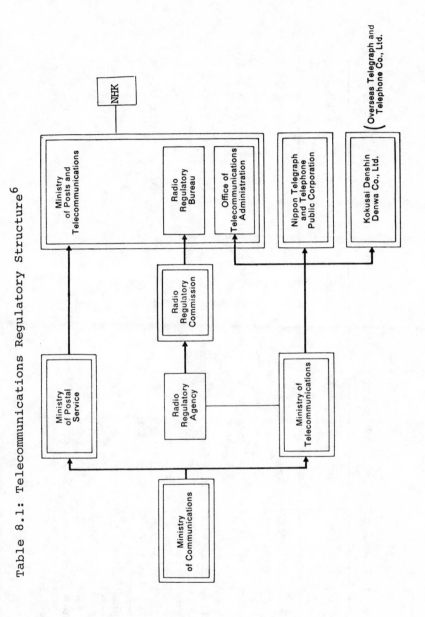

Table 8.2: Schema of Relationship between NHK and the Government[7]

Classification	Relationship with Government	Relationship with Diet	The Broadcast Law
1. Alteration of Articles of Corporation	Approval of the Minister of Posts and Tele-communication		Article 11
2. Appointment of members of the Board of Governors	Appointment by the Prime Minister	Consent of both Houses of the Diet	Article 16
3. Dismissal of members of the Board of Governors due to loss of qualification	Dismissal by the Prime Minister	Consent of both Houses of the Diet	Article 19
4. Dismissal of members of the Board of Governors due to ill health or their mis-conduct	Dismissal by the Prime Minister	Consent of both Houses of the Diet	Article 20
5. Carrying on of inter-national broadcasting	Expenses to be borne by the Government		
6. Designated research of broadcast and reception	Expenses to be borne by the Government		Article 34

Table 8.2: continued

Classification	Relationship with Government	Relationship with Diet	The Broadcast Law
7. Voluntary works on improvement and development of broadcast and reception	Approval of the Minister of Posts and Tele-Communication		Article 9, Item 10
8. Restriction of areas for repair of receiving equipment	Designation by the Minister of Posts and Telecommunication		Article 9
9. Revenue/expenditure budget, business plan	Opinion of the Minister of Posts and Tele-communication	Approved by both houses of the Diet	Article 37
10. Provisional budget	Approval of the Minister of posts and tele-communication	The Minister of Posts and Telecommunication reports to the Diet	Article 37-2
11. Business report	Submitted to the Cabinet by the Minister of Posts and Telecom-munication	The Minister of Posts and Telecommunication reports to the Diet	Article 38
12. Three financial statements	Submitted to the Cabinet by the Minister of Posts and Telecom-munication	Submitted by the Cabinet to the Diet	Article 40
13. Accounting	Inspected by the Audit Board		Article 41

Table 8.2: continued

Classification	Relationship with Government	Relationship with Diet	The Broadcast Law
14. Amount of receiving fees	Opinion of the Minister of Posts and Tele-communication	Approval of the budget by the Diet	Article 37
15. Contents of receiving fees	Approval of the Minister of Posts and Tele-communication		Article 32
16. Standards for exemptions from receiving fees	Approval of the Minister of Posts and Tele-communication		Article 32
17. Issuance of broad-cast bond	Approval of the Minister of Finance		Article 42
18. Transfer, etc., of broadcast equip-ment	Approval of the Minister of Posts and Tele-communication	Consent of both houses of the Diet	Article 47
19. Opening and operation of broadcasting stations	Supervision under the Radio Law, including permission of the Mini-ster of Posts and Telecommunication		Provisions of the Radio Law
20. Discontinuance, sus-pension of broad-casting	Approval of the Minister of Posts and Telecom-munication		Article 43

The general structure of Japanese Broadcasting as of 1981 is described in Table 8.3.

Table 8.3:[8]

NHK:	2 television channels:	(a) General (entertainment, news, cultural programmes)
		(b) Educational (85% instructional)
	2 AM radio:	(a) General (entertainment, news, cultural)
		(b) Educational (78% instructional)
	1 FM radio:	75% classical and popular music
Commercial:	97 stations:	36 TV and Radio (AM)
		61 TV only

The important differences in the general output of NHK compared with that of commercial television are presented in Table 8.4.

Table 8.4: Programming Categories for NHK and Commercial Television[9]

	NHK general TV	Commercial TV
News	32.8	11.6
Culture	24.8	24.9
Entertainment	26.1	47.1
Education	16.3	12.4
Sports	-	2.8
Other	-	1.2

Japan: Broadcasting in a New Democracy

Table 8.5 lists the kinds of television programmes watched by the Japanese audience.

Table 8.5: Types of Television Programme Frequently Viewed[10]

News, news shows	77%
Weather forecasts, information	61
Commentary programmes	20
Political, economic, social programmes	24
Extra/long talk shows	22
Hobbies, practical information programmes	21
Educational/cultural programmes	11
Study, vocational programmes	5
Home dramas, melodramas	40
Action, detective dramas	40
Costume dramas	39
Historical dramas	27
Theatre feature films	23
Stage relay programmes	15
Cartoons, animation programmes	14
Vaudeville, amusement programmes	30
Skits, variety shows	11
Quiz, game programmes	47
Japanese popular music, foreign popular music	42
Japanese Folksongs	27
Classical music programmes	5
Sumo Wrestling tournaments	37
Professional baseball games	41
Other sports programmes	21
Do not watch television, do not know, no response	1

Tables 8.6 and 8.7 and Figure 8.1 describe the revenue available to commercial broadcasters and NHK.

282

Table 8.6: Advertising Revenue in 1981 (Calendar Year)11

	Total amount	Television	Radio	Newspaper
Amount (yen)	2,465.7 bill.	838.9 bill.	126.4 bill.	757.2 bill.
Component ratio	100.0%	34.0%	5.1%	30.7%

Table 8.7: NHK's Revenue from Viewers' Fees in Fiscal 1981 and the number of Viewers' Contracts as of the end of the same Fiscal Year12

Revenue from viewer's fees (yen)	Number of viewers' contracts	
	total number of viewers' contracts	number of colour television contracts
273.0 billion	29.8 million	27.1 million

Figure 8.1: Trends of revenue from advertising (for commercial broadcasting stations), and the revenue from viewers' fees and the number of viewers' contracts for NHK[13]

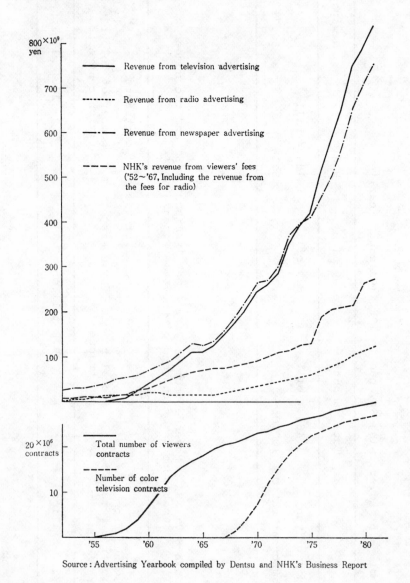

Source: Advertising Yearbook compiled by Dentsu and NHK's Business Report

As one commentator noted:

> Japanese commercial stations have engaged in
> fierce competition for high audience ratings
> reminiscent of the "ratings war" so familiar to
> the United States. In Japan, it has spurred an
> increase in vulgar programming.[14]

The problem for any public service organisation
is how to insulate itself from such pressures. Geller
also notes in this context that despite NHK's continuing reputation as the most credible news medium
and source of cultural programming, there are persistent criticisms from both inside and outside
broadcasting: 'it is apparent to all that NHK has
become more rating conscious'.

In this context it is interesting that NHK was
under severe competition from Asahi Television for
the broadcast rights to the 1980 Olympic Games. This
was a straw in the wind which has parallels in the
way in which the assumed right of the American networks to bid for the coverage of the Los Angeles
Olympics was very nearly successfully challenged by
a consortium of cable TV companies led by HBO. In
similar vein in Britain there is the continuing debate about the monopoly rights of the BBC and ITV
to certain sporting events.

NHK's own response to competition from commercial television has been more competitive scheduling
during 'the golden hours' (prime time). More
serious educational and documentary programmes have
been replaced by variety shows, cartoons and quiz-
shows, as well as the familiar slick, fast news
magazine programmes in the early evening.

Competition and financial stability are inex-
tricably linked. The Broadcast Law gives NHK the
task of ensuring that every part of the nation can
receive its signals. The same law also establishes
the right of NHK to collect receiving fees from
every household with a television set. The organisation employs about 7,000 people to collect the
receiving fees door to door. About 40% of households pay the fees by automatic bank transfer, while
another 47% pay a lump sum in advance to cover
either 6 months or a year. The intriguing, indeed
to a British mind bizarre, fact is that even if a
household concludes a receiving contract with NHK
there is no penalty for non-payment, and yet most
Japanese do pay with only about 4% of television
households refusing.

The preliminary indication of a financial

crisis for NHK emerged in the 1970s as the ownership of television sets reached saturation levels
and there was a slowing down in the increase of
colour television receivers:

> NHK's income from receiving fees reached its
> limits in fiscal 1973 and, in the wake of the
> oil crisis, the cost of commodities continued
> to soar to such an extent that the sharp in-
> crease in production costs could no longer be
> covered by income. NHK was forced to operate
> at a deficit. It had to take steps to stabi-
> lise its finance by raising the amounts of the
> receiving fees under authorisation from the
> National Diet.[16]

The fee was raised in 1976 by 54% for colour
sets and 33% for monochrome sets. In 1980 the fees
were increased by a further 24%. The difficult spiral
within which NHK is trapped is a familiar one. The
number of households that are concluding new contracts is diminishing, with the net result that
NHK's income has been increasing by about only 2% a
year. Costs, however, have been rising by more
than 10% a year. The end result is the cyclical
need of NHK to go cap in hand to the Diet, a position which is never good for the operational independence of any broadcasting organisation.
    It is in this fiscal relationship that a key
link between government and broadcasting actually
lies. It is not however just a question of setting
the level of the receiving fee. NHK also has to
send its budget and programme schedule to the Ministry of Post and Telecommunications. The Ministry
cannot change these, but it can comment when sending
them forward to the National Diet to be reviewed and
debated.
    There is a tendency for Cabinet and Diet mem-
bers to avoid openly criticising programmes. What
tends to happen is that politicians' relationships
with newspapers are exploited to raise issues about
broadcasting or to get party associates to complain
to stations as 'concerned viewers'. An example
quoted by Geller occurred during the Vietnam War
when NTV previewed a film of a South Vietnamese
soldier carrying the decapitated head of a North
Vietnamese. The Prime Minister's secretary raised
objections 'as a private citizen' and the film clip
was not shown. One commercial broadcaster is
quoted at the time as saying 'if there is too much
bias, a Diet member may take issue with it and a

harmonious solution is sought.' There was also a
case of a prominent commentator on the Tokyo Broadcasting System, Mr. H. Den, who was sacked as a
newscaster because of his critical views on South
Vietnam. Mr. Hata of Asahi TV was in turn dismissed
because of a hard-hitting news commentary about the
construction of the airport at Narita.

In a rather British way, the lines of both
political pressure and political resolution tend to
take place outside any legalistic structure. For
example, the legal prescriptions available through
the Broadcast Law of 1950 have never been used. In
Britain, of course, the powers of veto available to
the government have never in effect been utilised
either. In the Japanese system pressures are subtle, solutions consensual. As one commentator noted
about the relationship between Japanese companies
and the government;

> The last thing it does is file an application.
> The first thing it does is informally sound out
> every official involved. Only when everyone
> assents informally is the formal application
> made. This avoids the surprises and rejections
> the Japanese find so jarring.[17]

Occasionally major political pressures and scan-
dals have broken through the tranquil surface of os-
tensible political calm and consensus. In 1975, for
example, NHK's President Ono had to resign after it
was made public that he had paid a social call on
Mr. Tanaka, the Prime Minister, who was then under
indictment because of the Lockheed scandal. This
was felt to infringe Ono's, and therefore NHK's, commitment to 'neutrality'. What seemed especially to
stick in the public gullet of many observers was
that Ono had used an official car. He was especially compromised however by the fact that before being
appointed to NHK he had served as the Vice Minister
to Mr. Tanaka when the latter was Minister of Posts
and Telecommunications. During the Lockheed scandal
there were also many 'phone calls from Diet members
belonging to the Tanaka faction who said that they
would support a budget cut because of their 'personal' view that NHK's coverage of the affair was
'unfair'.

THE FUTURE OF BROADCASTING IN JAPAN

The traditional links between broadcasting organisations and governments have depended upon the extent

to which resources are influenced and political pressures applied. If there were a scale of those relationships with total independence at one end and total dependence at the other, Japanese broadcasting would be just off-centre on the dependent side. It would have as close neighbours such bodies as the BBC and IBA-ITN system of Britain, RTE in Ireland, and would be within hailing distance of Denmark's Radio and the ARD network in Germany.

In the future, just as much as for all those other systems, the conditions of broadcasting in Japan will be determined by a remarkable conjunction between the technological and ideological evaluation of the western industrial democracies. The president of NHK, Tomokazu Sakamoto, has called the period of the 1980s the 'new period of fruit-bearing for technological innovation'. And on the occasion of NHK's 55th anniversary he announced, with touching, if a trifle naive, optimism:

> The deeper we find ourselves plunging into what is variously called an "era of change" or an "era of uncertainty", the higher shall we raise the torch of public broadcasting with the un-flinching determination to overcome all diffi-culties that may await us in our future path. We will do everything in our power to contri-bute to the promotion of people's happiness and to their brighter future through our continuous efforts to safeguard the freedom of speech, as we keep on advancing with our eternal trust in mankind.

With the rapid developments in communications policy in Japan, as in all other industrial socie-ties, that 'eternal trust' might last another ten years, a generation at most. Consider the following developments which are either underway or at an ad-vanced stage of development:

1. An increasing emphasis of the conservative Liberal Democratic Party government of Mr. Nakasone on the virtues of 'liberalisation' (for which read deregulation) of communications and telecommunications policies

2. Its similar emphasis on the need to create a 'comprehensive' telecommunications policy within which broadcasting policy would be placed.

3. NTT's (the main domestic telecommunications

agency) INS (Information Network System): a digital, integrated, national data transmission network.

4.   KDD's (the international arm of NTT) *Venus* project: a digital switching network for overseas telecommunications.

5.   NHK's development of high definition television and teletext facilities.

6.   Increasing interest in the development of cable television to provide new entertainment channels, locally originated programmes and interactive services. The driving force behind these developments are the large railway companies and advertising agencies.

7.   A massive development of computer technology, including the likely creation of a fifth generation.

8.   'Request' type media: *Captain* (still picture transmission over 'phone line), Teletext and Video Response Systems (which transmits moving pictures through the telephone network, developed by NTT).

9.   'Participation' type media: for example, the CCIS (Coaxial Cable Information System) in Tama City; and the Hi-Ovis experiment (the Higashi-Ikoma Highly Interactive Visual Information System), involving the creation of a total 2-way, optic fibre-based communications system in a community south of Osaka.

10.   'Dialogue' type media: facsimile; data telephone; electronic mail.

11.   Direct broadcasting by satellite.

There is then a rapid development of communications and telecommunications policy in Japan. The net effects of this will be vastly to expand available sources of entertainment, thus undermining the whole position of existing broadcasting organisations of whatever complexion. Such developments will expand the ways in which other kinds of communication are undertaken by the Japanese public. In particular, the changes in the total structure and nature of communication will probably transform the kinds of

finance which are deemed appropriate to pay for
people's communication needs, from general payments
through a listening fee or subvention through advertising, to particular payments for particular needs
- of which education, information and entertainment
will be but parts. The real impact of politics on
broadcasting in Japan will lie in the fact that for
purposes of economic planning and growth, policies
will be embarked upon which will change all the
rules by which, to date, broadcasting in Japanese
society has been governed.

Japan: Broadcasting in a New Democracy

References

1. A. Briggs, *The History of Broadcasting*, Vol. IV.
2. Quoted in *Report of the Committee on Broadcasting*, 1960, Cmnd 1918, September 1962.
3. All the references in this section are taken from official SCAP documents 1945/1950.
4. CI & E Report, August 1 1946.
5. Judith F. Geller, *Japanese Public Broadcasting: A Promise Fulfilled*, Aspen Institute, 1979.
6. Ichiro Miura, 'System and Problems of Japan's Communications Administration', *Telecommunications Journal*, Vol 44, 1977.
7. Material for this schema was prepared by Chosei Kabira of NHK, and is quoted by Geller, *Japanese Public Broadcasting*.
8. Source: Mikio Shimuzi, '30 years of Japanese television in figures and tables', *Studies of Broadcasting*, Vol. 19, 1983.
9. Source: NHK (Radio and TV Culture Research Institute), May 1978; Office of the Director of Communications Policy Division, Ministry of Posts and Telecommunications.
10. Source: Jun Yoshida, 'Japanese TV' Audience as seen from Surveys', *Studies of Broadcasting*, Vol. 18, 1982.
11. Shimuzi, '30 years of Japanese television'.
12. *Ibid*.
13. Source: Advertising Yearbook compiled by Dentzu and NHK's Business Report, quoted in Shimuzi, '30 years of Japanese television'.
14. Geller, *Japanese Public Broadcasting*.
15. *Ibid*.
16. Chosei Kabira, 'Public Broadcasting: the issue in Japan', *Intermedia*, November 1980.
17. Andrew H. Malcom, 'US and Japan's Basic Conflict', *New York Times*, December 8, 1977.

291

NOTES ON CONTRIBUTORS

Muriel and Joel Cantor teach at the American University, Washington DC. Muriel Cantor is the author of *Prime-Time Television* and co-author of *The Soap Opera*.

Richard Collins lectures in the Faculty of Communications at the Polytechnic of Central London. He is the author of the BFI television monograph *Television News* and co-author of *WDR and the Arbeiterfilm*.

Richard Harding is Professor of Law at the University of Western Australia. He is author of *Outside Interference: The Politics of Australian Broadcasting*.

Raymond Kuhn lectures in the Department of Political Studies, Queen Mary College, University of London. He is the author of various articles on the politics of broadcasting in France.

Ralph Negrine lectures in the Department of Politics and Government, City of London Polytechnic. He is the author of numerous articles on broadcasting in Britain and is at present editing a book on cable television.

Don Sassoon lectures in the Department of History, Westfield College, University of London. A Specialist in Italian politics, he is the author of *The strategy of the Italian Communist Party*.

Michael Tracey is head of the broadcasting research unit at the British Film Institute. He is the author of several books on broadcasting including *The Production of Political Television*, *Whitehouse* and *Variety of Lives: a biography of Hugh Greene.*

Arthur Williams lectures in the Modern Languages Centre, University of Bradford. He is the author of *Broadcasting and Democracy in West Germany.*